COMING OUT

FROM BEHIND THE BADGE

The people, events, and history that shape our journey

Stories of success from police officers "out" on the job

SECOND EDITION
BY: GREG MIRAGLIA

CONTENTS

FOREWORD

I never had any desire to be in law enforcement. In high school, my dad called me a half-time student. He said, "David, you spend half of your time getting kicked out of school and the other half getting back in." My vice principal wrote in my senior yearbook, "Some bring happiness wherever they go, others whenever they go. Good luck; you'll need it."

I attended the University of Wyoming and majored in social work. I came out of that program with the attitude that there were two things wrong with our country: Republicans and police officers. Later, after taking a police test on a dare, passing, and getting hired at the Laramie Police Department, I quickly learned that I was wrong, and the two things wrong with our country were Democrats and social workers! It took many years and the death of a young man named Matthew Shepard to force me to realize that I had spent my life formulating my beliefs and opinions of others based on stereotypes rather than on an informed basis of knowledge through personal experiences.

On October 6, 1998, Matt Shepard was a student at the University of Wyoming. Matt was a loving son, brother, and friend. On the same day, I was the commander of the Investigations Division of the Laramie Police Department, and, in all respects, I was bigoted and prejudiced toward the gay community. Although I have never physically assaulted anyone I thought might be gay, I certainly teased those I felt could be and bought into all of the myths and stereotypes about homosexuals. I used all of the gross terminology and retold the jokes I heard, never stopping to think about who might be listening or who I might be hurting.

On October 7, 1998, Matthew Shepard lay dying in a hospital in Ft. Collins, Colorado. It was on that day that I began to learn so many things that have caused me to lose my ignorance; this has become profoundly important in my life. The investigation into Matthew's murder allowed me to meet many people from the gay community, which I knew existed in Laramie but had never experienced. I saw the terror in the eyes, the horror on the faces, and heard the fear in the voices of Matt's many gay and lesbian friends. The trauma and fear was causing kids to quit school or transfer to other universities. I quickly began to understand what a hate crime was and the profound effect this one had on the gay community, not just in Laramie, but in all corners of the world. I never realized the extent of this investigation's effect on our country. It was like throwing a stone into a pond. The stone struck Matt and his family, and, as the waves rippled outward, they struck his friends, his acquaintances, other gay people, the parents of gay people, their brothers and sisters, and beyond. These very same ripples are still impacting people all of these years later, and thank God that they are.

At the beginning, I never realized how personal this case would become. You see, Aaron McKinney, one of the two people who murdered Matthew Shepard, was my next-door neighbor for several years as he was growing up. Matt's uncle Steve and I graduated from high school together. Although we were not friends, I knew Steve, and it made the dynamics of this case much more intense. A volume could be written about the investigation itself. It was a year between the time Matt was killed and when Aaron McKinney was put on trial for Matthew's murder. Other volumes could be written on everything that has transpired since the day McKinney was convicted and sentenced to two consecutive life sentences in prison.

Although I never had the opportunity to meet Matt, meeting his family and friends was all I needed to make the decision to do whatever I could do to help, in any way possible, to move toward an understanding of tolerance and diversity in our country. Following the trial, I became involved in lobbying efforts, through the Human Rights Campaign, to support federal legislation by way of the Local Law Enforcement Enhancement Act. This act would give the same basic protections received by those based on race, religion, and national origin to those based on gender, disability, and sexual orientation. The legislation appeared to me to be a no brainer! After all, every major law enforcement executive organization in our country supported and endorsed the bill. I quickly found out how naïve I was, and now know that if sexual orientation had not been included in the bill, it probably would have passed in 1999 as the Hate Crimes Prevention Act.

Some years later, at a Human Rights Campaign banquet in Denver, Colorado, I was introduced to a group of gay and lesbian peace officers from the area. I was hugely impressed with their personal and professional demeanor and with their dedication to their chosen profession. It was also apparent that some administrators supported their officers, but that other officers were forced to remain hidden among the heterosexual officers they worked with. Even if that person was the best detective, crime scene technician, SWAT team member, or any other integral member of any department, he or she was subject to ridicule, harassment, and even termination, for no reason other than sexual orientation. Being a cop is tough; being a gay cop is tougher; being a gay cop having to remain hidden for fear of losing the profession he has chosen is incomprehensible to me.

It is incumbent on administrators across our nation to stand up and support their officers, without the prejudices toward gays and lesbians historically encountered in law enforcement. Administrators need to lead by example, provide training specific to prejudice and bias at all levels, formulate general orders as they pertain to prejudice and bias within the department and public we serve, and take quick and severe action against those who violate those premises.

They say a Democrat in Wyoming would be a Republican in any other state! Even in a conservative state and in a conservative profession, I never heard any disparaging comments toward my efforts to help others understand tolerance and diversity. That goes a long way toward showing others the caliber of the men and women of the Laramie Police Department, a group that I hold dear to my heart and would today provide backup for in any situation, regardless of the officer's race, religion, national origin, gender, disability, or sexual orientation.

David O'Malley

Sheriff, Albany County, Wyoming

DEDICATION

As this edition of *Coming out from behind the Badge* is published, I am preparing to retire from full-time work and reflecting on 35 years of experience in law enforcement. The list of people who have contributed to my success exceeds the space available in these pages. I will forever be grateful to the mentors, role models, colleagues, and precious friends I've made during my journey. I am humbled by their care and support.

This book is dedicated to men and women in law enforcement who shared their knowledge, experience, and friendship with me. Thank you for your inspiration and becoming a part of my work and my life.

The stories, history, and advice in this book would never have made it to print without the encouragement, love and support I get every day from my husband, Tony Pennacchio. Thank you for being such an important part of my journey and for continuing to be a core part of my life—I love you.

INTRODUCTION

Coming out from behind the Badge is a book intended to support lesbian, gay, bisexual, and transgender (LGBT) law enforcement professionals who are seeking a way to "come out" and be successful on the job. It is also intended to educate heterosexuals (persons attracted to the opposite sex) and cisgender people (persons who identify their gender in a way that is consistent with their birth sex) to better understand differences in sexual orientation and gender identity and how to support their colleagues. In addition, this edition of *Coming out from behind the Badge* was written to support students who are preparing for a career in law enforcement and those already in the field seeking a better understanding of a large segment of the community which law enforcement serves.

I will use the initials "LGBT" to refer to all non-heterosexual people and transgender people. I will also use "LGBT community" to refer to the social and political communities inclusive of people who are not heterosexual or cisgender. I do this not to be exclusive, but rather to simplify the reference to the populations described above. I also recognize that the terms people use to describe their sexuality, gender identity, and community affiliation are constantly evolving. I have included in this edition a more detailed discussion of sexual orientation and gender identity and how these two aspects of personality are related. Along with this explanation is a discussion of terms and why they are important to our identity.

I wrote the first edition of *Coming out from behind the Badge* in 2005 after my husband Tony suggested that my own story might be helpful to other law enforcement professionals who are struggling with "coming out." I was 41 when I came out, though I had known I was gay since about the seventh grade. It was 2004 when I finally got the courage to start living my life truthfully as an "out" gay man. One of the first things I did was to read the coming out stories of others. I found several anthologies with stories from college students, teachers, and others, but nothing with current stories specifically about law enforcement professionals who happen to be lesbian, gay, bisexual or transgender. The books I found with law enforcement related stories were over ten years old. They reflected the common struggles and failures many LGBT law enforcement people experienced in the 1990s and before. But 2004 was a different time and attitudes about LGBT people were changing quickly. It was this change I was witnessing that gave me the confidence to come out and I believed it was time to collect stories of success. These stories would hopefully inspire still closeted LGBT people working in law enforcement to come out.

I had no idea of how successful the first book would be. If I could inspire even one law enforcement officer like me to come out and start living life fully and truthfully then I would declare success and be happy with my efforts. In the months that followed the book's release, I received dozens of emails from officers all over the country. They told me how helpful it was reading the many stories of success, which gave them the confidence they needed to come out. I never believed that the book would be on anyone's bestseller list and I was humbled when it was selected for required reading in criminal justice classes. I didn't bank on my retirement coming from the profits of book sales, but I never imagined having the speaking opportunities that took me to many locations from coast to coast.

After hearing so much positive feedback, I embarked on a second book, *American Heroes Coming out from behind the Badge* with the hope of reaching out to not only more law enforcement personnel, but also to those LGBT people in the fire service and emergency medical services profession. Like the first, *American Heroes Coming out from behind the Badge* is an anthology with stories from police officers, firefighters, and paramedics from across the United States. Like the first book, this one focuses on how people "came out" as lesbian, gay, bisexual, or transgender, and remained successful on the job.

The sale of both books did generate revenue, which I immediately dedicated to a new non-profit organization called Out to Protect that my husband and I formed in 2009. We enlisted the help of a small board of directors and quickly established the mission of the organization to "create a greater awareness of the gay, lesbian, bisexual, and transgender professionals working in law enforcement and to support those pursuing a law enforcement career." We now provide two scholarships a year for LGBT students enrolled in a basic law enforcement training program. In addition, we offer grants for LGBT awareness training for law enforcement and copies of our books for public and department libraries. This was always my dream for the books and I'm thrilled that it has all come to fruition.

And now for this book. It's been ten years since I wrote *Coming out from behind the Badge* and so much has changed. In 2004, same-sex marriage was a pipe-dream former San Francisco Mayor, Gavin Newsome attempted to make real. Now, in 2015, marriage equality is the law of the land and same-sex couples can marry in all 50 states. We are finally really talking about non-heterosexuality and gender identity in schools, in the workplace, and even in law enforcement training. I've always said, and still maintain, that law enforcement is 20 years behind the rest of society in its acceptance and understanding of diversity. In the 1970s and '80s, it was racial diversity and women that were issues of struggle in law enforcement. Today, it's gay and transgender people. The good news is that change is happening.

I chose to produce a second edition rather than a third new book so I could update my own story and content in the first book in order to make it relevant for today. You will find some of the same stories as well as many new ones in this book along with a new section on LGBT history. I've included LGBT history that is relevant and important for law enforcement personnel to know. Like many minority groups that have had to fight for equality and civil rights, LGBT people have clashed with law enforcement. Over the last century and a half, LGBT people have been targeted by police in ways that have left scars and a lack of faith and trust in law enforcement. It is important for anyone in law enforcement to know the origins of these scars and of the events that contribute to the lack of trust many LGBT people still carry with them.

This book's subtitle, "The history, events, and people who shape our journey," captures my belief that who we are today is very much influenced by the history we witness, the events we experience, and the people we meet. All of us have a journey in life, and for LGBT people, "coming out" can be as significant a part of that journey as one's own birth. It is a life-changing event that is often surrounded by tremendous fear and shame. But coming out is so very worth it and the experience of having done it is one I will always consider the most significant of my life.

I hope that you appreciate and enjoy the stories contained in these pages. Most importantly, I hope you learn from the experiences of everyone who shared their journey. If you are searching for a way to "come out," look for it here. And if you are an ally, student, or colleague, I offer you an explanation and insight to the LGBT community. Thank you for taking the time to learn.

SECTION I

SEXUAL ORIENTATION AND
GENDER IDENTITY

There is a great deal of mythology out there about sexual orientation and gender identity and how these two aspects of personality relate. Unless you take a specific course of study on the subject, most people never hear any detail about what sexual orientation and gender identity are. The two are simply not taught in school, but we all have a sexual orientation and a gender identity and so do the citizens that law enforcement serves. So here are the lessons you should have received in school.

Your sexual orientation is about your attraction to someone else. It is not only the gender you are attracted to, but also the color, shape, age, size, and look. Sexual orientation is about the heart, who gets you excited, makes your heart pound, and who do you love. There is evidence of same-sex attraction and sexual activity throughout the history of mankind. However, science only began to examine human sexuality in the 1860s. In fact, German scientists were the first to define sexuality with terms to distinguish opposite sexual attraction from same-sex sexual attraction.

The word "homosexual" was first coined in 1869 by German scientists. Richard von Kraft-Ebbing and Magnus Hirschfeld were the two most notable scientists who first studied human sexuality, and they ended up disagreeing on whether homosexuality was a normal human difference or a mental disorder. Probably the most famous study of human sexuality was completed by Alfred Kinsey between 1948 and 1953. Kinsey's work showed that sexual orientation was not simply being heterosexual (straight) or homosexual (gay), but rather an infinite spectrum of naturally occurring variation. He created a scale based on sexual history data he collected that ranges from 0 (exclusively heterosexual) to 6 (exclusively homosexual). Kinsey proved that the variety found in human sexuality is similar to the varieties of hair color, eye color, and facial features, and is naturally occurring regardless of other group features, such as race, nationality, and birth sex.

Human sexuality (sexual attraction) is not something we choose. Although science has not found the gene or hormone that specifically determines human sexuality, it is widely accepted in the medical and psychological community that one's sexuality is definitely NOT a choice. Homosexuality can be found in over 1500 other mammal species. The one recognized difference in humans is our ability to choose whether we act on our sexual attraction or not. In other words, human sexual attraction is not a matter of choice, but how we act on that attraction very much is a choice.

Some gay men choose to live a "straight lifestyle" for many reasons including fear of coming out, fear of losing a career, family expectations, and other social pressures. Just because a gay man marries a woman or a gay woman marries a man, it doesn't mean that person chose to become straight. Their inherent sexual orientation does not change because of certain life choices. Unfortunately, in many cases like this, the urge to act on an inherited sexual attraction can be overpowering and has led men, for example, to look for one-time encounters in public restrooms or online. For proof of this behavior, all you have to do is search the internet for stories about politicians, religious leaders, and other famous people who have been "caught" with call-boys, prostitutes, or other anonymous sexual partners. No matter the person, this situation is always tragic for everyone involved and it can all be blamed on homophobia.

The opposite is also true. I know many heterosexual men who have chosen to engage in gay sex. It may be for money or for simply a lack of opportunity with an opposite sex partner. In prisons, when men or women only have access to members of the same gender, they may choose to engage in same-sex activity because it is the only source of sexual satisfaction available. That choice to engage in same-sex behavior does not make the person gay and it does not change their inherent sexual orientation. Younger men and women may experiment, most commonly in their teens and twenties, with members of the same sex either because their sexual orientation is somewhere in the middle of the spectrum or out of curiosity. Kinsey's research showed that 37% of men had had at least one homosexual experience that resulted in an orgasm. But this one-time experience doesn't mean that the individual is gay.

There are also many men and women who do not identify as being gay or lesbian, but who regularly or exclusively engage in sex with members of the same gender. Someone who is sexually attracted to others of the same gender identifies but as "straight" isn't really heterosexual. In communities of color and conservative faiths, identifying as "gay," "lesbian," or "queer" may mean rejection by family and excommunication by the church. For many individuals, they cannot see themselves in their own image of what "gay," "lesbian," or "queer" looks like. Choosing to identify as "straight" doesn't make a bisexual or homosexual person truly heterosexual. The identity, word, or label used has no impact on one's inherent sexual orientation and changing the word we use doesn't change who we are.

Kinsey's study was the first to provide data that 1 out of 10 people is homosexual. But later studies and surveys suggest that this number could be higher. In 2012, a total of 90,000 college students were asked to identify their sexual orientation. 17% identified a sexual orientation that was other than heterosexual. In 1948, when Kinsey conducted his research, homosexual behavior was illegal across the United States. Homosexuality was considered a mental illness and every religion considered it a grave sin. In addition, Kinsey's study measured self-admitted sexual experience, not self-admitted sexual desire. It's no wonder that the numbers vary so much from 1948 to 2012. In addition to homosexual behavior being decriminalized, being declared "normal" by the American Psychological Association, and being more widely accepted by society, the 2012 survey only asked people to self-identify a term for their sexual orientation and did not consider sexual history. Again, one's sexual desires may be very different from one's actual sexual behavior.

The important points here are to understand that sexual attraction is not a choice and that there is more variety in the spectrum of sexual orientation than we have words to describe. The terms people use to describe their sexuality are ever-changing as people try to find a word that best represents their sexual orientation and is comfortable to use. While science is responsible for creating the terms "homosexual," "bisexual," and "heterosexual," many other terms have been used to label sexual orientation. Many of the words have had negative connotations over the years and have been used as forms of violence against non-heterosexual people. This issue of language and social acceptance has also complicated the measuring of the variety of sexual orientation. For example, if someone is attracted to members of the same sex, but is not comfortable with the term "gay" or "queer," or doesn't see themselves in a way that they understand that term to mean, that person may deny being gay even though their sexual attraction leans in part or entirely toward members of the same sex. And because sexual orientation is not something you can see, it can be easily hidden.

The words we use to identify all aspects of ourselves are important and must fit our own understanding of that word. Terms are important, because they help us see how we relate to the rest of the world and how the world relates to us. Time has changed the meaning and social acceptance of words and this evolution even further complicates our ability to measure the real prevalence of various sexual orientations. There are certainly more slang terms people use to identify their sexual orientation and each has an important history.

The word "gay" has origins in the 17th century and meant, in words we know today, "happy," "joyful," or "care-free." A hundred years later, the word evolved to mean "uninhibited" or "addicted" and was used to label those who engaged in frequent sexual behavior. In the 1800s "gay" was used for prostitutes and to refer to, particularly, men who had sex with female prostitutes. In the early 1900s homosexual activity became more visible and defined and "gay" was the label for deviant, immoral, and illegal sexual behavior. Of course, today "gay" is a popular term used by men and women who are attracted to members of the same sex. It is also a term used to describe the larger non-heterosexual community—"gay community."

Women have long used "lesbian" as a term to describe their same-sex attraction. The word has origins in ancient Greece and the island of Lesbos. It is a word that has remained connected with women who are sexually attracted to women as well as with feminism. Although some women choose to use the word "gay" or "queer" to describe their sexual orientation, I've never met a man who has used the word "lesbian" to describe their orientation—except, perhaps, a straight guy who enjoys hyper-expressing his attraction to women!

"Queer" is a word that has long meant "odd" or "different." It too had a negative connotation in society in the 1900s and was only reclaimed by many younger non-heterosexuals in the 21st century. It is a useful term because it is inclusive of anything that is different from the majority. Homosexuals, bisexuals, or anyone in between can make use of this term because it simply means "different." "Queer" is also a popular term with those individuals on the gender spectrum or who identify as being part of the transgender community.

So what about those in between homosexual and heterosexual, gay and straight? The term "bisexual" has long been used to label that space in between 0 and 6 on Kinsey's scale and for those who "switch-hit" or who "play on both teams." Bisexuality is complicated and even doubted by some gay people, who believe bisexuality is only a state of indecision or confusion. Science and research, though, show otherwise. The word "bisexual" doesn't work for some who have found a closer identity with words like "pansexual" and "omni-sexual." These words relate more to an overall and more inclusive attraction, that which is beyond physical attraction. But where does bisexuality end and homosexuality begin or, on the other end, where does bisexuality end and heterosexuality begin? The truth is that there isn't one definition that works for everyone.

Asexuality is hard to place on Kinsey's scale, or any other spectrum of sexuality that considers a gender attraction. Asexuals are not attracted sexually at all. But like sexual orientation, it's not an "either-or." One way to consider the asexuality spectrum is by considering it as a vertical scale against the otherwise horizontal scale of sexuality. Asexuals have a lessened or non-existent attraction to anyone. Because asexuals are another type of sexual minority, they are often included in the LGBTQQIAA community alphabet (lesbian, gay, bisexual, transgender, queer, questioning, intersexed, asexual, allies).

Words and labels are simply a matter of language. No matter how many new words we create, it won't change what has existed through the history of man. Whether we label it as something good or something bad, same-sex attraction has always existed in every society, culture, race, nationality, and ethnicity. It is part of who we are as humans.

The research about gender and gender identity is much more recent, still evolving, and much less abundant. Perhaps the most harmful and most untrue stereotype about LGBT people associates gender identify with sexual orientation. For example, a common stereotype about gay men is that they really just want to be women and gay women want to be men. Sexual orientation has little to do with how a person sees themselves in terms of gender. Gender identity is a different and separate part of who we are, but socially and politically, the transgender community has been associated with the gay community in part because of the commonality of our fight for equality, and because of the way gay and transgender people have been victimized, often violently, in history.

What is known is that about 98% of the human population sees themselves as male or female, consistent with their birth sex (the genitalia they were born with). But for the remaining percent, there can be an inconsistency between one's birth sex and how the person sees and knows themselves mentally in terms of gender. The medical and psychological professions have most recently termed this condition as "gender dysphoria." Gender dysphoria can occur naturally or can be caused by a necessary decision made by doctors at the time a person is born when the genitalia develops with both a penis and vagina or some combination thereof. Persons born with this kind of physical development are known as "intersexed." The dated, and now viewed as offensive, term for this condition is "hermaphrodite." If a baby is born intersexed and the genitalia are such that the health of the baby's development and growth could be compromised, doctors have to decide how to correct the situation, sometimes by making a complete vagina or a complete penis. This correction leads to determining a birth sex of either male or female, but of course, does not reflect mentally and psychologically how the child will grow. There is a 50/50 chance this medical decision could be wrong and cause gender dysphoria.

What we also know is that gender is defined on many levels and includes physical characteristics, such as genitalia, physical attributes, personality, behaviors, speech patterns, clothing, likes and dislikes, and so much more. A vast majority of these attributes have been defined by society and generalized into categories of maleness and femaleness. Like sexual orientation, we now know there is a wide spectrum of gender and gender identity. It's not simply a matter of what genitalia you have or one clear inconsistency with birth sex and mental gender identity. How one sees oneself in terms of society's definition of gender has an infinite number of variations and both science and society are finding ways to allow people to make changes in order to bring more harmony to whatever level of gender dsyphoria might exist.

The term "transgender" includes everyone from those who cross-dress in opposite gender clothing to those who have a clear case of gender dysphoria. Men and women who cross-dress do not necessarily experience gender dysphoria. Many men and women cross-dress for entertainment purposes or to challenge gender stereotypes, but the transgender community is inclusive of both. It is also important to know that a transgender person may take no action to make physical changes to the way they dress or to their physical body. Fortunately though, medical science has found new options for transgender people to bring about a full physical change of gender for those who wish to make that change. These surgeries are extremely expensive and take years to complete. In the end, though, they can bring lasting peace for an internal and painful conflict that many experience for decades before "coming out" as transgender.

There are many incredible books that have been written about gender identity and the transgender community, and this book is not intended to provide all there is to know about gender. In fact, our focus is much more on sexual orientation than it is on gender identity. What is important for law enforcement officers to know is that no matter how one dresses or behaves in relation to gender, or what physical changes a person decides to make, everyone deserves the same level of respect and understanding from law enforcement. And don't be surprised if a co-worker, someone you might never even suspect, reveals they are transgender. Gender dysphoria is nothing new, but the ability to "come out," especially in law enforcement, is new, and is extremely challenging for people.

There are some truly offensive terms that no one, especially law enforcement, should ever use. Don't ever call someone a "tranny" or a "he-she." These words, and other forms of them, are highly offensive and completely inappropriate. A "transvestite" is someone who dresses in opposite gender clothing for sexual or emotional gratification. This is different to gender dysphoria and not a word that should be used. A "transsexual" is someone who has had gender re-assignment surgery and now has genitalia consistent with their gender identity. But none of these words are even necessary for a law enforcement officer to use when interacting with or referring to a transgender person. Simply use the pronoun "him/his" or "her/hers" as you would for anyone else. If you are not sure how a person is identifying themselves in terms of gender, do the polite thing and ask: "How would you like me to refer to you?" or "Which pronouns do you prefer to use?" It's a simple gesture that can go a long way to easing tension and demonstrating basic human respect. This practice has already started in some colleges and universities. In fact, at Santa Rosa Junior College in California, students and staff are allowed to change their name in the college system to one that reflects their gender identity. If a co-worker comes out as transgender and wishes to be referred to with a different pronoun or name, there is no better way to demonstrate support than by honoring their wishes and using their preferred pronoun and name.

Another important fact to understand about gender identity is that one's sexual orientation will not change with a change of gender. For example, if someone has a birth sex of female, but then later identifies as male, the gender they are attracted to will not change because of this change of identity. The same is true with a physical change of gender. If someone has sex re-assignment surgery, who they are attracted to will not change. For example, if a person has a penis, has a gender identity of a female, is sexually attracted to females, and has sex re-assignment surgery to replace their penis with a vagina, their attraction to females will not change. In this case, however, the person may change their sexual orientation identity from straight to lesbian. Of course, the opposite is true and, yes, people can, based on their physical gender and the way they identify their gender, end up changing their sexual orientation identity from straight to gay or from gay to straight. What is important to know is that sexual attraction is not determined by gender identity. The words we choose to use to describe our sexual orientation can be impacted by a change in gender identity.

What is also important to know about both sexual orientation and gender identity is that in today's world both are becoming more fluid than ever. Young people are finding less necessity is claiming a word or label for either who they are attracted to or how they identify their gender. As mentioned before, the word "queer" has a great deal of utility because it is inclusive of a very broad spectrum of gender and attraction. It is no longer an offensive word as it once was and might even help others to better understand the rather vague and fluid place on the spectrum another person might be. The key with all words and labels is to be respectful. If you are not sure how someone identifies, either sexually or with gender identity, simply ask. Recognize the words that are truly offensive and should never be used, such as "fag," "faggot," "tranny," and "he-she." If someone tells you that they are offended by use of a particular term, respect that person and don't use the word.

LGBT HISTORY IN RELATION
TO LAW ENFORCEMENT

The history of lesbian, gay, bisexual, and transgender people begins with the dawn of mankind. In fact, we know that non-heterosexuality exists throughout the animal kingdom. But the words we use to describe sexual orientation and aspects of gender identity are all relatively new to this history. Volumes have been written on LGBT history, documenting and interpreting cultural and societal customs and practices dating back centuries. While this can make for fascinating study for those interested, it isn't necessarily relevant for today's law enforcement officer. Like other racial and ethnic minorities, LGBT people have not had a long-term positive relationship with law enforcement. The history of this relationship has shaped many LGBT people's views of law enforcement. It is helpful to know some of that history and why LGBT people may not feel at ease with or even trust law enforcement officers. I offer you a very abridged discussion of LGBT history as I believe it best relates to the law enforcement profession.

From the time the 13 colonies were formed here in the United States, same-sex sexual acts were considered illegal, immoral and a grave sin against the church. In fact, any sexual act committed outside of marriage and not for the purpose of procreation was at least a sin, if not a crime. These laws were known as "sodomy laws" and included any sexual act between two people, regardless of gender, outside of marriage. In fact, consensual sexual intercourse was the only legal sexual act between two people. Sodomy laws were established in every state and prohibited oral sex, anal sex, and intercourse outside of marriage, even it was consensual, regardless of the genders involved.

There was no understanding of sexual orientation differences or gender identity. In fact, it wasn't until 1869 that terms to distinguish and identify sexual orientation were defined by science. What is important to know is that attitudes about same-sex relationships and same-sex sexual behaviors were considered wrong on all levels since our country's birth, and attitudes about same-sex attraction have been evolving slowly ever since. But at no time in the history of the United States have attitudes shifted more dramatically than in the last half century. We have come a long way, but as you will read, we still have a long way to go.

I will begin when science began studying human sexuality and defining terms to describe sexual orientation in the 1860s. Here in the United States, focus was on reconstruction, the 13th Amendment, and the abolition of slavery. Of course, there was no internet or news wire, so research, like that being done on sexuality in Germany, was slow to reach the United States. Karl Heinrich Ulrichs, Magnus Hirschfeld, and Karl-Maria Kertbeny were three of the most famous "sexologists" who studied same-sex attraction at that time. There is some disagreement about which of these individuals actually "discovered" homosexuality as a sexual orientation, but suffice it to say our definition of homosexuality was born in 1869. It was also at this time that disagreement about how "normal" homosexuality is erupted within this scientific community. Urichs and Hirschfeld theorized that same-sex attraction was a naturally occurring variation of sexual orientation, while many others argued that it was an illness and a mental disorder. Both Urichs and Hirschfeld argued before legislatures that laws criminalizing same-sex sexual acts should be eliminated, but their efforts failed. In fact, homosexuality became recognized as not only criminal, but also formally as a type of mental disorder that warranted treatment and correction.

By the time the American Psychological Association was created in 1892, homosexual conduct was still illegal across the country, still viewed by religion as a grave sin, and now in addition also as a mental disorder by medical science. This formal classification played out in the first half of the 20th century in brutal ways. It included institutionalizing those caught engaged in homosexual acts and subjecting them to brutal treatments of correction, including electro-shock therapy and frontal lobotomies. Of course, none of these treatments made someone a heterosexual, but they did often result in catatonic states or suicide.

During the industrial revolution of the late 1800s and early 1900s, large cities, such as Los Angeles and San Francisco were being built by men who traveled from rural America to find work. Women were not allowed to work. In places like San Francisco, men far outnumbered women, so there were limited opportunities for heterosexual activity. Workers were housed in shared facilities that rarely offered private bathrooms. A new business provided much needed bathing facilities and they were known as public bath houses. The baths served a true practical purpose in providing a place for people without showers or bathing facilities to wash up. But as you probably can already imagine, they also provided a place for men to meet. For perhaps the first time in their lives, men discovered their true sexual attraction to other men. Imagine for just a moment living in a rural environment your entire life, attending a school with less than 50 students, having no television, radio, or other contact with the media and having only your parents and other adult family members as role models. If you were gay, how would you ever know it? Now imagine walking into a facility with a group of others you are attracted to. It's no wonder that bath houses attracted a gay following.

Society and law enforcement both took notice of what was becoming visible. As concern for preserving public morality and decency grew, law enforcement took an active role in the enforcement of sodomy laws. It quickly became a known fact that getting caught violating sodomy laws, especially with another of the same gender, carried great risks. In addition to getting arrested, police would commonly post pictures of those arrested in the newspaper calling out their behaviors. Someone arrested for such a crime would quickly lose their job, be excommunicated from the church, and rejected entirely by their families. And this is all in addition to any punishment doled out by a criminal court, including commitment to a mental institution.

Men found other places and other ways to meet. Parks, such as Lafayette Park located directly across from the White House in Washington DC, were a hot spot at night for gay men to meet. Men would meet in certain theater districts and wear a certain color tie that matched the scarf in their coat to catch the eye of other gay men in the area. Because every corner of society disapproved of same-sex sexuality, gay men had to sneak around their wives and the rest of straight society to find each other.

The situation was a bit different for women. Because women were not accepted in the workplace at the time, it was not entirely uncommon for women to share a house or living facility. Unmarried women could live together in a "Boston Marriage" without raising too much concern. Lesbians have always enjoyed a bit less scrutiny, although sexual acts between two women were just as much a violation of the sodomy laws as acts between two men. And there were plenty of women too who were subjected to institutionalization, either by their families or the courts, to correct their disordered sexuality.

By the end of the 1920s and the start of the great depression, pressure against gay people began increasing exponentially. Under Hitler's rule, Germany, which had once eased sodomy laws, re-enacted them. By the end of World War II, 100,000 homosexuals had been murdered in Nazi gas chambers. Magnus Hirschfeld, one of the German scientists who studied homosexuality and believed it to be a naturally occurring variation of human sexuality, just happened to be in the United States speaking on the subject when the Nazis burned his books and research materials.

In the United States, laws were expanded to prohibit the wearing of opposite gender clothing and the serving of alcohol to known homosexuals. This meant that everyone had to wear at least three items of gender-consistent clothing at all times. Police in major cities focused on men who dressed as women. In San Francisco, if a man wore lipstick or had a traditionally female hairstyle, he could be arrested for impersonating a female, which was a public decency crime. It was also illegal to hold hands and to dance with members of the same sex in a bar. For those bars where gay people tried to gather and meet, couples had to be very discreet. This was to avoid detection by undercover officers who were looking for homosexuals and transgender people visiting these bars.

The United States military also took an interest in homosexuals within the rank and file of all branches of the military. Service members discovered to be gay or who engaged in same-sex sexual conduct were dishonorably discharged. They were issued a special blue colored sheet of paper documenting the reason for discharge as being "homosexuality." This type of branding set discharged members up for failure. Imagine being a 20 year old in the early 1940s from middle-America and being dishonorably discharged for being gay. What were your chances of returning home with that branding from the US government and being accepted by your family? What chances would you have for a job? By this time, being labeled a homosexual in society meant that you were a deviant, a pervert, and of course, a criminal.

Port cities, like San Francisco, were dumping grounds for men discharged for being homosexual. For the reasons described above, many men chose to remain in San Francisco and found community there. This is one of the reasons San Francisco emerged as a "gay city" and ultimately became the birthplace of the modern-day LGBT civil rights movement. New York and Washington DC also had large gay populations that faced similar scrutiny and brutality from law enforcement. This scrutiny would only get worse as the fear of communism, brought about by people like

Senator Joe McCarthy, began to grow in the post war times of the late 1940s and early 1950s.

High school history books commonly include descriptions of the "red scare" and the fears of communist infiltration in society and the United States government. The Federal Bureau of Investigation, under the leadership of Herbert Hoover, actively investigated suspected communists throughout the United States, but this activity was most concentrated in large cities, like Washington DC, New York, Los Angeles, and San Francisco. But by 1950, it became obvious that the number of actual active members of the communist party in the United States was more paranoia than reality. To save face, another enemy had to be identified. Homosexuals were a perfect target. The "red scare" shifted to be the "lavender scare."

McCarthy and Hoover both shifted the focus of their investigations from communists to homosexuals working in government. Both believed that many homosexuals were also communists and were particularly dangerous to national security because they could be blackmailed. Hoover was one of the most infamous leaders of the FBI and was believed to be a closeted gay man himself. Rumors about Hoover's lovers have circulated for many years, but he always kept himself well insulated and if he was truly gay it was never formally discovered.

Sodomy laws were firmly in place in every state and actively enforced by local police. The medical and psychological professions still believed that homosexuality was a mental disorder. Research on how to correct this disorder was still actively being pursued and experimented with using actual human beings believed to be gay. This is all to say that being caught carried with it the risk of either incarceration in prison or commitment to a mental institution with torturous medical procedures, thus the risk of blackmail.

In 1948, Indiana State University professor, Dr. Alfred Kinsey, published his study of human sexuality that was focused first on males in a book called *Sexual Behavior in the Human Male*. His research included data from the sexual histories of thousands of men from across the country, of every race, and of every age over 18. Kinsey showed that 37% of all men had had at least one sexual encounter with another man that resulted in an orgasm. His study showed that 1 out of every 10 people is homosexual and that sexual orientation includes a spectrum of naturally occurring variation. Kinsey advocated for the abolition of sodomy laws. His work and his advocacy caught the attention of the FBI and tremendous pressure was put on him to stop.

Despite Kinsey's revolutionary research, fear of homosexuals working in government continued to escalate through the 1950s. On April 27, 1953, President Dwight D. Eisenhower issued Executive Order 10450, which ordered all department heads to rid the government of known threats to the security of the United States. This included the firing of all federal government employees who were known to be "sexual perverts," meaning homosexuals, alcoholics and neurotics. The FBI led the internal investigations and would regularly bring employees suspected of being homosexual into an interrogation room. Investigators would question the suspected employee and essentially extort a confession and resignation. Sometimes the evidence would be as slim as a co-worker who came forward with mere suspicions. But the fear of being arrested and institutionalized was so great that those confronted with an accusation chose to resign rather than face prosecution.

Executive Order 10450 remained in place until July 3, 1973. Over 5,000 federal employees lost their jobs for being a suspected homosexual. The impact of this order wasn't limited to the federal government. Many private corporations followed the government's belief that homosexuals were really sexual deviants and a threat to society in general. Of course, local law enforcement carried the same beliefs and, because homosexual sex was a felony crime, the possibility of being employed in law enforcement in any capacity didn't exist.

By 1957, gay people had had enough and things were about to change. LGBT people were not going to stand by and be treated like second-class citizens and criminals. In response to being terminated from federal employment for being gay, Frank Kamney led the first organized protest for gay rights in front of the White House in 1957. Gay men marched in suits and lesbian women in conservative skirts, but both genders carried signs demanding equality.

The 1960s brought many kinds of change to the United States. The Vietnam War, feminism, and the black civil rights movement put law enforcement at odds with many groups. Civil unrest of all kinds occurred and LGBT people were not to be left out of the picture. Young people lead the pushback and challenged gender stereotypes in hairstyles and clothing. A period of sexual liberation emerged. For the first time, science began to understand and talk more about gender identity. The idea that was being discussed was how someone might understand their gender differently from their birth sex. The increasing visibility of LGBT people only fueled law enforcement's efforts to preserve public morality and to protect citizens from the dangers posed by sexual perverts. In fact, the Inglewood, California, Police Department and Inglewood School District produced a crime prevention documentary called *Boy Beware*. Today you might recognize it as a "stranger-danger" type of program, but this one contains a clear message that homosexual men are pedophiles and a danger to young boys. It is an example of the kind of harmful message about gay men that fueled stereotypes that are still believed today.

Mainstream media was also starting to talk more openly about homosexuality. In 1967, CBS became the first television network to produce and broadcast a documentary about homosexuals. Mike Wallace, who later hosted the long-running series *60 Minutes*, narrated the documentary. This documentary furthered the belief that homosexuality was a sickness and a disorder. The piece opens with lines read by Wallace that include:

"Americans view homosexuality more harmful to society than: adultery, abortion and prostitution."

"Most Americans view homosexuals with disgust, discomfort, or fear."

"1 out of 10 views homosexuals with 'hatred'"

"Vast majority believe homosexuality is an illness."

"10% say it is a crime—and yet, and here's the paradox..."

"A majority of Americans favor legal punishment even for homosexual acts performed in private, between consenting adults."

The good news about this documentary is that it put the issue of homosexuality in front of the American public and began to make it more visible. It reflected just where our country was with homosexuality just prior to the Stonewall riots.

The Stonewall riots were credited with being the start of the modern-day gay rights movement, but there were other notable uprisings before Stonewall and one worth mentioning here. As already mentioned, law enforcement used a variety of legal justifications for regularly raiding bars and other places where LGBT people gathered. The beatings, arrests, and publication of names with pictures to humiliate LGBT people was commonplace. By the mid-1960s the LGBT community in San Francisco was sizeable. In fact, when the Navy veteran and now famous drag queen Jose Saria first ran for public office in San Francisco in 1961, he earned over 5,000 votes. Saria didn't win a seat on the Board of Supervisors, but he did make the gay vote visible for the first time. The LGBT community at the time was centered around Polk Street in an area known as the "Tenderloin." One of the places drag queens used to hang out, especially after the bars closed, was known as the Compton Cafeteria. It was a cafeteria style restaurant that was open all night. Like the gay bars, police raided the Compton Cafeteria and regularly arrested men dressed in drag for the crime of "impersonation of a female." Patrons were used to the routine and conceded to the order of police until one August night in 1966 when the "screaming queens" had enough. That night they fought back and resisted being arrested. They demanded that the police leave them all alone to be who they were and to dress as they wished.

A similar, and now more famous, situation occurred in New York's notoriously gay district at a bar known as the Stonewall Inn. The bar was opened by the mafia in a building that had once been horse stables. Like every other major city, in 1960s New York, serving alcohol to anyone know to be a homosexual was a crime and cause for a liquor license to be suspended or revoked altogether. The mafia provided a "safe place" for gay people to meet and have a drink of the "bath-tub" booze employees made in the backroom. Although police still raided the bar, the mafia paid-off the police to keep them away. When the police did raid the bar, the same scenario as described in San Francisco occurred at the Stonewall. On June 28, 1969, the patrons there too had had enough. That night the police raided the bar and the drag queens fought back. At one point, the police retreated into the bar and barricaded the front door for their own safety until backup arrived. The riots continued for two nights and protest marches followed with hundreds of gay New Yorkers demanding equal rights and to simply be left alone.

Unlike the riots at the Compton Cafeteria in San Francisco, the press covered the riots at the Stonewall Inn and the riots that followed. The riots drew the attention of LGBT people across the country and a cry for liberation was sounded. The following year, gay liberation marches happened in New York and San Francisco to commemorate the Stonewall riots and to call attention the abuse by police and injustices suffered by the LGBT community. Gay liberation marches turned in theme to gay rights and, today, we call them Gay Pride Parades.

Stonewall will likely always be the moment in history documented as the turning point of the gay rights movement in the United States. It is viewed by many other regions in the world for the same reason. It was the turning point when things began to change ever so slowly, starting with law enforcement backing off of the raids and beatings that had become commonplace. In fact, the San Francisco Police Department was the first to create an LGBT liaison officer back in 1962. Officer Elliott Blackstone made it his personal mission to learn as much as he could about sexual orientation and gender identity. He worked to mend relationships between the police and LGBT people despite the ongoing raids and beatings.

Finally in 1973, following the work of Dr. Kinsey and other psychological and medical researchers, the American Psychological Association removed homosexuality from its diagnostic manual (known as the *The Diagnostic and Statistical Manual of Mental Disorders*, Second Edition) as a mental disorder. No longer could gay, lesbian, or bisexual people be committed to institutions and subjected to corrective treatments. Imagine, one day being considered ill by the medical profession and 24 hours later being considered normal. Of course, public opinion didn't change overnight and the existing sodomy laws were still in place in most states. But this change was huge and set a stage for great change for law enforcement internally and externally.

In the 1970s, state sodomy laws began to be repealed and legislatures began considering consensual sexual acts between anyone to be a matter of privacy. In San Francisco, Sheriff Richard Hongesto and San Francisco Police Chief Charles Gain were the very first to openly recruit gay and lesbian people to be deputy sheriffs and police officers. Both of these progressive leaders realized that San Francisco had a large LGBT population and that law enforcement's relationship with the growing LGBT community was horrible. Women and racial minorities were also making a debut as law enforcement began the very slow process of diversifying its ranks. The existing rank and file was less than accepting of this diversity and for LGBT people that struggle continues today.

The decade following the Stonewall riots was a good one for the LGBT community. Being a non-heterosexual was no longer a mental illness. Engaging in consensual sex other than intercourse with your opposite sex spouse was no longer illegal in many states. Law enforcement was backing away from raids of gay establishments and gay ghettos emerged in every major city. Gay bars became visible and safe for LGBT people to meet one another. Gay bookstores sprung up and offered a place for young LGBT people to learn about themselves, how to come out, and to see themselves in the experiences of others as written in books and magazine articles. Gay liberation was being realized as more LGBT people could be out, visible, and free to live their lives.

One of the most famous gay ghettos was San Francisco's Castro District. The neighborhood, which was once occupied primarily by white Irish Catholics, was being revitalized by gay people who were moving up from the Tenderloin area and from over all parts of the United States as word of this place where gay people could be free to be themselves spread. One of those people who moved to the Castro was Harvey Milk. Harvey opened a camera store on Castro Street and quickly became involved in local community issues. He was instrumental in forming a merchants' association for the newly established gay neighborhood. Harvey was also interested in bettering the lives of gay people and fighting for gay civil rights.

As he became more involved with the local community, Harvey decided to run for a seat on the San Francisco Board of Supervisors. After two failed attempts, Harvey Milk was elected to the Board of Supervisors in 1977 and he became the first openly gay elected official in the country. Among many other issues, Harvey worked to improve relationships between the police and the LGBT community. He was instrumental in moving the police away from bar raids and getting them to respond to more important issues such as the gay bashings that were taking place in and around the Castro.

The year 1978 was another big one for the LGBT community. Harvey Milk gained national notoriety after being sworn into office that January. In preparation for the Gay Pride celebration that year, Harvey and others enlisted the help of a local artist named Gilbert Baker to create a special banner for the parade. Gilbert was not only an artist, but also a flag maker who studied flags and their meanings from around the world. The banner he created was actually a flag with eight colors, each with a specific meaning. Each colored band was hand-dyed and hand-sewn together. Gilbert chose a rainbow of colors to symbolize the diversity of the LGBT community worldwide. The colors appeared in order with the meanings as follows:

- **hot pink** for sex,

- **red** for life,

- **orange** for healing,

- **yellow** for sun,

- **green** for serenity with nature,

- **turquoise** for art,

- **indigo** for harmony, and

- **violet** for spirit.

The flag flew for the first time at San Francisco's Pride celebration that year and became an instant success. Demand for copies of the flag exceeded Gilbert's capacity to produce them. Commercial flag makers couldn't duplicate the pink color, so Gilbert made the decision to eliminate the pink and turquoise bands, resulting in what we know today as the rainbow flag with six colors: red, orange, yellow, green, blue, and violet. This flag has become an international symbol for the LGBT community. Since that time, many other versions of the flag have been created to represent bisexuals, transgender people, and other segments of the LGBT community.

During his short time in office, Harvey also took on the "Brigg's Initiative," which was a proposition put on the ballot by then Senator John Briggs. This initiative would have made it illegal for any public school to employ anyone who was gay or lesbian. Harvey Milk was unabashed and totally courageous, speaking out openly about being gay and confronting all of the stereotypes and misinformation used by Briggs to scare voters into supporting his proposition. Fortunately, Harvey and the campaign were successful in defeating Prop 6. Harvey Milk was seen as a hero and an icon for the LGBT community. There was a sense of hope and promise for the future and what he could bring. It was all very short lived.

When Harvey was elected, a man named Dan White was also elected to the Board of Supervisors the same year. Dan was a former San Francisco Police Officer and a San Francisco Firefighter. White grew jealous of Milk and his ability to get the attention of the media. From the very beginning, Milk had the media's attention, not only because he was the first openly gay man elected to office, but because of his outgoing charismatic personality. White grew disgruntled and resigned from office, but then changed his mind days after. San Francisco Mayor George Moscone denied White's request for reinstatement to the Board of Supervisors and sought a replacement. On November 27, 1978, White concealed a handgun and entered San Francisco City Hall using a non-public entrance in order to bypass the metal detectors. He went first went to the mayor's office and assassinated George Moscone. White then walked across City Hall to Harvey Milk's office and assassinated him, shooting him at close range in the head.

White fled, but was arrested soon after and charged with both murders. He claimed his judgment was impaired by his diet and the fact that he consumed too many sugary foods, like Twinkies. The jury believed him and convicted him of manslaughter instead of the double first-degree murder he was charged with. He received seven years and eight months in prison as his sentence. The night the sentencing was handed down, the LGBT community erupted in marches and protests. Protesters stormed San Francisco City Hall and over-ran the police, who were severely outnumbered. The "White Night Riots" resulted in broken windows and burned police cars as people expressed their anger at the obvious injustice that had been done. White committed suicide shortly after being released from prison.

The 1970s ended not only with the tragic murder of Harvey Milk, but the gay sex revolution was soon to end. In 1981 news of a rare and deadly "gay cancer" appeared in major newspapers across the country. On June 5, 1981, the United States Centers for Disease Control published an article about a rare lung infection that was showing up in young gay men in Los Angeles. Similar cases were found in San Francisco and New York. Within days, reports surfaced about various opportunistic and, to date, very rare infections that were being discovered in gay men. And then the deaths began. By the end of 1981, 121 gay men were dead. Just four years later, over 12,500 people had died from what we now call AIDS (Acquired Immune Deficiency Syndrome).

The United States government, and the rest of society for that matter, were slow to acknowledge the epidemic. Because it was primarily gay men who were dying, many wrote off the deaths to an immoral lifestyle. In the early years of the disease, no one knew exactly how it was transmitted, but everyone knew getting it was a death sentence. There was no test and there was no cure. In 1983, law enforcement training in California prescribed wearing masks and donning gloves before touching someone believed to be gay or who was bleeding. Local governments responded by closing public bathhouses in order to stop the spread of the disease. President Regan was in office at this time and didn't even mention AIDS until seven years after the disease was first identified. Ten years later, over 156,000 people had died from AIDS.

In 1987, motivated by the lack of acknowledgement and response by the government to the AIDS crisis, an organization known as ACT UP (AIDS Coalition to Unleash Power) was born to bring attention to the problem. Once again, the LGBT community was at odds with law enforcement. There were protests, demonstrations, and acts of civil disobedience all intended to draw public and governmental attention to the now hundreds of thousands of people who were dying. Funding for research was slow to come and it wasn't until 1994 that the Federal Food and Drug Administration finally approved a drug called AZT as treatment for AIDS. By then, over 309,000 people were infected with HIV and over 234,000 had already died.

AIDS impacted the ranks for law enforcement too. By the mid-1980s, progressive departments like San Francisco had hired a large number of openly gay men, but of course, there were many more gay men working in law enforcement who were not "out." San Francisco is one of the departments who lost an entire generation of officers to AIDS. It was one of the most significant killers of law enforcement personnel in those years, but one rarely talked about or publicized by law enforcement leaders.

While many states had already repealed their sodomy laws, in 1986, there were still plenty of other states that not only kept them on the books, but enforced them with vigor. Gay people were ready to challenge these laws in court and one of the first ones of this era made it to the United States Supreme Court that year. Bowers vs. Hardwick was a case involving two gay men who were arrested in their private home while engaging in consensual sodomy, a felony crime in the state of Georgia. The plaintiff, Michael Hardwick, asserted that the Georgia sodomy law violated their constitutional right to privacy and free association. The United States Supreme Court disagreed in a 5 to 4 vote and upheld Georgia's law.

This case was considered a major defeat for LGBT people, but was adjudicated right in the middle of the AIDS crisis and well before any solid treatment for this disease had been identified. Of course the Supreme Court didn't cite AIDS as any part of the reason for their decision, but they simply said that the United States Constitution does not guarantee any right to commit sodomy.

By the start of the last decade of the 20th century, ACT UP and others had finally motivated the government to start heavily funding AIDS research. The disease had started to impact people outside of the gay male community as well. A young hemophiliac named Ryan White died and the famous basketball player, Earvin "Magic" Johnson, came out publically as being HIV positive. Science discovered how HIV was transmitted and massive education campaigns were underway. The number of deaths began to slow and fear receded. The LGBT community was bouncing back, but it would never be the same as it was in the 1970s.

Gay Pride Parades continued to highlight the demand for equal rights and issues such as employment protection and even gay marriage. There was also a demand for hate crimes laws to be expanded to include sexual orientation and gender identity. LGBT people were regularly "bashed" by thugs who would travel into areas known for being gay neighborhoods to physically assault their victims. In 1996, the FBI recorded 1,256 hate crimes committed in the United States that were motivated by the victim's sexual orientation. Many of these crimes were brutally violent, but few caught the media's attention like the one reported on October 7, 1998.

On the evening of October 6, 1998, a 21-year-old college student named Matthew Shepard left a student group meeting at the University of Wyoming and went by himself to the Fireside bar to have a beer. This was a bar frequented by university students and was the kind of place young people would go to hang out and even sing karaoke. Two other 21-year-old males were at the bar, Russell Henderson and Aaron McKinney. Neither had ever met Matt, but both saw him sitting at the bar and made the assumption he was gay simply because of the way he was dressed. Henderson and McKinney approached Matthew and told him they were gay and invited Matt to go and "party" with them. Matthew left the bar willingly with both men, but things changed quickly.

Shortly after driving off, McKinney told Matthew they were not gay. McKinney pulled out a large revolver and started hitting Matthew with it while demanding his wallet. They drove Matthew out to an open area behind the neighborhood where McKinney grew up. Both men tied Matthew to the base of a fence-like structure. McKinney struck Matthew in the head over 20 times, fracturing his skull and rendering him unconscious. Both left Matthew there to die.

Eighteen hours later, another young man riding a mountain bike discovered Matthew and called police. Within 24 hours, the world's media was focused on Laramie, Wyoming and questioning the amount of violence and hatred focused on this young gay man. Matthew was still alive, but unconscious when transported to the hospital. Word of his attack spread throughout gay communities worldwide. Vigils sprung up everywhere while police worked diligently to track down his attackers. Both Henderson and McKinney were in custody within 48 hours. Matthew Shepard died five days later with his family at this side.

The murder of Matthew Shepard started a new conversation about hate crimes, LGBT equality, and the effort law enforcement must make to investigate hate crimes. The primary investigators in the Shepard case, now Sheriff David O'Malley and Under-Sheriff Rob Debree, did an outstanding job investigating Matthew's murder. They both became outspoken advocates for expanding federal hate crimes law to include sexual orientation and gender identity. They were among the first law enforcement leaders to step forward and ended up testifying before Congress on the need for hate crimes protection. It took another nine years for what is now known as the "Matthew Shepard-James Byrd Jr. Hate Crimes Prevention Act" to be passed by Congress and signed into law by President Barack Obama.

Hardly a discussion about gay rights goes by without some mention of Matthew Shepard. He became an icon in the LGBT civil rights movement. No matter what your feelings about non-heterosexuality are, there was strong agreement that this kind of brutal violence directed at anyone was unacceptable. But even more than that, Matthew's murder caused mainstream society to think of non-heterosexuals and transgender persons as actual people. By the dawn of the 21st century, attitudes were changing quickly, especially among young people.

By the year 2000, police officers in San Francisco were no longer raiding bars and beating gay people, but instead were marching alongside them in the annual Gay Pride parade. The same scene was being played out in New York, Los Angeles, and many other larger cities. In many states, sexual orientation and gender identity had not only been written into hate crime laws, but also employment law. LGBT people in these states could no longer be fired from their jobs simply because they were gay. The conversation about marriage came up almost every year on Valentines Day with activists who would intentionally go to a city clerk's office to get a marriage license in order to be denied and to call attention to the disparity. And, perhaps based on fear that it could actually happen, state legislatures started passing laws to narrow the definition of marriage to that of a man and woman. Federal law had already been modified back in 1996 by the Federal Defense of Marriage Act. Although laws relating to marriage reside primarily at the state level, several key legislators and President Clinton acted to protect federal recognition of marriage from any change states might make in the future. The Federal Defense of Marriage Act recognized only marriages as between a man and a woman. This act impacted some 1,138 federal rights and obligations related to marriage.

Sodomy laws were still in place, but came before the United States Supreme Court once again in 2003, this time from a case in Texas. John Geddes *Lawrence* and Tyron Garner were arrested in Houston after engaging in consensual sex. Like Bowers 17 years before, they appealed their case all the way to the Supreme Court. This time, the court ruled in favor of privacy and overturned their decision from 1986. On June 26, 20013, the court ruled that consenting adults have a constitutional right to privacy and that sodomy laws regulating the consensual and intimate sexual relationships of adults are unconstitutional. This case, Lawrence v. Texas, became a landmark decision favoring gay civil rights and set a strong legal foundation for LGBT civil rights moving forward.

In 2004, then San Francisco Mayor, Gavin Newsome, decided it was time for change. Newsome declared that denying same-sex couples a marriage license was a violation of the constitution and as a public official who swore an oath to defend the constitution, he could no longer deny same-sex couples a marriage license. Newsome ordered the San Francisco city clerk to immediately begin issuing marriage licenses to same-sex couples. There was a collective uproar on both sides of the marriage aisle. Gay couples from all over traveled to San Francisco for the opportunity to marry while religious leaders and many elected officials called on the courts to stop the weddings. Almost immediately, the California Supreme Court stepped in and ordered the marriages to stop and voided all of the marriages that had already taken place. It was in May that same year when the State of Massachusetts became the first to enact a law permitting same-sex couples to marry. Between Newsome's move to issue licenses despite state law and now Massachusetts legalizing same-sex marriage, it was clear that marriage equality would be the next push in the LGBT civil rights battle. This is when the true battle for marriage equality began.

Almost immediately, two opposing movements happened around the country. Legislatures, primarily in northern states, were passing laws permitting civil unions or, in some cases, full marriage equality, while opponents of marriage equality in other states were getting state constitutional amendments passed that would permanently ban same-sex marriage. These voter initiatives passed one after another while the courts began to rule otherwise. In California, the State Supreme Court declared California's state law limiting marriage to one man and one woman unconstitutional. Marriage equality became legal in June of 2008, but opponents saw this decision coming and put Proposition 8 on the ballot the following November. For the first time in our country's history, voters amended the state constitution such that the right to marry was taken away. In all previous cases, amendments were put in place by voters before the right for same-sex couples was even an option. Some 18,000 couples had married during the brief period same-sex marriage was legal in the state.

That following year, film director Rob Reiner assembled a unique legal team comprised of David Boies and Ted Olson to challenge Proposition 8 in federal court. The belief was that Proposition 8 (and theoretically every other ban on same-sex marriage) violated the 14th Amendment's equal protection and due process clause. A full trial on same-sex marriage was held in federal district court in San Francisco. Judge Vaughn Walker ruled that Proposition 8 was indeed unconstitutional and violated the

14th Amendment. The sponsors of Proposition 8 appealed all the way to the United States Supreme Court, losing their case each step of the way. Finally, on June 26, 2013, the US Supreme Court ruled that the sponsors of Proposition 8 had no standing to appear in the first place. This resulted in Judge Walker's ruling being upheld and marriage equality resumed immediately in California.

On that same June 26th, the United States Supreme Court rendered a decision in another case involving same-sex marriage, but this one challenged the Federal Defense of Marriage Act of 1996. The court ruled that the federal government could not discriminate against same-sex couples whose marriages were legal and recognized by a state. This decision was huge because it instantly made available 1,138 rights and obligations for married same-sex couples across the country. It also opened the door for the federal government to provide benefits for federal employees in a same-sex marriage, which were previously not provided.

The Proposition 8 case was of particular importance because the arguments made by Boies and Olson along with the decision written by Judge Walker served as a foundation for more legal challenges across the country that banned same-sex marriage. One by one, over 30 courts ruled these bans unconstitutional and marriage equality quickly became available to the vast majority of same-sex couples in the country. One district court in the South ruled in support of same-sex marriage bans and set into motion an ultimate appeal to the Supreme Court.

In April 2015, the question of same-sex marriage reached the highest court in the land. On June 26, 2015, in a 5 to 4 vote, the United States Supreme Court ruled that same-sex couples have a fundamental right to marriage and that marriage bans violated the 14th Amendment's equal protection and due process clause. Marriage equality became the law of the land across all 50 states.

As you can see, the last week of June has a great amount of historical significance for the LGBT community. It marks the anniversary of the

Stonewall riots as well as three landmark Supreme Court decisions favoring LGBT civil rights, all of which were released by the court on a June 26th. Winning the right to marry is a cornerstone of equality, but it doesn't mean LGBT people have arrived at the same table as heterosexuals. As I write this chapter, it is still legal in 29 states to fire someone for being gay, lesbian, bisexual or transgender. A gay person could get married on a Sunday and be fired the very next day after their boss finds out they are gay. Discrimination in housing based on sexual orientation and gender identity is not currently protected nationwide. It's fair to say that employment and housing are just as important to the security of a family as marriage can be.

So why is marriage equality an important issue for law enforcement? First of all, marriage is a special relationship with legal tenets that provide security for families. Family structures provide security for spouses and children. Without legal marriage, same-sex couples, including those in law enforcement, lack security. An officer who has a same-sex partner and children and who is killed in the line of duty will not have any survivor benefits passed on to the survivors without legal marriage. This is only one very significant example of why marriage matters. In law enforcement, we value family and we rely on our spouses and families for emotional support during those tough times on the job. Legal marriage provides a kind of security and support not available in any other type of relationship.

Employment protection is of equal importance. Our LGBT co-workers deserve the same kind of employment protection as the heterosexual majority. A successful and hardworking officer who happens to be gay should not be able to be fired simply because a police chief doesn't like gay people. Our co-workers should never have to worry about facing discrimination in a community they work so hard to protect as a law enforcement officer. But the reality is that homophobia continues to be pervasive throughout the law enforcement profession.

The University of California's Williams Institute published two studies of law enforcement attitudes and behavior toward LGBT people. The first study published in November 2013 looked at LGBT issues within the law enforcement profession. The study found an overwhelming amount of evidence of homophobia throughout the law enforcement profession. Much of the evidence was based on litigation involving outright discrimination and harassment of LGBT law enforcement employees. A second study was completed in March of 2015. That study looked at relationships between law enforcement and the LGBT external community. This study also offered vast amounts of data showing homophobia to be pervasive throughout law enforcement. These studies make visible the void within law enforcement that exists between laws and policy and behavior. Police in major cities may be marching in Gay Pride Parades today, but attitudes about LGBT don't seem to have changed enough. There is clearly a tremendous amount of work that needs to be done to eliminate homophobia within the profession.

HOMOPHOBIA IN LAW ENFORCEMENT

As far as we have come, as visible as we think we are, there is an ugly truth that we cannot ignore: Homophobia is still pervasive in law enforcement. It is true; we have "out" gay men and women serving as chiefs of police and in all ranks below. LGBT recruits are coming out during the police academy, transgender men and women are coming out and being recognized by their agencies and society for their capabilities and talents. In 2015, a trans-woman was named supervisor of the DC Metro Police LGBT Liaison Unit and San Quentin State Prison in California fielded its first trans-woman in the facility. But the ugly truth is that homophobia continues to be pervasive within the law enforcement profession as evidenced by recent events at San Francisco PD and the UCLA's Williams Institute study published just this month titled, "Discrimination and Harassment by Law Enforcement Officers in the LGBT Community."

The San Francisco Police Department has long been perceived as being one of the most diverse organizations in the country. The department serves one of the most culturally diverse and politically challenging communities in the country. I know from experience that they have been leaders in providing diversity training, in recruiting diverse candidates, and in promoting acceptance and inclusion. And even in an organization like this, evidence of intolerance, bigotry and a perception of racism exists. In this week's news, the department announced the investigation of ten police officers who are accused of exchanging text messages with racist and homophobic language. San Francisco PD's Pride Alliance (the LGBT employees association) condemned the actions of these officers in a press release and demanded a full investigation. An attorney for one of the officers said his client didn't really mean what they said, but that they were "just blowing off steam."

Shouldn't officers be entitled to privacy in their communications with one another? And what about an officer's First Amendment rights? We wouldn't be hearing about this story if it were private citizens involved, right? In my mind, police officers are public officials who are empowered with the responsibility and authority to protect the constitutional rights of all. This responsibility includes providing due process and equal protection of all people in accordance with the 14th Amendment. No, they don't have a right to use or utter racial or homophobic slurs, even when "blowing off steam."

The conversation today about racism and bigotry within law enforcement in this country is lively. I do sincerely believe that the lion's share of law enforcement professionals working the street are hardworking people with a good heart. Unfortunately, the actions of a few end up casting a dark shadow on the many and we don't seem to be able to rid our profession of these unprofessional and unworthy members. What I find most disturbing is that stories like the one above are not isolated and that, despite how far the rest of society has come in its acceptance and understanding of LGBT people, law enforcement continues to be way behind.

In March of 2015, UCLA's Williams Institute released another study on homophobia within law enforcement. You might recall the study they released in the fall of 2013 highlighting homophobia within the law enforcement workplace. This new study looked externally at how law enforcement treats citizen members of the LGBT community, and the results are very similar. Here are the first two paragraphs from the executive summary.

"Discrimination and harassment by law enforcement based on sexual orientation and gender identity is an ongoing and pervasive problem in LGBT communities. Such discrimination impedes effective policing in these communities by breaking down trust, inhibiting communication and preventing officers from effectively protecting and serving the communities they

police. While a patchwork of state, local, and federal laws provides some pro-
tection against certain forms of discrimination, there is no nationwide fed-
eral statute that comprehensively and consistently prohibits discrimination
based on actual or perceived sexual orientation and gender identity.

...Data from a wide range of sources show that such harassment and
discrimination is greatest for LGBT people of color, transgender persons and
youth."

— UCLA Williams Institute, March 2015

Like the report on homophobia within law enforcement published two years ago, this one is just as damning. Both demonstrate that homophobia is a pervasive problem, but this one goes a step further in linking race as an associated problem. The data suggests that racism and homophobia are connected and so I don't believe we can talk about one problem without including the other.

San Francisco Police Chief, Greg Suhr, responded to the allegations against his officers with an appropriately strong statement that included a commitment to fire the offenders if the allegations were proved true. And while this kind of administrative leadership and commitment is important, the damage to community trust has already been done. That damage extends well beyond the borders of San Francisco just as does the damage done from incidents in Ferguson, New York, and every other place where racism is at least perceived to be.

The question now is, what is to be done? As stated already, the fallout is a loss of trust between the police and the citizens they are paid to protect. Trust is something that can be compromised with one action, in just seconds, or with one text message. But trust takes years to rebuild and reclaim; just ask LAPD following the traffic stop in 1991 with Rodney King. The UCLA study suggests that a federal non-discrimination law that includes sexual orientation and gender identity is one way to combat homophobia, but from my experience, laws and policies are really only useful for punishing offenders after the damage has been done. These laws are important, but they don't make people whole after being victimized.

The Williams Institute identified training as being one of the recommendations for remedying this problem. They also recommend that departments reach out to LGBT communities and establish liaisons with this community. In my mind, these are the two most effective ways to change hearts and minds and to build relationships between police and the citizens they serve. Training on differences such as race, sexual orientation, and gender identity need to be ongoing and part of the "perishable skills" inventory of training. Cultural diversity training has never been viewed as being of the same value as officer safety and tactics, but it should. How an officer relates to others who are different is at the heart of this issue and, in my mind, there is a very close correlation between relating effectively and preserving safety.

Homophobia and racism are very much the same thing and originate from ignorance and fear. The prescription for dealing with homophobia in law enforcement remains the same and includes a heavy doses of education and awareness. As LGBT members of law enforcement, we can take an active role in helping our profession evolve by being "out" and by sharing our stories.

We need to evolve the hearts and minds of every law enforcement professional so that, even when "blowing off steam," the utterance of a racial slur or homophobic term never even comes to mind. We need to train, constantly, our officers how to maintain a clear and conscious awareness of the individual biases we all have. When we know our biases, we will always be in a better place to monitor how those biases impact how we see others and how they impact our decision-making with those we come into contact with. This is critical, because the decisions law enforcement officers make every day involve our civil rights and the protection of those rights—a responsibility that is at the core of every law enforcement officer's job.

SECTION II

"CELEBRATING PRIDE: THE PEOPLE, EVENTS AND HISTORY THAT SHAPED MY JOURNEY."

BY GREG MIRAGLIA

We all have a journey in life that is shaped by the people we meet, the events we experience and the history we witness. Sometimes years go by before we realize the real impact of these meetings, relationships, and life experiences and how they contribute to the person we have become. In 1963, I was born into a world, a culture, and a society that considered consensual same-sex sexual behavior a felony crime. Homosexuality was considered a mental illness and cause for commitment to a mental institution where torturous procedures, such as electro-shock therapy and frontal lobotomies, were used to remedy the illness. Every major religion considered same-sex attraction immoral and homosexual sex a grave sin. It was illegal for the federal government to employ a homosexual. Society at large considered gay people perverts and sexual deviants. These beliefs, attitudes, and legal circumstances all shaped the way my family and friends thought about the person I would eventually become. The messages in the media, on the playground, and in the social circles I became part of, all influenced how I would see myself. I began to feel fear and shame about being gay.

"Gay" was never a term of identity I related to until much later in my life. As I look back at my childhood now, without the fear and shame clouding my view, I can see the attractions I had to male friends that were really "crushes." These were similar to what heterosexuals have in elementary school. There was Ricky in third grade, an older boy, who I remember wishing was my brother. Then there was Vince in sixth grade who attracted the eyes of every girl in my class and me as well. I think for most young people, middle school is when sexual attraction begins to bud and grow and it was no different for me.

I remember my first day in seventh grade at Joaquin Moraga Intermediate School in Moraga, California. This was the first year I experienced multiple classes with different teachers. My very first class on that first day was with a teacher named Ray Lippincott who taught social studies. He had a big smile and was a wonderful storyteller as any good history teacher should be. For my last class of the day, I had introduction to drawing with Walter Mast. He was every bit of an artist that you could imagine. His hair was Irish red and he had a mustache that was waxed and curled up around both sides of his mouth. He spoke with a low tone and slow pace and when he got frustrated, I noticed that he would role his blue eyes. He was as stereotypically gay as one could be. There was a group of eighth grade boys in the class who were ruthless in their taunting of Mr. Mast. I knew he was gay, but what I didn't know until decades later is that he and Ray Lippincott were partners and had been together for 40 years until Walt passed away in 2003.

In 1976, there were no "out" gay teachers, no gay-straight alliances, and certainly no other gay students who would even think of coming out. In fact, shortly after meeting Ray and Walt in their classrooms, California State Senator John Briggs launched a campaign to promote Proposition 6, an initiative that would have made it illegal for any public school in California to employ an LGBT person. Had the initiative passed, Ray and Walt would have lost their jobs and any chance of being role models for young students like me. In 2013, I reconnected with Ray and shared with him a copy of my first book. He died a year or so later and before we could ever meet up in person.

Although I didn't know about the incredible relationship shared by my two teachers, it didn't stop me from discovering who I was back in seventh grade. But it was probably in sixth grade that I began to realize that

I was physically attracted to men. It was never a conscious or deliberate choice I made, but rather a strong internal natural feeling that was part of my personality. I've always known that sexual orientation is not something you can choose. It's like hair and eye color. The gender you are attracted to is part of who you are, how you are made, and who you were made to be. To the heterosexuals reading this book who doubt this fact, ask yourself: could you choose which gender to be attracted to, like you would consciously choose an item to eat from a lunch menu?

The names being thrown around on the school playground changed during the seventh and eighth grade from "skinny," "shorty," and "fatso" to "homo," "faggot," "queer," and "you're so gay." I didn't connect my attraction to men to me being gay at that time. I knew being gay was a bad thing and would subject me to daily bouts of ridicule and physical violence. I hated being called a fag and a queer, but almost everyone at school was called a fag or faggot regardless of whether or not they were perceived as such. If you wore an odd item of clothing or did something stupid, the likely feedback you would hear from other kids was, "That is so gay!" I don't think I exhibited stereotypical gay behaviors, but every time I was called a fag or a queer, I felt the negativity and the pain. No matter how hard you try, it's really hard to let "sticks and stones break your bones, but not let names ever hurt you." As I began to realize that I was gay, the force and impact of being called a fag took on an entirely more powerful meaning for me. Every time I heard that name, it reinforced the reality that I could never disclose this part of my life. How did they know? I think kids have the ability to sense weakness and fear in others and in that struggle for social acceptance and status, the kids battling for the top label the weaker kids in an effort to keep them down. It was at this same time in my life that I stepped into the closet and locked the door behind me. Although degrading labels like "fag," "faggot," "queer," and "homo" were commonplace in the school hallways, I never once used them.

My first real teenage crush came in seventh grade on a guy named Ritchy. I knew for sure I couldn't tell him I was attracted to him, so I just tried to get close to him as a friend. Not being honest may have protected my feelings and emotions, but it never really got me anywhere. The purpose of sharing my story in this book is not about exposing my sexual escapades, so I won't go into detail about what I wanted or tried to do with Ritchy. But, just like any other eighth grader with a fresh set of hormones, I was eager to explore. Imagine being back in the eighth grade and having feelings for someone, but not being able to pursue them out of fear of rejection or much worse. When it came time for school dances and other social events where boys were supposed to go with girls, I always found an excuse not to go. Although I knew I could not ask another boy to go with me, I never once considered trying to "fake it" with a girl just for the sake of not missing out on a dance. I didn't attend a single school dance, including my junior or senior proms. It was actually easy because I never got pressure or was questioned by anyone, including my parents, about not participating in these kinds of events.

From the time I can remember, I always wanted to be a teacher. I saw myself in the shoes of just about every elementary and junior high school teacher I had had since kindergarten. In fourth grade, we were told to write a letter to ourselves describing what we would be doing in life at the age of 30. In my letter, I wrote that I would be a school teacher living in Lake Tahoe. Much of that dream came true later in my life, but not without a detour through law enforcement. My dad was a firefighter and had many friends who were in law enforcement. I met several of them over the years and at age 14 was invited to go on a patrol ride-along with one of them. To this day, I can remember every minute of that ride-along. I remember the deep rumbling sound of the 1978 Dodge Monaco patrol car as it accelerated. I remember the first traffic stop, responding to a silent alarm call, and the sound of the dispatcher on the other end of the radio. I knew from the moment I got out of the patrol car at the end of the shift that I wanted to get into law enforcement!

I got a police scanner for my next birthday and listened to it in my room anytime I was at home. I used to leave it on all night even while I slept. Occasionally, I would be awakened by the scanner with the sound of sirens blaring in the background during a high-speed pursuit. I imagined myself both as the dispatcher and as the cop in the field. My dad told me about the police explorer scout program and introduced me to a police dispatcher who worked at the same department that hosted the explorer program. I remember observing in the dispatch center, watching emergency calls come in, listening to the teletype machine click and clack away, and watching the dispatcher work in the center of all the action. I also remember attending my first meeting of the police explorers. I was still 14 years old, but you had to be 15 in order to join. Every one of the mostly male group was between 16 and 20 years old. The officer and advisor for the group was a motorcycle officer. I remember meeting him as he walked into the run-down portable building used for shift briefings, meetings, and also as a locker room (there were no female officers at the time). He had a great welcoming smile and made me feel right at home. On my 15th birthday, I put on for the first time my new and freshly pressed police explorer uniform. We had an assignment that day to go out and canvas a neighborhood with fliers about the "east bay area rapist" who had recently attacked a woman in the region. I was so jazzed to be part of this "big operation."

As I mentioned at the start of my story, I believe that the history we witness often influences our lives in very significant ways. While I don't have any recollection of when the American Psychological Association removed homosexuality from its list of mental illnesses in 1973, I do remember when Harvey Milk was elected to the San Francisco Board of Supervisors and became the first openly gay man to be elected to public office in 1978. I remember distinctly the news coverage and the general criticism of the City of San Francisco for being so openly gay. I also remember the news coverage when the President of the Board of Supervisors Diane Feinstein announced to the world that Supervisor Harvey Milk and Mayor George Moscone had been shot and killed in City Hall and that the suspect was former Supervisor Dan White. The fact that White was a former police officer and that he received such a light sentence for murdering a gay man communicated to me that society simply didn't value gay people as they did straight people.

That same year, I started my freshman year at Campolindo High School. Students from several junior high schools merged together to form our freshman class, so there were many new faces and a lot of kids who were trying to figure out who they were and what they would become. It was also the same year that the guys with stereotypical feminine behaviors became more obvious and were permanently labeled as "faggots." They were often the target of name-calling, a friendly punch, an extended leg intended to trip, or degrading graffiti on their lockers. Fortunately, for my own ego, I was spared from most of that ridicule. I spent most of my time in the marching band and found acceptance there. I befriended a junior in the band named Sean who happened to be one of the trumpet players. It was not at all a likely friendship, but I thought he was very good looking and a pretty nice guy. I spent many Saturday afternoons with Sean talking about the band and listening to his sexual encounters with various girls on campus. Sean was the first guy to offer me marijuana to smoke. Although tempted, I turned him down and settled for watching him get high. I remember him telling me the graphic details of a time when he had sex with a girl in a house that was under construction. I also remember having to be careful not to show him how excited I was to hear of his exploits. The reality was that none of the guys I was attracted to ever knew of the attraction and few of these friendships ended up ever being very real.

High school was a fun time, but only because of weekends I would spend working as a police explorer at the department, doing ride-alongs, helping out in the booking room, or sitting in the dispatch center helping out however I could. My ideas about gays not being accepted in law enforcement were reinforced daily by the comments I heard from my peers as well as from the officers. There was a gay bar in the city I worked in and periodically I would hear officers talking about the faggots they had to deal with at this bar. I'd never been in a bar of any kind before, but I was always curious about what went on in that gay bar.

I also had a part-time paid job as a janitor for the local school district. I cleaned the district office building, which was located across the street from the post office. It was sometime during this period of my life that I first discovered gay porn. By the age of 16, I had a post office box and a steady stream of the latest gay adult movies on VHS tape. I saved up my money and bought a VCR, a new piece of technology at the time, selling for $1,000. I had a stash of tapes from George Higgins and Catalina Video that would rival most adult theaters. It was through watching these tapes that I learned about gay sex. Now I'm sure that if my parents understood what was really going on, they would have made a gallant effort to teach me about the male birds and male bees in a more appropriate way.

The reality at the time, and in most cases still today, is that the sex education provided by schools doesn't include enough about same-sex attraction or behavior. In seventh and eighth grade when Ruth and Peggy taught sex education to us, they couldn't even mention homosexuality. Society still considered it immoral and a perversion. It simply wasn't acceptable for children to have or express a same-sex attraction, so therefore it wasn't necessary to talk about. The absence of information along with what I heard and what I saw around me reinforced the idea that my attractions and orientation were wrong. How different it would have been for me to hear from Ruth or Peggy that is okay for boys to like boys and for girls to like girls.

Junior prom and senior prom came and went and no one ever questioned why I didn't want to go, because I was always involved working at the police department every weekend. My parents did try to dissuade me from law enforcement one time. They had a good friend of my dad's, who worked as a state drug enforcement officer, come to talk to me about how dangerous law enforcement work was. The plan backfired in a big way. I left dinner that night more excited than ever before with the intent of getting into law enforcement as a career. But how could my parents really complain about having their kid spending Friday and Saturday nights at the police station … on the outside of the jail?

By the spring semester of my senior year, I was already working 40 hours a week for a burglar alarm company in addition to the 16 hours a week at the police department. The combination of the two jobs gave me the perfect excuse for avoiding all of the normal boy-girl social events. I graduated in 1981 sick of high school and ready to move on with my life. I landed a full-time job as a dispatcher my first year out of school at the same police department I worked for as an explorer scout. I can remember the phone call from the captain offering me the job and how excited I was. I was pretty popular with the officers and most of the dispatchers in the department. I had a lot of support through my training program and I quickly proved myself to be one of the best dispatchers on the radio. I worked graveyard shift and went full-time to a community college in the mornings. I buried myself in a very busy schedule and earned my Associates Degree in just two years. This was also the year that I ventured out to explore my sexuality away from the VCR.

One night while working for the alarm company, I was sent to a store called "Bachelor Books." It didn't dawn on me until I pulled up in front of this business that I was about to walk into an adult bookstore for the first time. My heart just about beat its way right out of my chest. I was excited and scared at the same time. I ended up coming back to this store days later in a moment of courage and bought my first gay magazine. I read about an adult theater in San Francisco that featured live dancers. Of course, you had to be 21 to get into this theater, but I already looked to be in my late 20s, so I figured I'd never be questioned … and I was right. It was also in a similar magazine that I found a personal ad for a guy named Marc. Marc was a guy in his late 20s who lived in Oakland and who offered to coach me in the finer aspects of gay sex. He wasn't particularly attractive, but for whatever reason, I felt safe with him. Marc treated me very well and allowed me to experience at my own pace. I saw him maybe a half dozen times over a five-year period and never told him my real name or of my law enforcement connections. I used a fake name and started to develop a cover story to keep my real life protected from any crossover that might give me away as being gay. This was all okay for me and I simply accepted the fact that being gay and being in law enforcement didn't mix at all. I never felt a conflict, hesitation, or disappointment about not being able to be me. I accepted it as a reality and kept moving forward because I truly loved police work.

In 1984, at the age of 21, I completed my academy training and was hired as a reserve police officer. A reserve officer is a part-time peace officer and usually not paid. I worked on the street as a reserve officer 16 to 24 hours a week on top of the 40 hours a week work as a dispatcher. I saved up enough money to buy a townhouse and moved out on my own. I made periodic trips to the movie theater in the city, but never ventured into any of the gay clubs or bars. Imagine being less than one hour from "the Castro" in San Francisco—the "gay Mecca"—and being too afraid of being found out to even go there. I was so afraid of being seen, I wouldn't even drive down Castro Street to look. It was about this same time that the second gay bar opened in the city that I was working for and now lived in. I was so curious about what this club was all about, but I distinctly remember hearing my fellow officers talk about the "flaming faggots" that they saw inside while doing bar checks and responding to calls there. The need to protect my life from mixing with my sexual orientation was again reinforced every time I heard such a comment. It hurt deeply, but I played the part of a "straight cop" perfectly. I invited female co-workers to various work-related events and every time I was working with another officer and we saw a good looking woman, I'd be sure to comment about how "hot" she looked. Of course, what my partner didn't realize was, I was really looking at the "hot" girl's boyfriend. I maintained the perfect cover, complete with a fictitious girlfriend and stories to match any others.

One night while working in a patrol car by myself, I drove through the parking lot of the new gay bar. I found a guy face down and passed out in the bushes. I went to wake him up by rolling him over onto his back. WOW! I recognized him as a guy from my high school and someone I used to be an altar boy with at our church. I smiled to myself and thought, just for a moment, that maybe I could meet up with him or talk to him, or even date him. He was the first guy I knew from my regular life who was gay. I don't know if he recognized me or not, but I gave him a ride to the Denny's Restaurant nearby, sat him down in a booth, and told him to drink coffee until he sobered up. I did leave him my card with a phone number, but never saw or heard from him again.

The excitement I experienced from working patrol on the street was more than I can describe and I got into my share of trouble—in a good way, of course. I did tend to spend more time in the captain's office than even he did, but I learned so much and wouldn't trade even one moment of my celibacy at the time for any of it. There was also an excitement in making some of the best friends of my entire life. Friends who 20 years later I would sit down with over a glass of wine and finally share my most protected secret. By this time, my dad moved in with me and became a roommate while my parents completed their divorce. It was strange having him as a roommate and it certainly limited my social life at home. However, I discovered I really liked living with someone rather than living alone.

After my dad moved out, I looked for a friend to be a roommate and to avoid being alone. There were two friends in particular, both of which became roommates at different times, with whom I developed very close friendships and even fell in love with. One of the many negative and difficult aspects of keeping things separate was that I found myself having sex with guys I never exchanged real names with and falling in love with guys I could never get physically close to or really share my entire self with. It wasn't at all psychologically healthy and certainly never truly fulfilling. But I did experience twice what it's like to be heartbroken with these same two friends. Yes, it is true that you can love a friend regardless of gender, but it is particularly difficult when one is straight and one is gay. The level of love that the two end up sharing is finite. But, as much as I loved them both and as close to them as I felt, I never considered telling either of them about me. In fact, I covered up my sexual orientation with them the same way as I did with everyone else; even through the entire time we were roommates, because I didn't want to take the risk of losing them as a friend. I came to find out later that both friends had their suspicions about me, but not for any reason other than I never had any close relationships with women and because I showed an unusual amount of care for each of them. Through all those years, neither of them said a word about it to me.

Throughout my 20s I was asked to participate in five weddings, including two as the "best man." One of the weddings I was best man for was my father's marriage to his second wife. I was always a bit envious of the relationships my heterosexual friends had and all the celebration and happiness that went along with a wedding ceremony. Each time I tried to see myself in their shoes, I had to remind myself that trying to marry a woman would be a huge lie and would only bring the opposite of what I wanted. I never imagined I would ever get the chance to experience the mutual love and dedication that comes with an intimate relationship.

In 1988, I turned 25 and made a decision to move on from the police department I had grown up in. It was so tough to leave my friends and mentors who were now everything in my life. My new department offered me a promotion, more money, and a chance to really grow in my career. The position I took was to supervise a 9-1-1 emergency dispatch center with a staff of 19 women. I was very successful right away. Two years after being hired, I was promoted to a middle management position with responsibility for overseeing not only the dispatch center, but also the training and personnel unit for the entire department. I managed a staff that included two police sergeants, three police officers, a fire captain, a firefighter, two civilians, and the 19 dispatchers I started with. An entirely different book could be written about all of my experiences over the ten years I was at this department.

One of the things I quickly realized about this new police department is how behind the times they seemed to be in almost every respect. Every day I worked, it was like stepping back in time ten years from what I was used to. The level of professionalism, education, and attitude was very different from my first department. If I had to choose a slang and derogatory term that best described this department's personality, I would have to use the word "redneck," and that isn't a good thing for a department serving a community where Caucasians are in the minority. Racial slurs and ethnic jokes were commonplace even in the chief's office. If there were any gay or lesbian employees, none of them were out and I doubt the environment would ever tolerate an out gay or lesbian employee. In addition to the usual negativity about homosexuals commonly found throughout law enforcement at the time, this department had a large contingent of openly "born-again" Christians. The chief who hired me was one of them. I found him to be much more subtle about his religious values than some of the others, but nevertheless, I've found no other intensity of homosexual bigotry greater than that found in certain factions of Christianity. It exists at a deeply personal and emotional level much deeper than most other types of bigotry.

Of course we all did the requisite sexual harassment training, but it had little or no impact on preventing inappropriate jokes and comments because managers and supervisors from the chief's office down engaged in the same behavior. Because there were no "out" visible lesbian or gay officers, the assumption was that no one could possibly be gay so there was no need to even talk about it. I remember a sergeant who made a comment to a female officer on his squad about her hanging around with all of her "dyke friends." The City settled with the female officer out of court and she left the department. The sergeant was promoted within five years to the position of police captain.

When I was promoted, I was re-assigned to work under one of the three assistant police chiefs. This guy was deeply religious and one of the "born-agains," known for pinching pennies, being unable to make a decision, and frankly, someone who was afraid of his own shadow. We got along fairly well, but I really intimidated him. I knew how to work an issue with him to get the right thing done without him ever realizing what I was up to. One of the sergeants who worked for me had also become a new roommate after leaving his wife. We were very good friends, shared a lot of the same beliefs, and definitely believed in always standing up for what we thought was the right thing to do. Like the other roommates I had, this sergeant also had no idea about my sexual orientation. It wasn't that I never dated men, it was simply that I never brought a date home. I continued to be an expert at playing the part of a "straight cop," and never let the two parts of my life mix. Little did I know, many of my co-workers, especially many of my peers who didn't like me, were starting to get very suspicious behind my back.

And then it happened… I had a conflict with a police lieutenant over a training issue. This lieutenant was the same individual who did my background investigation when I was first hired. Admittedly, I didn't handle the situation in the best way that I could and I was successful in making this lieutenant look like an ass in front of the chief. He was so angry. The next thing I knew, my boss, an assistant chief, called me into his office and told me to shut the door. I could tell from his facial expressions something was wrong. He told me that this same lieutenant had come to him to "express concerns about my lifestyle." He then asked me about all my male roommates and what that was all about. I thought I was going to throw up all over his desk. I could feel my entire body heat up and my face get red. I felt a type of pain, anger and fear all at the same time like no other point in my law enforcement career. I knew exactly what he was implying and I could feel his next question coming; "So, are you gay?" But I never game him the chance. I leaned forward in a very calm and cool voice and said, "You are walking down a very dangerous path with these questions. If you say one more thing about this to me, I will take everything you own … your house, your car … everything. This conversation is over with!"

I got up and walked out of my boss's office and marched directly into the chief's office shutting the door loudly behind me. I told him everything that had just happened and said that I was not going to tolerate it. I could tell he was stunned, but then he said, "Well you know if you are gay it would definitely impact your ability to be a leader in this department." I felt my stomach sink and again felt as if I was going to throw up. I saw my entire law enforcement career about to crumble. He asked me what I wanted him to do. I replied simply, "Don't let it ever happen again." I told him I was leaving and would come back when I was good and ready. I couldn't believe what I just heard from the chief and it hurt so much, especially because, to that point, I had respected him a lot.

I ended up going to our department's employee assistance service and spoke to a psychologist I knew and respected. I told him exactly what had happened, but adamantly denied being gay. I think maybe he knew otherwise, but didn't push me at all. He let me vent and I ended up going back to work the next day. My roommate, the sergeant, was also upset by this incident, but for a different reason. He wasn't as much upset about me being attacked as he was about the inference that if I was gay, he must be gay too and must be involved in some sort of a relationship with me. After all, he did leave his wife to move in with me. It took some time before I got past the idea that "everyone at work was looking at me." I was totally uncomfortable at work and now truly understand how devastating work-place harassment can be. Things did return to normal, at least to my face. What I found out later on was that other managers and supervisors talked about me being gay on a regular basis. One sergeant referred to me as a being a "fucking faggot" to a manager from a neighboring department. I never got used to hearing those words. Ironically, this sergeant's grand-daughter became a student of mine in the police academy many years later after I came out.

The last three years of my time at this department were the worst years of my life to date. I hated my job, didn't like all but three of my peers, and used to get physically ill while driving to work. Each morning, I would have coffee with one of the lieutenants, a friend who would later become chief, and I would start out the conversation with, "This department is so fucked up." He would nod his head and say, "I know, I know…" I didn't have a true social life and I continued to meet guys using different names and never experienced a relationship beyond the superficial level. Once it got too close, I ended it. But personal life aside, I knew it was time for a change and I knew in my heart that I needed to be in the classroom doing what I knew I always wanted to do long before that first patrol ride-along. I needed to be a teacher.

A couple of years before leaving my first department, I started teaching part-time at two police academies; one in the Napa Valley and the other in Pittsburg, California. One of my many mentors got me a two-hour block of instruction on radio procedures. I had always enjoyed training, but there was something about being in a classroom in front of a group that really energized me. All of the negativity and bitterness I felt at the police department seemed so far away when I was teaching. I took on more classes, went to more instructor courses, and started using all of my vacation time to get away and teach. I knew my career at the police department was doomed, so I made a decision to go back to school, finish my degree, and to do whatever it took to get a full-time teaching job at the academy.

Senior instructors I worked with used to joke about having to wait at least two hours after graduation before being able to have sex with the female students. They never said anything about the guys, but somehow I knew it would never be a good thing to date a police academy student. I always wondered in each class if there were any gay students and speculated to myself which ones could be. I was never attracted to uniforms and the power of the job did nothing for me. One day, a male student in a class I was coordinating came forward and complained about another male student who propositioned him in the restroom. I met with the offending student and asked him to tell me what happened. He denied most of it, but he did tell me that he thought I was cute and said that he planned to ask me out some time. I froze for a moment, stuck with two competing desires. I respected my teaching job so much, but I wanted so badly to meet a guy that I could relate to and who could relate to me. The temptation was so great, but I didn't give in. I thanked him for the compliment, but said I wasn't interested. Months after he graduated, I did end up going out with him for a drink and enjoyed the most amazing night at his place. What was disappointing in the morning was finding out that he was living with his boyfriend who happened to be gone for that week. They had been together for many years and he had just cheated on him with me.

In 1998, my dream of becoming a full-time teacher came true and I left the police department I had grown to despise so much. I actually got to say the words I had rehearsed so many times in the shower. "Chief, I quit!" The last three years there certainly destroyed all the good of the first seven, and they almost destroyed me. In my first full-time academy job at the Los Medanos College Public Safety Training Center, I worked directly for the academy director, Gretchen, and had full responsibility for managing the basic police academy program. Gretchen was a new-age academy director well ahead of her time. She was an educator first and a cop second, which, in a training setting, isn't necessarily a bad thing. I thrived in this new job and took every chance I could get to be in the classroom. A student in my first class at this academy ended up coming out to me about six years later. I heard a comment or two speculating that he might be gay, but I never believed it. He told me he knew I was gay the moment I walked into the classroom. He told me it wasn't anything I said or did, he just knew. I think there is some truth to the myth about "gaydar." As much as I tried to keep it a secret, many of my students knew all along.

My plan was to stay at this academy forever, but it lasted only a year and a half. I was living in Napa at the time and the Napa Valley Criminal Justice Training Center was looking for an academy director. I put my application in just on the chance that I would at least get an interview. By this time, I had started work on my master's degree, but was still a year away from graduation. I not only got an interview, I got the job. On my last day of work, Gretchen took me out to lunch to give me some "director to director" advice. She told me that I might have some obstacles to overcome. Despite my successful career and reputation as an excellent teacher, she said, "some people have questions about your sexuality." I was stunned and immediately lost my appetite. I know Gretchen wasn't trying to be mean or hurtful. It just felt like an intrusion and a violation of my own personal security. I didn't say anything and she didn't push the question. In the back of my mind, I knew that I would not have been hired in either of these two teaching jobs if I had been "out." Law enforcement just wasn't ready for a gay academy director. Even today, after having been "out" and successful for over ten years, I don't believe in 1999 I would have been hired in such a politically visible position.

I was now in my 30s and still hadn't brought home a nice girl to meet the family. My mom asked me only once when I was going to get married. I used my parents' divorce as an excuse and skirted the question. Friends, of course, would ask all the time if I was dating anyone. I did participate in the sexual story swapping that guys do with each other. I simply changed the gender in my story to fit the company I was with, and I was really good at it. My married friends, especially, used to tell me that they would live vicariously through me since they were no longer able to have wild sex like I was having. It all seemed perfectly all right to lie because I was simply trying to protect my friendships. I was afraid that I would lose my friends if they really knew the truth about me.

The job of academy director is similar to that of a school principal. I hired staff, created and managed curricula, managed a classroom facility, handled student discipline, and provided leadership to a staff of over 100. I was one of only 39 academy directors in California. The academy is located on the Napa Valley College main campus and is part of the college organization. I always felt comfortable at this college and believed it was the place I would retire from. It is here in a place of higher education and learning that my journey of coming out began.

By now, I was hearing periodic rumors and speculation about me being gay coming in from all directions. I was very well respected and no one ever said anything to my face, but I knew what the "word on the street" was. Still I persisted in protecting my true identity. I found out quickly that there are many gay and lesbian employees who work and teach on the campus. My fear of coming out was all centered on how my law enforcement colleagues would view me. The academy director job is somewhat political and coming out was definitely something I feared could impair my ability to lead our organization. A year or so into my tenure, a local police chief was forced to come out after rumors began to run wild about him. There was lots of press coverage and exposure that I'm sure was very difficult for him to deal with. I never wanted that to ever happen to me and the fear of being forced out made me even more protective of my true self. My love for teaching continued to outweigh the importance of my own personal happiness and, after 20 plus years, I still wasn't willing to let the cat out of the bag.

In 2000, I was hired as the deputy police chief for a small railroad police department. I was once again out on the street driving a black and white and loving every minute of working patrol. I really think working patrol is the best job in law enforcement. It is truly and literally where the rubber meets the road. Railroads are unusual organizations. The one I worked for is very unusual because it operates the "Wine Train," which offers a gourmet dining experience on a passenger train. One of the first days I was doing a walk-through of a passenger train, one of the female staff members I used to joke around with told me that one of the other wait-resses on the train was asking her earlier that day if I was gay. I immediately felt sick to my stomach, but in the same moment asked myself, "How in the hell could she have come up with that?" I had only talked with this waitress a few times. It must have been another case of natural "gaydar." Of course I denied being gay entirely and ended up becoming close friends with this suspecting waitress. She started to fall in love with me and there were times when I had a hard time keeping her an arm's length away. I later learned that I was the second guy she had started to fall for who turned out to be gay. She is still a wonderful and supportive friend.

Like my experience early in law enforcement, I found out quickly that this railroad organization was also very homophobic. I heard the president of railroad operations use the phrase "little faggot" regularly, especially while referring to the executive chef on the train. I remember the executive chef telling me about how he was being teased by another old time railroader for the type of chef pants he was wearing. He complained bitterly to me about being called "fairy" and wanted me to know, as he said, "I ain't no faggot!" The kitchen staff, mostly Spanish speaking with English as a second language, would regularly call each other "fag" and "faggot" all day long. It just didn't make for a welcoming and safe-feeling work environment. No one ever attacked me verbally, probably because of my uniformed status, but I lasted only seven years there before finally deciding to leave so that I could concentrate fully on teaching.

Overall, my time working on the train and in a patrol car for the railroad was an amazing experience. In addition to being a police officer, I was trained to work on board the train. I had always liked trains as a kid, so being able to work as a conductor and engineer on a real one was a "dream come true." It also felt really good to be back in a patrol car and to be able to prove that I could do the job, even as a gay man. Many of our academy graduates went to work in Napa County and it was always an honor to back them up on a car stop and see them on the street putting to use the training we had provided. In 2015, I returned to ride the train as a passenger with my husband Tony. The same executive chef was there. I introduced Tony to him and he greeted us both with a warm hug as if we were family returning home. The railroad has become a regular donor to the Matthew Shepard Foundation and a place that I feel welcome.

The first few years of my tenure at the academy were very busy and, again, I was able to immerse myself in work 50 to 60 hours a week. I was still living alone and had bought a house in the mountains about three hours away. I avoided loneliness by working until I was so tired I couldn't keep my eyes open. My friends and family all knew what my schedule looked like and no one ever questioned why I never had women in my life. But at that time, unbeknownst to me, I was about to start on a personal journey that would lead me out of the closet. The feeling of being lonely was one I dreaded. I began to pray regularly for someone to come into my life to love. The prayer never included coming out, but I was really starting to think about wanting something more to love than just my career.

In January of 2000, I remember sitting at home alone watching MTV and a documentary they produced called "The Anatomy of a Hate Crime." It was a story about the murder of Matthew Shepard. In 1998, when Matthew was murdered, I remember a lot of conversation in gay internet chat rooms about what happened, but never really paid close attention to the case. I watched the documentary and remember breaking down in tears. I was stunned and amazed at the level of violence and hate involved in Matthew's murder. As soon as the documentary was over, I went online and searched for an email address for Matthew's family. I sent a letter to the Matthew Shepard Foundation and talked about what we were doing at the police academy to combat hate crimes. I also praised the documentary and said that I wanted to show it to our students. I received an email back from a film producer who was working with Matthew Shepard's mother, Judy Shepard, on another documentary. He invited me to lunch and six months later, I was in Los Angeles attending a training program presented by Judy Shepard, Brent Scarpo, the producer of a documentary titled, "A Journey to a Hate Free Millennium," and an amazing and beautiful vocalist named Randi Driscoll. I ended up booking all three of these people to speak at Napa Valley College for a community-wide presentation.

This presentation was my debut in the community as a champion for hate crimes education and prevention. I hosted Judy, Randi, and Brent for the weekend and began developing a friendship with them that would impact me more than almost any other in my life. Randi Driscoll wrote a song after Matthew's death titled, "What Matters." She donates all of the proceeds from this single to the Matthew Shepard Foundation. The song is about the loss of Matthew Shepard and unconditional love. Randi sang it live during our program at the college. I listened to this song and Randi's words over and over again and found it motivating and very re-assuring. By the end of the weekend, I had made two life-long friends who would prove to play the key role in my coming out.

I stayed in touch with Judy Shepard and the Matthew Shepard Foundation and looked for every opportunity to be involved. A year later, I traveled to Laramie, Wyoming, the place where Matthew Shepard was murdered, and met Chief David O'Malley who was the lead investigator in Matthew's case. He took me to the crime scene and told me as much about the case as we could fit into a weekend. Chief O'Malley was transformed by the murder and is now a champion for hate crimes legislation. He was later elected as Sheriff of Albany County, Wyoming.

I decided to celebrate my 40th birthday by hosting a fund raising dinner for the Matthew Shepard Foundation. I invited 60 of my closest friends and family to dinner and a private concert by Randi Driscoll. Judy Shepard was there and we raised $4,500 that night for the foundation. Even after all of the acceptance and joy that I felt that night, I still hadn't considered even the possibility of being able to come out. In the months that followed, I stayed in close touch with the foundation and was active in teaching hate crimes prevention classes at high schools, junior high schools, community groups, and at the college. I heard Judy Shepard speak at a couple of locally hosted events and I remember her making an appeal to closeted gay and lesbians in the crowd to come out and be role models for the world. I began to think inside about how desperately law enforcement needed good gay and lesbian role models in order to overcome the prevalence of homophobia that I saw in the profession. I was also thinking more and more about growing old alone and how great it would be to truly love and to be loved.

In late 2003, we had an opportunity to grow at the academy significantly by starting a new training program in corrections. Unfortunately, there was no money available for program development, so I made the decision to take on a second full-time assignment as a recruit training officer for one of our academy classes. We would then use the salary savings to hire a corrections expert to develop the program we needed. I had been a recruit training officer for many years while working as a part-time faculty member and got more satisfaction from doing that job than any other I had in law enforcement. I saw this opportunity as a "good excuse" to do something I really loved and to get back into the classroom on a more regular basis. It was unheard of for an academy director to also act as a recruit training officer and it was never in my plans to go back and do this, but is just felt right—like it was meant to be. My staff was not overly enthusiastic about this idea because it meant more work for them as well. Just before our winter break, I worked with my staff to plan this special assignment to begin for an academy class that would start in April. At the last minute, we had to make a change and I had to take on the class starting three months earlier in January 2004.

Usually a return from four weeks off during winter break is a slow process for me. But, this time, with all the anticipation of having my own class of academy cadets, I was fired up and ready to go. The class started out with nothing unusual in sight for me. No one really stood out as being obviously gay and I kept my distance so that the drill instructors could do their work with the class. I hosted study-sessions every Sunday morning that were open to everyone in the class to help them prepare for the written exams that were scheduled almost every Monday morning. It was a good time for casual exchanges and some humor away from the regimen of drill and ceremony. During the fifth week of the academy, I presented my usual hate crimes class that included a detailed overview of the Matthew Shepard murder case. There was a student in the class named Martin who showed a lot of interest in this topic. Martin was an "all American" looking kid with short blond hair and a friendly smile. He was generally very quiet in class, but we talked several times during breaks from class in the days that followed and I began to think that he might be gay. There was something different about Martin that I couldn't put my finger on. One Sunday morning, Martin showed up for a study-session. Martin showed up with his hair spiked into a "faux-hawk," with earrings in both ears, and wearing a black and silver studded belt. Now I knew: he had to be gay.

I've always maintained an approachable, but professional relationship with my students. Many great friendships develop out of the classroom, but while in school, I know that a distance has to be maintained.

Like before, I again experienced a tremendous internal conflict between wanting desperately to find another guy to connect with and protecting my secret. I thought about approaching Martin to see if he would come out to me and thought about what it would be like to come out to him; to finally tell someone. It was a crazy thought with so much at risk, but something inside me told me it was all right. I'm a true believer that, in life, everything happens for a reason. I also believe that we are all very much in control of our own fate, but people come into your life for a reason and I knew that Martin had come into mine for an important and good one. I knew that I had taken on this assignment and that my class was switched at the last minute for a purpose. What I had been hoping for, for so long, could be a reality if I simply took a chance and exercised faith in what I believed.

After some sleepless nights, tossing and turning ideas back and forth in my mind, I sent Martin an email suggesting that we seemed to have many experiences in life in common and asked him if he would like to meet up away from class to talk. He agreed right away and we set a time to meet for dinner—March 10, 2004. I was nervous about this meeting in every respect. If it went sideways, I knew that I could easily lose my job. If someone found out that I had met with a student for dinner, it could compromise my ability to be objective and subject me to even more rumors. As I drove to the Applebee's Restaurant, where we had agreed to meet, my heart was pounding uncontrollably. I knew it was wrong and a huge risk to take, but at the same time, I knew it was right for this moment and that it was going to work out just fine.

We sat down and started off with small talk, both of us eagerly waiting for the real conversation to unfold. I found out later that Martin knew all along the purpose of our meeting. In fact, he had a bet with his room-mates at the time that I was going to come out to him that night. I started and said, "So, tell me about your story." Martin told me that he was gay and how he grew up always knowing he was gay. He told me how he arrived at the academy and about what he wanted to do after graduation. Then, it was my turn. I took a deep breath and started to explain that what I was about to tell him, no one had ever heard. I asked him for his confidence and promised him mine. I said for the first time, to anyone, "I'm gay and I've known it my entire life. I've kept it a secret and you are the first person I've ever told." Martin wasn't surprised to hear that I was gay, but he was stunned to find out that he was the first person I ever told. He promised me his confidence and offered his support. My life changed forever that night, and all for the better. Next to telling my parents, coming out to Martin was the hardest thing I've ever done in my life and I had never been more scared of anything than I was that night. Once it was over, I felt more relieved and more free than at any other point in my life. I felt an exhilaration and joy that far surpassed that call from the captain offering me my first job as a dispatcher or that time I told the chief of my second department that I quit.

The rest of the time with this academy class was a rocky road for me as I began to tear away at the wall of separation in my life that I had built over the last 25 years. Martin and I stayed in close contact during the academy, trying not to compromise our professional relationship. Although many rumors about us surfaced during and after the academy, we were never ever romantically involved. Our friendship was growing and he was a tremendous help to me as I began the endless process of coming out. After telling Martin, I didn't tell anyone else for more several months. I decided to go slow and to be strategic about who I told and when I told them.

After graduation, Martin took me to the Castro in San Francisco, because I had never been there before. This area of San Francisco is known as the "gayborhood," because of its many gay bars, gay stores, gay restaurants, and gay people who live there. In the Castro, there is nightlife for gays every night of the week. I was still extremely nervous on this first trip because, other than Martin, I hadn't told a single person about me. I was fearful about someone seeing me there. We parked my car and started walking down the hill to the first bar. All of a sudden, I heard a crash. I looked back to see my truck shaking after just being hit by another car. Martin and I ran back to the truck and saw a cab drive away having just scraped my back bumper. Without even thinking, we got into my truck and went after the cab. At that time, I had emergency lighting in my truck because of my job as deputy chief of the railroad police. I stopped the cab at 16th Street and Noe, right in the heart of the Castro, and confronted the driver. We exchanged information and I let him go all without even thinking about where I was and what I was doing. And then it dawned on me. I was going have to call my chief and let him know about the actions I just took and also explain what I was doing in the gayest part of California. I made the call and told him what had just happened and that I was "in the City." He never asked where and simply congratulated me on catching the suspect. I was very relieved.

One thing I learned early on is that telling each individual friend or family member requires special attention and a customized approach. Martin told me a story about a friend of his who came out to his family over a Thanksgiving dinner. It went something like, "Hey Mom, can you pass the mashed potatoes, oh, and by the way, I'm gay." I laughed so much at the story that from that moment on, between Martin and me, the phrase "passing the mashed potatoes" meant coming out to someone. I also learned that you can't make it a guessing game and you should never tell someone in a group setting. I made that mistake with the very first friend I told. Tom was an officer I worked with at my first department and was a roommate for a brief period of time. I told him on a boating trip with ten other people on board. There was no place to talk and no place for him to react. I had him trying to guess my news for several hours before I finally broke it to him. I learned my lesson with Tom and decided to do it the right way with my friend Mark.

Mark was an instructor at the academy and a very close friend. We would typically get together for dinner and drinks three or more times a month. He is a former Marine whose only experience with gay men was what he saw on television broadcast from the San Francisco Pride Parade. Mark used the phrase "that's so gay" a lot and I wasn't sure how he would respond, but he was a close friend and a good place for me to start. I took him to lunch and decided to tell him the story of how Martin and I met over a bowl of cream of potato soup. I'll never forget the look on his face. After letting the news settle in, he smiled and said, "So dude, I want to know, what's your type?" Mark asked a million questions about being gay and about my experience. Since that day, Mark's entire perspective about homosexuality has been changed. Judy Shepard was right: sharing your personal story is the best way to change hearts and minds. Later that same year, Mark chose to spend his 30th birthday with his wife, Martin and me in San Francisco, partying at gay bars in the Castro.

I had such great success telling Mark, that as soon as we returned from lunch, I told my friend Damien, an instructor at the academy and a long-time friend from my first police department. Damien teaches human relations and community policing for the academy and succeeded me as Napa's academy director. He was with me for the training I attended with Judy Shepard in Los Angeles. Damien thought for a while I might be gay and had been waiting for me to tell him for at least three years. He too was incredibly supportive and wondered only why I hadn't trusted him until now. I began to realize quickly that everyone in my life that I continued to keep in the dark about my life was someone I was lying to. I could no longer lie about having a girlfriend or play the role of the "straight cop." I also knew that I couldn't keep this secret from my family for much longer. If my family was going to find out, I wanted to be sure they heard it from me first.

My sister is five years younger than me. As kids, we were never very close, but since the birth of my nieces, our relationship has grown and I respect her so much for the amazing job she is doing as a parent raising her two kids. I decided that she would be the first family member I would tell. I used the same approach with her, telling the story of how Martin and I met. Martin came down with me to my sister's house and, after one glass of wine, the cat was out of the bag. My sister was so excited and could hardly wait to find me a good man to be with. I suggested that we wait on any match making activity until I told my parents. My mom figured it out without me having to tell her. After meeting Martin and talking to my sister, she knew, but moms always know. She was totally accepting, supportive, and ready for me to find happiness. My sister told my aunt, on my dad's side, for me. My aunt was a school teacher and retired after 30 years in the classroom. I knew that she would be the most open and accepting of me given her vast life experience with people. The real challenge for me was going to be my dad.

Homophobia in the fire department is so much worse than in a police department. My dad has a strong Catholic faith and I was worried that he would not be able to reconcile the conflicts between his faith and me being gay. I was also concerned that he would somehow think it was his fault. I talked with my mom, aunt, and sister about how to approach my dad and none of them could predict how he would react. Although I never liked the popular idea of using a letter to share such personal news, I decided it might be the best approach for him. It would allow me to provide some answers in writing right up front to the many questions I knew he would have. The letter was sincere, concise, and in some places humorous. Some of the things I said in the letter included:

- I've known that I'm gay since junior high school. I've never struggled with it other than being afraid to tell anyone for fear of being rejected or it preventing me from being successful in law enforcement.

- Nothing in my life caused me to be gay. I was born this way and it's always been the way I am. Being gay is not caused by anything and it's clearly not a choice people make.

- I am very happy with my life. I made a conscious choice not to tell anyone because I thought I would be able to keep my family and professional life separate from my life in a relationship. There are huge and obvious limitations with this thinking.

- Being gay isn't a bad thing. I feel very good about who I am. I hope that you will be happy for me too.

- Nothing about me has changed … other than I'm happier than I have ever been and I feel much more at ease. My interests, personality, hobbies, and dreams for the future have not changed at all. I've simply decided to share with you and others close to me something that has always been part of me ... you just never knew for sure.

- My journey through the coming out process really began after meeting Judy Shepard and Randi Driscoll. Judy's message and the words to Randi's song carried me forward. Martin's friendship gave and continues to give me invaluable support. Why come out? Because not coming out feels like lying.

- Don't expect to see rainbow flags or a large banner at the academy with this news. Although it's an important part of who I am, it is a very private and small part of who I am and something I plan to share only with those who are closest to me.

- No, that's not why I don't go to church ... my faith in the Catholic Church has never been stronger. I've prayed for someone like Martin to come into my life for years and believe that my prayers were answered. Being gay has never created a conflict for me with what I know the truth in the Bible to be. Of course, the fact that the Catholic Church has such a high number of gay priests and lesbian nuns helps a little.

- No one should feel guilt. I certainly don't. And I won't accept that from anyone in my life who really cares about me. Love me for who I am and be happy that I can finally be myself and share with you all aspects of my life including who I may love.

- Don't worry about me. Being gay isn't new for me, perhaps only new for you. I'm savvy as to the realities of the world. Fortunately, I'm in a very good place professionally and the law is clearly on my side. Besides, it's trendy these days to be gay.

I also found a book for him to read titled *Is it a Choice?* by Eric Marcus. I sent him a copy and asked him to read the book and to think of it as an "owner's manual" for his gay son. I sent the letter overnight mail because the thought of waiting for a standard delivery was something I couldn't deal with. The next day, I sat waiting for the phone to ring. My dad did finally call and said, "I got the letter. The only thing I regret is that you are not right here so that I could hug you and tell you that I love you." That was all that I needed to hear. I immediately hung up and drove down to his house, which was about an hour away. We hugged and then sat and talked about how I got to this time and place in my life. I told him a little of what I wrote in this book, but not *everything*.

In the months that followed, I continued coming out to close friends and now began my totally open search for someone I could date and hopefully settle down with. Unlike many gay men who come out later in life, having never had an experience with another man, I already had way more than my share of one-night stands. I could now use my real name and share my whole entire life. My life was getting back to normal and friends began to notice that I was more relaxed, more easy going, and happier. I was still not out at work, but I was definitely headed in the right direction, gaining more and more confidence every day. I began using a variety of online services, including "gay.com," to meet people. I went to clubs frequently, but never seemed to find the right crowd in which to meet someone.

That summer, I decided to travel back to Wyoming to visit my friends from the Matthew Shepard Foundation and sit down with each of them to share my story face to face. I told Randi Driscoll and thanked her for writing the song "What Matters." I told her it was her words that inspired me to come out. Chief O'Malley was surprised, but was happier for me than I think even I was. I drove to Casper and told Judy Shepard. I thanked her for telling me how important it is to come out and to be a role model. I also told her that it was Matthew and his story that brought us together as friends and that I owe so much of my journey to him. I often describe Matthew as "the best friend I never knew." Thanks Matt.

The very next winter break, I decided to spend much of my vacation out meeting people. Friends told me that love never comes when you are looking for it, but I wasn't going to waste any time. I dated a number of guys I met, but didn't really click with any of them. I talked regularly with some guys online and quickly discovered my experience coming out late in life was not unique. In fact, I talked with several guys who had been married and who had kids. I met other teachers and even other cops, but never just the right one for me. Almost everyone who I initiated conversation with online had a picture posted. For the first time in my life, I actually posted a real picture of me.

I remember seeing this one guy who I was attracted to. He had a great smile in one of his pictures. I noted that he lived about an hour from me and I started off with the usual, "Hey, what's up?" I did this on several occasions before and he sort of blew me off each time, but I was persistent and eventually found out that he too was a teacher. On the day after Christmas in 2004, I saw him online again and typed, "Hey Tony, what's up?" He typed back and told me that he was just relaxing while enjoying the winter break from school. We typed back and forth a bit more and I finally asked him if he would like to meet up sometime. Tony replied, "Sure, how about dinner tonight?" We met at a restaurant near his house and have been inseparable ever since that night. He told me later he knew there was real potential for something more than a one-night-stand after I served him first the Cesar salad we split at dinner. Who said chivalry is dead? I never knew how happy I could be having someone who is intimately involved in every level in my life. I soon realized how great it felt to look forward to seeing someone special every Wednesday night and on weekends. Tony and I began traveling together and found out that we really enjoyed each other's company but didn't need to be doing everything together all the time.

Tony had been out for about ten years before we met. He had a sense of confidence about him that inspired me. I was still struggling with coming out at work and especially to one of my co-workers. He was a "born-again" Christian with some very strong beliefs about homosexuality. I respected this co-worker very much and we got along very well. I was struggling with the fear of jeopardizing our working relationship if I came out and with continuing a lie that was quickly becoming bigger if I didn't. It was almost a year after meeting Tony that I officially came out at work. I invited Tony to our office Christmas party at a local restaurant. I remember walking up to the front door of the place and feeling almost sick to my stomach. Tony said, "We are going in and you are coming out!" I had never said anything to anyone ahead of time. It wasn't a huge surprise, but there was definitely an uncomfortable moment when we first walked in together. But it became fine and we enjoyed conversation over dinner like everyone else. Tony taught me something about coming out that I discovered to be very true that night: other people will be as uncomfortable with it as you are, but if you are uncomfortable, others will be as well. I left that night felling really great and was set to leave with Tony for Hawaii!

Now, with coming out to my co-workers behind me, I could focus on my special plans for Tony in Hawaii. By this time, we had been seeing each other regularly for just about one year. I knew he was the one I wanted to spend the rest of my life with. Several months before this trip, I had a special ring made just for him that has two emeralds, two diamonds, and two rubies in order of the colors of the Italian flag. Since we are both Italian, I thought this would make the ring extra special. When I had the ring made, I hadn't thought about how or when to give it to him, but I brought it along to Hawaii figuring that I would find the perfect time and place. It was a full moon on our first night on the big island. There was a huge open lawn area above the place we were staying. We took a walk up the hill to look at the full moon and I knew this was the time and place. There are not rules or traditions for gays to ask each other to become life partners. At the time, the idea of being able to marry wasn't even on my radar. I decided to use a traditional heterosexual tradition of getting down on one knee and proposing to Tony and, as I had hoped, he said, "Yes." The rest of the vacation was magical and was something I never dreamed of experiencing.

Over the next year, I began to meet other gay cops, including one who came out during one of our academy classes. I met his partner, who is now also a gay cop who is out, months before. Tony and I became good friends with this couple and had the honor of hosting their engagement to each other. I learned about other former students who came out years after graduating from the academy and who are enjoying very successful careers in their police departments. I had the occasion to help another student who was just coming out after a horrible experience in the military. I learned all about the devastation our country's "don't ask, don't tell" policy has on individuals who serve our country with honor. This guy was forced to lie to his parents, friends, and to everyone close to him until he was finally "outed" by one of his best friends. Despite his distinguished record, the military tossed him out like a criminal all because of who he is. Fortunately, most of my reunions with former students who are gay have been full of positive experiences and even some surprises.

One day a student from seven years before came to the academy to do a recruiting presentation for his department. I remember him because he started his career much like I did as a police explorer with the same department. He was hired as a police officer and sent to our academy by my first department and I remember being proud of his accomplishments. He graduated at the top of his class. I never even considered that he might be gay. On the day he returned, we chatted briefly and he told me how he was thinking about leaving the department for a job at San Francisco PD. San Francisco … why? He told me that he wanted a "big city" experience and that he was tired of everyone at his department being "all up in his business." He added that he was planning to move to the city as well. I told him my story and of my experience as an explorer and shared with him that I had just come out a couple of years ago. To my surprise, he came out to me and told me about his partner. I could tell he was still struggling, but understood every bit of the challenge he faced. I encouraged him to be who he is and to continue on his journey of coming out. To date, it's all gone very well for him. He's enjoying a great career as a field training officer and member of the SWAT team. When he did finally leave his department for San Francisco, he literally got a standing ovation from the chief, captains, and many of his peers as he walked out the back door on his last day of work.

All of these amazing people have become an important part of my life and hopefully I have become an important part of theirs. I've learned that an important part of coming out is building a close and reliable network of gay friends. There is a unique bond between cops already, but finding other cops who are also gay to share stories with and to talk about the challenges of being gay in law enforcement is invaluable.

In the summer of 2006, Tony and I took a cruise to Alaska. Before booking the cruise, we talked about having a family party to celebrate our lives together. We didn't consider having any kind of ceremony, because marriage was not a possibility or even on the horizon for California. We didn't want to present something that would not be real in a legal sense. Sure, we could have had a ceremony of our own and exchanged vows, but it just didn't fit for us. Instead, we decided to forego the party and take a cruise. We set sail from Vancouver, Canada, where anyone can get married. We talked about the idea of getting married there after the cruise, but it wasn't until we were actually on board the ship that our talks became a serious reality. We returned to Vancouver on a Saturday and got married on the roof-top garden of the hotel we were staying in. Two friends we made on the ship served as our witnesses. We got our marriage license and certificate just like anyone else and returned to the United States a married couple, but with a marriage that our own state and the US Federal government would not recognize.

The next summer we followed through with our initial plans for a family party, but we called it what it was—a wedding reception. My good friend Randi Driscoll flew up to attend and to perform that incredible song that lead to my coming out, "What Matters." Tony and I each prepared a slide show of our lives showing the journey that had brought us together. When the slide show ended, I looked back at the friends and family who had come to our wedding reception not knowing what was in store for them. I saw my straight friends, gay friends, and both Tony's and my family, clapping, smiling and loving us unconditionally. What they experienced was probably much the same feeling that they would have at any other wedding reception. It was another very surreal experience that I never imaged would have been possible.

Today I'm often asked how coming out impacted my career. Despite all of my fears, I always answer, "It changed my career in ways I could have never imagined and all for the better." Did people talk about me behind my back? At first, of course they did, but I discovered quickly that the truth isn't nearly as interesting as a rumor. In law enforcement, I think it is hard to let go of a lie someone is perpetuating even if it's about themselves. After the initial "story" that likely went something like, "Hey, did you hear Miraglia is gay?" I started hearing less and less rumors. Frankly, no one ever said a negative word to my face and, if anything, colleagues spoke only in support of my decision to come out.

Tony was the one who first inspired me to write the first edition of *Coming out from behind the Badge.* I had read several books after coming out that included coming out stories from teachers and other professionals, but I couldn't find any examples of positive coming out stories from law enforcement officers. In fact, the two books I did read, with stories of LGBT officers, all contained stories of loss and tragedy, but both of these books were published prior to 1995. It was now more than decade later and times were changing quickly. The experience of sharing my story and seeing the attitudes of my friends and colleagues change was still so fresh in my mind. Tony suggested that I share my story in a book so other LGBT officers across the country might be inspired to come out as well. I wrote my story line by line and then saw it was published for the world to see in the first edition of this book. Talk about an uncontrollable coming out experience!

Unless you are a famous author, no one makes a lot of money selling books, but the wealth of experience and friendships I've earned from sharing my story has changed my life forever. I've had the honor of speaking to LGBT law enforcement groups all over the United States and in Canada. Most notably, I had the honor of speaking to an LGBT federal law enforcement group, facilitated by the FBI, at their first LGBT Pride celebration held in a federal courtroom in San Francisco. A few years later, I was invited to speak at a similar LGBT federal law enforcement Pride celebration held at the Hoover building in Washington DC. This is the same building that 50 years earlier was the place where suspected homosexual federal employees were interrogated and forced to resign from their federal employment. The LGBT law enforcement conferences and these two special events will always be highlights of my career. The release of the first book and all of these speaking invitations reminded me of my passion for activism and gave me the opportunity to become part of the LGBT civil rights movement.

Activism can take many forms and for me it meant making myself visible as a law enforcement professional who happens to be gay. When I first came out, I told my dad in the letter I wrote that being gay was a small part of who I am and that I didn't see myself flying the rainbow flag everywhere. But I've learned since that letter that being gay is a huge and important part of my life and that the rainbow flag is something I'm truly proud of. Attending Gay Pride celebrations became very important to me. Tony and I started marching annually with San Francisco Police Department's Pride Alliance in the annual San Francisco Pride Parade. I'll never forget the feeling of walking out onto Market Street holding Tony's hand while in full uniform and hearing the cheers from the literally million people who lined the parade route. I've made it a goal to bring a new officer to the parade every year to experience this feeling.

Pride has real meaning for me and I'm grateful to be living in a time when these parades are about celebrating who LGBT are more than they are about fighting for basic human rights. In 2014, I was invited to speak at the International LGBT Law Enforcement Conference hosted by the Toronto Police Service. This was in conjunction with the 2014 World Pride

Celebration hosted by the City of Toronto. I can't express enough how well we were treated by Toronto Police and everyone involved in the conference. Canada is truly decades ahead of the United States in its support and acceptance of LGBT people. We rode on the Toronto Police float down the parade route while the department "DJ" played dance music for a crowd that was crazy for the police. The conference presentation was "first class" with no detail overlooked. It was another highlight that I would have never experienced if still in the closet.

Beyond all of the speaking opportunities, nothing has been more rewarding that what coming out has done for me and my work at the academy and the college. In 2000, I created a cross-cultural research project for academy students as part of the mandated cultural diversity training. Students are required to research a culture they are unfamiliar with and to prepare a presentation about that culture for the rest of the academy class. The culture could be based on nationality, race, disability, sexual orientation, or gender identity. The research requires students to conduct at least three face-to-face interviews with members of that culture and to become immersed in the culture. I had been co-teaching cultural diversity and facilitating this project with my good friend Damien, who is now the academy director. This platform provided me with an opportunity to really focus on homophobia along with other forms of bias in the room.

In 2008, I started coming out to academy classes as part of my regular introduction. I'll never forget the first time I did it and how sick to my stomach I felt. Even having been out for four years, standing in front of an academy class and telling students I am gay felt very uncomfortable. As time went on, it began to feel routine. In fact, my introduction sounds like every other instructor's except for when I share who I am married to. I don't say that I'm gay, I'm simply include that I'm married and that my husband's name is Tony and HE is a fifth-grade school teacher. There is usually a pregnant pause of uncertainty and then the questions begin. I think this disclosure is important because, for just the reasons that we offer female instructors and instructors who are different races and nationalities, we also need to present instructors who identify as other than straight. Over the years, I've come to know that there is at least one LGB or T student in every academy class, and these students need to see themselves represented just like everyone else.

Every time a student comes out after the academy is over, I'm reminded how important it is that we have a visible and out gay role model in the classroom. But no one made this clearer to me than a young student named Anthony. His academy class started like any other. I did my introduction, talked a bit about my experience, let students ask questions about my experience and then moved on. Anthony approached me after class that day and asked if he could speak with me. I offered him lunchtime or after school as options. He showed up at my office at lunchtime and sat down. I could tell he was very nervous, more so than a typical first-week academy student. His lip was quivering slightly and I asked if he was okay. I closed the door and asked what was wrong. Anthony told me he is gay and wanted to know if he stood a chance getting hired as a police officer. I told him that in some departments it still might be challenging, but that things were changing quickly in favor of LGBT officers. I asked him how long he had been out and Anthony replied that I was the very first person he had ever told. Now I recognized the fear I was seeing.

I was so humbled that he trusted me, especially given how early into the academy training program he was. Anthony said that he hadn't told anyone else ever in his lifetime and that he planned to wait until after he was hired and off probation to come out. I assured him of my confidentiality and offered my support. He told me later that he never expected to meet an "out" gay officer as a teacher in the academy, but that because I came out as part of my introduction, it gave him a sense of security in the program and hope for success in the future. That's all I needed to hear to know that every time I share my story with a class it has the potential to unlock a closet door. Anthony didn't wait until he was hired to come out. In fact, within four weeks, he came out to his brother and parents. And eight weeks later, he came out to his academy class during his cross-cultural research project. He got a standing ovation and lots of congratulatory hugs of support.

All of this led to creating an optional field trip for interested academy students to San Francisco's Castro neighborhood. This trip includes a walking tour and to sit with a panel of LGBT law enforcement officers. I'm grateful for the team of over 40 officers I now have who are willing to give their own time to share their stories. We sit and the students hear the coming out experiences of officers from around northern California of various ages and rank. The students can ask any question they want. It's an amazing training experience for both panel members and students. And because we do it in the Castro, the students learn about the LGBT community through an immersive experience. The feedback we get is consistently positive and some students have even said the trip is one of the best parts of the academy.

In 2009, I also started hosting an LGBT news radio program on public radio station KRCB in Santa Rosa, California. Becoming a radio personality and hosting my own show has been a joy. This opportunity too has led to me meeting some amazing people, many of who have been instrumental in advancing the LGBT civil rights movement. I remember being on the air the day the United States Supreme Court announced its decisions on California's Proposition 8 and on the Federal Defense of Marriage Act. Everyone at the radio station was elated as the news came in and we shared it on the air with our listeners.

Also in 2009, the media began sharing stories of young LGBT people who were committing suicide in response to years of bullying. This wasn't a new phenomenon, but it was new that the press was paying attention. Much conversation started at Napa Valley College among the faculty about what the college was doing to support our own LGBT students. The fact was we weren't doing anything. I saw a wave of support coming and decided to put forth my own two ideas. The first was to create a Safe

Space program for our campus that included a two-hour LGBT awareness training for participants and signs throughout our campus complete with a rainbow colored triangle and the college logo. I secured approval to build the program and launched it in 2010, hoping that I could eventually get 20 employees to participate. Over 100 signed up during the next two years to complete the training. This led me to my next idea, which was to propose an LGBT Studies Program for our college curriculum.

By the time all of this came to be, we had re-organized and expanded the police academy program. I was now a dean and my former colleague Damien was hired as the academy director. My role as a college dean made me much more visible. More people across the campus were learning about me being gay. In fact, when I became a dean, my supervisor at the time had no idea. Ironically, she also promoted another dean at the same time who she had no idea is a lesbian. I did a good amount of research on LGBT Studies Programs before submitting my proposal formally. I knew that only one other existed at a public college in the nation. I feared pushback and resistance from the faculty. I thought they would question the need for such a program as well as why a former police officer from the police academy would be developing and teaching such a program. I was completely wrong and just the opposite happened: there was some jealousy around me being chosen to develop the program, but in the end, I got 100% support from my faculty colleagues.

In the fall of 2012, I taught the very first Introduction to LGBT Studies course at Napa Valley College. The program ended up being a fully accredited certificate program accepted for transfer by the California UC and CSU system. The first class had 45 students and a waiting list. I distinctly remember the surreal feeling I had that first night of class. I was standing there talking openly about being a gay man working in law enforcement and at the college. The program has since become widely popular. I was also invited to teach the class on a local high school campus for high school students. Never in my wildest dreams did I ever see myself in front of high school students teaching a college class about the LGBT community. Creating and now teaching this program is one of my greatest accomplishments as a teacher and is among the top five programs I'm most proud of. But nothing like this comes without a price.

As comfortable as I have always felt at the college and as visibly welcoming as it claims to be, it is not free from homophobia. The details of what happened are not as important as what I learned from my experience. Like that day, long ago now, when I was called into the assistant chief's office at my second police department and questioned about my sexual orientation, I found myself in situations that felt just as threatening to my job as well as to me personally. At the police department, while I did stand up for myself, I never thought I took a strong enough stand and I certainly didn't walk away from that situation with any kind of pride. In fact, the feeling I was left with was just the opposite. Today, though, is a different story and I learned that I can never again allow anyone to attack me for who I am and get away with it.

Fortunately, we have laws in California that protect employees from harassment and discrimination based on sexual orientation. These laws are in place for a reason, but they can't be exercised if you don't stand up for yourself. Victims of harassment and discrimination often rationalize away their experience for the sake of not making waves or being a complainer. Victims often fear retaliation or further harassment and discrimination. This is exactly what I did years ago and how I have felt on several occasions since then. The difference today is that I am out. I committed myself to holding offenders accountable for their actions and I will never again back down. This too is being a role model for others who face the same kind of experience and I have learned that no matter how inclusive and accepting an organization may seem, homophobia can be brought into the culture by anyone working there.

People have asked how coming out has impacted my life and career. Despite some bumps along the way, my career and my life exploded with opportunity. It's opened up a whole new aspect to my law enforcement and education career that would have never been possible if I was still in the closet. I've met people and witnessed, in a very intimate way, achievements in the LGBT civil rights movement that I never thought possible. I've been able to witness and take part in historic moments, like the one on June 26, 2015, when the United States Supreme Court made marriage equality a reality for the entire United States. Tony and I were in the Castro that day and participated in the celebration on the same street and place where, decades ago, Harvey Milk led protests against the police, the Briggs Initiative, and countless other LGBT civil rights issues. I've received so much more than I think I've given as an activist and it continues to motivate me every day to continue pushing.

As I look ahead at the next phase of my life and my career, I also have to pause to thank all of those people in my past. I am grateful for the events I've experienced and the history I've witnessed that have all made up my journey. Positive or negative, each person and event has shaped who I am today and who I will be in the future. With as far as we have come since 1978 when I started my law enforcement career, my experience has shown me that we have a long way to go. I'm looking forward to moving away from my role as a dean and working full-time to combat homophobia in law enforcement. This includes collecting stories of LGBT law enforcement professionals and sharing them in order to change the hearts and minds of those who still don't understand. Matthew Shepard and his family will always be a big part of my life and I will continue supporting the Matthew Shepard Foundation as long as it exists. I will continue to fly a rainbow flag outside my house with pride because I am truly proud of who I am.

FROM LT. GREG LEMKE, FARGO POLICE DEPARTMENT

I remember that when I was in sixth grade, about 12 years old, I felt *different*. Other boys in my class were talking about having girlfriends and going on dates. I felt no attraction toward girls and, in fact, felt drawn to a couple of my male classmates. I didn't really know why I was attracted to them; I just wanted to be around them and spend time with them.

I did try to have a girlfriend. My best friend had a girlfriend, and I hung around with her best friend, but nothing ever came of it. I went to a Catholic school, and thus it was instilled in me at a young age that being attracted to members of the same sex was a sin. I spent most nights praying the Rosary that my feelings would change and go away so that I would not be sinful.

No matter how hard I prayed, those feelings would not go away. Of course I did not tell anyone about my feelings for fear that I would be disowned by my family and beat to a pulp by the other boys at my school.

My first year at a public school was in ninth grade. It was the worst year of my life. Somehow, the other boys in the school picked up on the fact that I was different and began threatening me and calling me a "faggot." There were four boys, who I still recall by name to this day, who would harass me on a daily basis. They would threaten to beat me up after school, and I would go out different doors every day, hoping to avoid them. They never did beat me up, but they would get in my face, yell, taunt, and follow me.

I never talked to a family member, teacher, counselor, or anyone else, for fear that things would only get worse. The environment was not friendly. Once I went to the high school, things were a little better, as there were a lot more students and it was easy to get lost in the crowd. I still had a lot of fear for my safety. There were more people, but there were also more people who were bullies. My high school years were not very pleasant.

It was during these years that I also had my first sexual contact with another male. It took place with a couple of older neighbor boys and was quite awkward. Of course, it was never acknowledged or spoken of afterwards. During this time, I also began to come to grips with my sexuality and realize what this *different* feeling I was experiencing actually was.

Because I felt scared and left out during these years, I developed a sense of wanting to fight for the underdog, feeling, of course, that I was one. I grew up in a home that was very vocal politically, with strong union Democrats, so as a young teenager I went to work for the George McGovern presidential campaign. I began to think that I wanted to be a politician. I wanted to help the underdog and the little guy. I set my sights on going to college for political science and then becoming a politician so I could help others.

After high school, I planned to attend a local college in the fall. I was working at a local restaurant and befriended several of the girls and was attracted to a few of the guys. A local gay bar opened, and I remember being so excited and afraid at the same time. I spent more time driving around the block prior to entering the bar than the actual time I spent inside. I was very paranoid and afraid. It was a small place, with not many people inside. I hated walking in and seeing everyone in the whole place turn around to see who came in the door. It was nice, though, to have a place to go where I didn't feel so different.

I began to make a few friends and go to a few parties. During this time, I had moved out of my mother's house and into an apartment with a co-worker. He was one of the ones I was attracted to. I also had my first sexual encounter with another man. He was a stranger I had met at the bar, and, in hindsight, it was not a very fulfilling experience. I never saw the guy again.

It was also during this time that a female co-worker and friend told me she had romantic feelings for me, so I felt forced to tell her I was gay. It wasn't long before it was pretty common knowledge at the restaurant, even though I personally only told a handful of people. My roommate and I discussed my orientation and my attraction to him, but he turned out to be straight. He was a very nice guy and not bothered by the conversation, but it was clear there was no chance for a relationship beyond friendship. I became very depressed during this period in my life and contemplated suicide regularly, but only took an overt step once. My attempt was interrupted by a friend knocking on the door and saying she wanted to talk.

While attending college for political science, it became apparent to me that I was not going to graduate and magically become a politician; reality set in. I began to look for something real I could do, and becoming a police officer is something I had thought about since childhood. Two years after I started college, I dropped out and went to a technical college to earn an associate's degree in law enforcement. The school was one hundred miles from home, so I had to move. I roomed with an old co-worker and his friend. We lived like three strangers, and I hated it! I felt the one roommate was a real macho tough guy, and I was terrified that he would find out I was gay. I found myself living in fear once again.

Occasionally, I would travel home on the weekends to go to the gay bar. I started to see a guy regularly, and we dated off and on for about a year, but it never went any further. I began to spend more free time in Minneapolis. It was a gay boy's heaven, or so I thought at this stage of my life. I found myself really feeling like I was connecting to every guy I met and hooked up with at the bar. Obviously they were better at the one-night stands than I was. I would drive home Sunday nights, thinking that I would go back and see this person again and we would live happily ever after. I was so naïve.

My two years of school for law enforcement were very tense and stressful. The two men who were in charge of the program were ex-Marines and ran the school as though it was boot camp. Comments and jokes about queers and fags were made openly and certainly not discouraged. During this time, I also worked part-time at the local shopping mall. I had gotten my left ear pierced when I was 18 and wore the earring when not in class. One day at school, the physical training instructor called me into his office and asked if I wore an earring while working at the mall. I told him I did, and he simply told me not to because people would think I was queer. This made things even worse because I felt I could not even be myself away from school. It was a very lonely time and a real struggle for me to get through. I was basically by myself and would leave town to be able to relax and be myself as much as possible.

Once I finished school, I went to work part-time in a small town in Minnesota as a part-time police officer and ambulance attendant. I liked the people I worked with but was very afraid to let them know I was gay. There was one officer there who I was strongly attracted to. He was the local ladies' man. Once again, this was a lonely existence with few friends and nobody I dared get to close to for fear they would find out my secret and reject me.

After nine months there, I was offered my first full-time law enforcement job in Fergus Falls, Minnesota. What a hell-hole. It was a small town and very unfriendly. I felt that if you were not born there, you had no business being in their town. Most of the officers were elderly and had been there forever. They did not like outsiders and were not afraid to let you know that. I hated working there and can honestly say that I made no friends there; there was nobody I would ever go out with or do anything with away from work.

I spent all of my off days either back home or going to Minneapolis. It was, once again, a very lonely existence. I was having one-night stands, but really searching for that Mr. Right. I thought I had found him on many occasions, only to be let down and heartbroken time and time again. I don't know what kept me going through this time period in my life. It was really horrible, lonely, stressful, and dreary. When I look back, I think it had to be my mom and my two nephews who kept me wanting to live and to move forward.

In 1986, I was hired by the Fargo Police Department. *Finally*, I thought, *back home, to a place where there is a gay bar and more than ten thousand people.* I was so excited and hopeful. What I didn't think about was that now I was back where people knew me and where I was a police officer. I now had to be even more careful when going to the bar. The department was made up of mostly middle-aged, white, straight men, who were not afraid to tell a joke about some minority group or to make fun of you if they felt like it.

I thought this would be the answer for me and that I would meet Mr. Right and settle down. Boy, was I wrong. It was even more stressful, because each day at work, I was afraid someone would say something about having seen me going into the gay bar. I also observed gay people being treated badly by some of our officers, and I heard negative comments about gay people from supervisors. I went further into the closet. I had also gone to a local counselor during this period in an attempt to deal with anxiety and stress. When I told him I was gay, he pulled out his Bible and gave me a list of scriptures that I should read before our next appointment. Needless to say, that was my first and last appointment.

Police departments tend to be close-knit and used to be pretty con-servative and militaristic. Fargo Police Department was no different. I was fearful that I would be outed and have to quit or would lose my job, as there are no protections for GLBT people in the state of North Dakota. My being closeted was affecting my work. I was always tense, on edge, and quick to anger. When I was hired, there was a group of us that started at about the same time. We were all pretty close. There was a group of us that spent a lot of time socializing, and there was always talk of women. Of course, I played along to some extent, feeling terrible for doing so.

Problems started to arise when we began to hang out more regularly. When we became more comfortable with one another, people started asking more personal questions, driving me further away from the group. This caused people to think I was stuck-up and not being friendly. It caused problems for me at work and socially. I really disliked it, but I was afraid to come out, not knowing how it would change things for better or for worse.

I was still heading down to Minneapolis on occasion to go to the bars, and on one of those trips, I finally met Mr. Right. We met at a bar—how clichéd—and have been together for 18 years. Shortly after we met, he moved to Fargo, not knowing anyone but me, and started his life over. When he first moved here, he would ride along with me a lot at work, and that was dangerous. I told people he was my friend, my roommate, or anything else but the truth. That was very hard on both of us. We never went to department functions as a couple, and I quit going altogether. This caused people to think even more that I was not being friendly or that I thought I was better than them.

We functioned like this for several very stressful years. It was tough at work and at home during these times. The gay community here was pretty close-knit and closeted, and if you were not in the in crowd, you couldn't penetrate it and were left out. Those were some very lonely years.

The work environment was terrible, mostly because I was hiding and putting the stress and pressure on myself. I became close friends with one of the officers and his wife. We did a lot of things together socially. These were the first work-related people I came out to. I found out this officer had a sister who was a lesbian, so he did not have any issues or concerns with my being gay. One down! What a relief. I felt as though a small weight had been lifted off my back, but there were still over 100 co-workers who had no idea.

Because of my drive to stand up for the underdog and my political involvement, we decided that I should run for the North Dakota state legislature. If red signifies conservative states, North Dakota is crimson. The Democrats would be moderate Republicans in many other states. I was again terrified that my sexual orientation would be found out and become an issue during the campaign, but fortunately, it never came up as an issue. I was running for one of three spots. There were two strong incumbents and four newcomers, including me. I finished fourth overall and first among the Democrats. It was a good experience, albeit frustrating.

Work was going about the same. I hadn't told anyone else nor had my friend. He said that he had been asked by co-workers and he always said, "I don't know. You should ask him." Nobody ever did. This at least told me that others suspected I was gay, and I thought that would make it easier when the time came to come out.

Two years later, I ran for the state legislature again. I must have enjoyed the punishment. This time, I asked for the support of the Gay and Lesbian Victory Fund. I received a generous donation from them, but one of their stipulations was that I had to acknowledge the donation in all printed ads. I was really afraid of this, so I listed them as "GL Victory Fund" in my ads. What a coward! I ran against the three incumbents and lost again. I realized my political future would not be in the state of North Dakota.

Mark and I had decided to move back to Minnesota, to a more progressive state with actual protections for GLBT people. Prior to this happening, we split up, as Mark continued to struggle with my being closeted and him not being treated as an equal in our relationship. This broke my heart, but it shows how fear can control us. I loved him with all my heart but was willing to lose him so that I could stay in the closet. It was all pretty selfish as I look at it now. We were apart for about six months, and began to talk and visit back and forth as he had returned to the Minneapolis area. We decided to get back together and to buy a house in Moorhead, Minnesota. One of the stipulations was that I had to come out to my family.

I was terrified once again, but also determined. I first told my sister, who is two years older than me. She said she had an idea already. She said that she had gay and lesbian friends and it made no difference to her. One more down, and a good response. I was starting to see a pattern. I told my oldest niece and received the same good reaction. I asked her to tell her mom, my older sister, as I was being a coward again. The reactions continued to be positive, but I was afraid, most of all, of having to tell my mom. My parents divorced when I was very young, and my dad was out of the picture. My mom had always been there for me; she was always supportive, loving, and caring. She was a strong Catholic also, so I feared she would think of me as a sinner.

Telling my mom was probably the hardest thing I had done up to that point in my life. I went to her house one day, intent on telling her. I was there for a couple of hours and never able to say the words. Then came time for me to leave, and out in the driveway, I just blurted out, "I'm gay."

She hugged me, we both cried, and she said, "I know, and it doesn't matter to me. You are my son and I love you." *Wow!* Now a ton of bricks had been lifted off my shoulders, and I felt light as a feather and ready to take on the world.

Well, needless to say, once I returned to work after that, reality set in and I wasn't feeling so brave anymore. There was nobody in a position of leadership at the department who stood up against jokes about minority groups and women. It's sad to say, but they often participated. It was not a safe, welcoming environment. Once Mark moved back to the area, we bought our house and started our family of two collies, Kate and Kirby. Things were good on the home front, but work was still a problem.

I had gone from patrol to teaching DARE in the schools and loving it. It was a positive environment, and I was working on my own. I had very little contact with the other officers. What a relief. During this time period, the Defense of Marriage Act was being enacted in states across the country, and, of course, ND was right there in the front of the line. There was some debate in the area about its passage, and one letter to the editor really got me angry. A person was claiming that he was gay, closeted, and worked for the church. He advocated that all gay people should stay in the closet, because then they would be accepted and could do more good. This made me furious and, in a fit of anger, I fired off a letter to the editor, outing myself. After mailing it, I was not so courageous. I truly hoped they would not print the letter, but, of course, they did.

I tried to control the fallout that I perceived would be coming my way. I took the paper and, at the end of the work day, I laid it on the desk of co-worker and asked her to read it. She was a great lady but also a bit of a gossip, and my hope was that she would pass it on. My drive home from work was 10 to 15 minutes. Before I got home, she called my cell phone to tell me she read it and that it made no difference to her. She passed it on to my sergeant and lieutenant. Mission accomplished.

It was done; I was out of the closet. I didn't sleep too well, not knowing what the reaction would be. Going to work the next day was difficult; I felt like a child going into that big school for the first day. For the most part, people acted as though nothing was new, and that made me wonder if they knew or not. Now I was getting disappointed a little bit since there was little to no reaction from many. The few I heard from at work were very supportive and encouraging. I received calls at home and a few cards from co-workers. I felt good about the reaction but still had some fear about how others would react. I heard secondhand that some of the older, more veteran officers did not take the news so well and they made derogatory comments. None of them were said to my face. I heard that one officer said he would not go around the corner to help me if I was in need of assistance. That is pretty scary in our line of work. It is also one of the reasons some officers are afraid to come out, but certainly not enough reason to stay closeted. Overall, the reaction I received was overwhelmingly positive.

I realized I wasn't giving people enough credit. I was projecting what their thoughts and feelings were toward gay people. I was stereotyping, something I was trying to fight against for the gay community. I went to one of the deputy chiefs to discuss the potential problems I may have in the schools. I was concerned about the "old gay equals pedophile" theory some ignorant people have. He told me that I was well respected and well liked in the schools, and the department would only base my staying in the schools on my work, not my sexual orientation. Once again, I experienced a good reaction and even got support.

I was asked by one officer why I even had to tell people I was gay; why couldn't I just leave it private? I respected him for at least talking to me about it. I told him that he flaunted his heterosexuality all the time with the pictures of his wife with the talk of their trips, telling other people what he and his wife were doing and where they were going. He seemed to understand my feelings when I put it to him that way. I had one other officer—again, who I respect for having the courage to talk with me in a civilized manner—who said he did not agree with my lifestyle and did not want to work with me. I thanked him for his honesty but told him that was his problem, not mine. We have been able to have a good working relationship over the years. (Since I became the GLBT liaison officer for our department, he has sought out my advice regarding his lesbian daughter.)

People became more sensitive around me as far as the off-color jokes were concerned. I did not hear them anymore. I truly think that, for most people, their fear and maybe even disapproval of gay people comes from ignorance. They don't know any out gay people. I think it is so important for gay people to come out of the closet, especially when they are in positions where they can make a difference. Law enforcement is one of them.

While things were going well in the work environment, I decided to try my hand at elected office again, this time in Minnesota. I ran for the city council in Moorhead and have been elected twice. I've served six years so far. My sexual orientation was never an issue discussed at any of the candidate debates nor did I hear any secondhand comments; it was a non-issue.

During my time on the city council, I sponsored a change to our Human Rights Ordinance to include sexual orientation as a protected class. This had been attempted twice before in the city of Moorhead but was unsuccessful. This time, I lined up several supporters to attend the meeting and speak out. There was no opposition; it passed 8–0. Once again, I anticipated the worst and planned for it, only to be met with no opposition. I really started to realize that my sexual orientation is not that big of an issue for most people. For a vocal minority it is, but for the majority of society it isn't. I sometimes get tired of having to educate people all the time. For instance, getting invites to events for city council that are addressed to "Greg Lemke and Spouse." I always say, "Isn't Mark invited?" The response is usually, "Of course he is." I point out that the invitation does not include him, and for a while, things change to "guest" or "significant other." I wonder if I am being too picky, but I think that people need to be reminded to make sure they are inclusive. The police department environment is worse, and I often don't correct their indiscretions as they are too frequent. When I do, the response is usually, "I'm sorry. You are right." People seem to have short memories, though.

The environment at work changed for the positive when the city hired a chief from Michigan. He was very supportive and pro-active regarding minorities and making inclusive policies. He even supported my request for domestic partner benefits from the city. He is now gone, and that battle is still being fought. It took me in excess of five years to get our pension plan changed so that money can be left to someone other than a spouse. Change moves very slowly, but if you are persistent, it can be accomplished.

Our department has seen a lot of change since I started. We have a lot of new, younger, well-educated officers, who seem to be more liberal in their thinking, at least as it pertains to gay people. A couple of years back, the local paper was doing a story on gay and lesbian people in the community, and Mark and I were featured on the front page, in a lengthy story, one Sunday. It was kind of like coming out all over again.

During the course of the story, the reporter and a photographer were following me around at work. Not many people asked what was going on, but those who did seemed pretty quiet after I told them the subject of the story. Several photos were taken and used in the story. There was no way to know which ones would be used, so it was a surprise when completed. I asked a couple of officers if they received any negative comments about having their photos in the paper regarding a story on a gay cop. None of them said they did.

I was really surprised and somewhat disappointed at the lack of any reaction from co-workers. I thought there would be several people who would at least say they read the story, even if they did not comment further. It really showed me that even though people treat me well to my face and seem to at least be tolerant, talking about sexual orientation is still a taboo for many people. It seems that the support, for lack of a better tem, may be wide but does not appear to be very deep.

I have been able to work my way up through the ranks of my department even though I am openly gay. I was promoted to sergeant, and four years later—just this month, in fact—I was promoted to lieutenant. This, to me, is evidence that coming out of the closet in a law enforcement environment does not have to have negative effects on one's career. At my recent promotion ceremony, my partner, Mark, attended, and I was amazed at the number of people who came up to him afterwards and introduced themselves. It really did not appear to make any difference to people that I am gay.

By not staying in the closet, I hope that I have been able to make some positive changes for gay people in our community. I have tried to show that being gay is just one part of the many things that make up the kind of person that I am. Because I was a hard worker and was promoted, I have had the opportunity to try and influence others. I have been able to teach a Sexual Orientation Diversity course to our new recruits and to speak at the local colleges and assist other agencies in developing a GLBT liaison position.

None of this would have happened had I not come out of the closet. I only regret I did not do it sooner. I would strongly suggest that if you are in law enforcement and still in the closet, you take that giant step out. If things don't go well, it means you should not be working at that agency in the first place. I have also found that I have underestimated people time and again, preparing for the worst only to find it wasn't necessary.

Know that there are others out there in your shoes and that things will not get better unless you dare to take the step out. You are not alone. Living in the closet is horrible and it takes its toll on you daily. It can affect the way you interact with the public and, in the long run, your safety. I have no regrets about my decision and hope that I have helped others along the way.

I have tried to live my life guided by a quote from Robert Kennedy, who said, "Some people see things as they are and ask, 'Why?' I dream of things that never were and ask, 'Why not?'" I think we, as gay people, have to dream a lot and ask, "Why not?" a lot. Why don't we have equal rights? Why don't we have the same protections as others? Start asking, "Why not?" Start demanding a place at the table. Don't let fear rule and ruin your life!

FROM AN OFFICER ON THE EAST COAST

When I was first asked to write my story regarding being an openly gay law enforcement officer, I first thought of telling all the stories of discrimination and hate brought on by a straight-male-dominated workforce. In many ways, I wanted to treat those guys like they treated me. I wanted to show the world their intense hate for persons of different sexual orientations. But, as I thought more and more about the pain I endured and those few months of hell I went through, I came back to the conclusion that two wrongs never make a right.

I was once told by a high-ranking official in the North Carolina Highway Patrol that being gay was only a phase I was going through. He said that I was too much of a man's man to be gay. Coming to understand the mindset of the whole gay issue in law enforcement has been a learning experience. I've found that people are more scared of the unknown than they are of the fact that someone they work with is gay. I've enjoyed teaching others that their perception of normal isn't always what they first expected. In the end, I've found great satisfaction in changing the minds of not only my co-workers, but of everyone I have touched in my law enforcement career.

"For you have taken a road less traveled; taken only by a few; hated by many; but admired by most!"

Politics, law enforcement, and religious discrimination were all points of discussion for my friend Kelly and I this evening. Kelly's father was a former state governor. Kelly is currently serving as councilwoman with a local town. Kelly is married to her partner and has become a role model for me. She is someone I deeply respect and admire. Kelly grew up in a conservative family similar to my own. She truly understands the ins and outs of our state politics and of right-wing conservative views. Kelly has been fighting her own urge to come out of the closet. I've been out for over five years now. The following is a bit of a discussion I had with Kelly, while at a local wine bar in downtown Raleigh, about the pros and cons of being gay in American today.

Me: "I don't know. Coming out has its pros and cons. I mean, don't get me wrong, I am sure glad it is over with for me and that I no longer have to deal with hiding my relationships. But, on the other hand, people see you differently and look at you differently, and it is almost shameful at times. Plus, for you it will be a different story, totally different. My family was full of farmers and businessmen, not politicians. You grew up in the spotlight. I grew up working hard and hoping one day to just be able to get out from behind my parents' shadows to make my own life."

Kelly: "Well, first of all, this hate is all brought on by the Southern Baptist agenda to not only excommunicate all the gays, but to exterminate us from American society. Their vote the other day confirmed every belief I have ever had. It all comes back to one thing: hate."

Kelly has always had the utmost class and sophistication. Her style has always impressed me from day one. The person who used to never admit she was gay was now fired up by right-wing conservatives. These are the same people who raised her and helped her become the incredible woman she is today. Now she is trying to fight back by showing that it is possible to be both conservative and gay.

Me: "Exterminate, yeah. Let's kill off all the gays and get rid of them once and for all. Hell, they tried to do that to me when I worked at Fuquay, and they didn't get what they wanted. They would have loved to see me get killed in the line of duty and then would have said, 'See that is why gays don't need to be in law enforcement or the military. They are a risk.' But if I were you, I wouldn't come out, at least not yet. I mean, there needs to be more people like you coming out. That would really help the gay cause in

America. You know what would help the most, well at least for the guys—to have a big-name person, who is very masculine, come out. We need a major league ball player or big-name football player, someone who is still playing, who is big, to just come out."

Kelly: "Well, I am ready to do a press release and get it over with. Show them that even a famous governor's daughter can be gay and fit into mainstream society. On the other hand, I know that will not help my career. So, I will sit back quietly. Rumors are already ramped about me. Just go online, see pictures of my father and me during my campaign for the commissioner's seat, comparing me to Mary Cheney. I mean, come on. I am not anywhere close to Mary Cheney. Plus, my father is long retired, out of the spotlight, and out of any influence on government legislation affecting gay men and women. The worst part is, the gay population is spearheading all the propaganda about my sexuality. They should be the ones supporting me. Instead, they dredge up old quotes from my father. Yeah, he was very outspoken, but he was a great governor and a great man. I could do a lot to help the gay population in this area, but they insist I not be elected."

Me: "I have always said I was too gay to be straight and too straight to be gay, but in the end, I found that there are more of us in the same boat than I have ever thought. There are extremes everywhere, from conservatives to liberals; we just have to find some middle ground. Well, I used to say I wanted to sit back, but then I was forced to deal with it. You will be, too; maybe not this next election, but soon. And when you do—I know you so well—you will do it with style and sophistication, in old Kelly fashion. But believe me, it's hard …

"I started at Fuquay-Varina Police department on January 2, 2001. I remember that day as if it was yesterday. I recall the sick feeling of when your nerves seem to take over your entire body. I remember realizing that the academy was over and now it was time for me to put all of the training I got to work. It just hits you like a freight train, and my training officer didn't make it much better. As a former army drill instructor, he knew how to make a new recruit feel like a piece of shit. He had the reputation of driving off more new hires faster than anyone else. If he knew my biggest weakness, there would have been no way I could have made it through field training.

"I knew I was gay at the early age of 14. I knew I was different and that I wasn't like the other guys. Girls just didn't seem to interest me. As I got older, I found myself forcing myself to date girls and trying so hard to please my family, friends, and others around me. The struggle sent me into a severe depression, which, in turn, took a toll on my studies and social life. After college I went to the police academy. The pain of my sexuality really turned me into someone with low self-confidence. I was in the job I had dreamed of, and I still felt an empty feeling inside. Somehow, deep inside me, I thought becoming a law enforcement officer would make me straight or at least take away the urges I was feeling. It was almost two years before the gay issue came up. I seemed to bond with all the guys I worked with. We became a very cohesive unit. Then it fell apart, with two little words: 'He's gay.' I had two choices: admit I was gay or deny I was gay. After a conversation one night with my best friend, who was also a deputy, I realized admitting I was gay would work much better than living a lie. I decided that the ones who truly cared about me would stand by me. I just didn't know he would be the only one.

"You get that 'oh shit' factor, you know, when you stop a car, and, on the approach to the driver's door, you see a weapon. You call for backup and no one answers. Yeah, the 'oh shit' factor hit quickly! I suddenly realized the true reality of homophobia within law enforcement, and now I was on the receiving end of it."

Kelly: "Well, homophobia is everywhere, from law enforcement to the courtroom to city hall. You remember the nice speech one of our councilmen gave a few years ago, wanting each town in the county to denounce homosexuality and same sex benefits?"

Me: "Oh yeah, I remember. I wrote a nice letter to him the next day. It went something like, 'You know, I give my life daily so you can sleep soundly in your bed at night. Firefighters come to your rescue when you have a fire in your home or place of business, and the gay paramedics come to your rescue when you need medical help. We don't discriminate against straight people; we actually care about everyone. And you know what? We are the best damn officers, paramedics, and firefighters in the city. We live our lives for our community, and our personal lives never interfere. It has to take a back seat just for your safety. Now, sir, if you get rid of us, we can find other cities and towns to take us, and Raleigh will be left unsafe.'"

Kelly: "Well, I see you told him. Maybe you should have told him about one of your fellow councilwomen and asked if he wanted to get rid of her too."

Me: "Ha, ha, now he can't do that. I should have. But they don't think like that. Hate fills their being. They see hate as a way to attack us. We, as a community, need to band together more. Stereotypes hurt us greatly; they always will. We need a great public relations company to change our image. 'The New Gay American' with a picture of a pro football player on it, like some famous quarterback from an NFL team, or a famous major league baseball player. But we both know that will never happen anytime soon, and if it does, it will be long after their careers are over."

Kelly: "Yeah, you kept seeing hate while you worked, didn't you? I mean, it wasn't just one or two incidences, was it?"

Me: "Oh no, it was months of pain and suffering. At one time, I was so depressed, I contemplated suicide; but with the support of my best friend, I found strength. Many times it seemed like no one was there for me, but when I asked for help, someone always showed up. I should have sued the department and the town, and, if it wasn't for my family, I would have. I mean, I was written up consistently, daily I mean, over stupid stuff. One time, I was written up because tires on my patrol car were dirty. Another time, it was for using improper radio traffic. The list goes on. I never did anything that was out of line or against departmental policy. I was a great asset to the department. Their only goal was to get rid of me. And to this day, they still brag about it all the time; they ran the gay boy off. My goal is to one day be their chief and not fire a single one of them. I want to watch them kiss my ass so much, daily, and then kill them with kindness. They think they have won, but we both know how the gay mafia works."

Kelly: "Ha ha! Well, that is why I just can't see myself coming out. You see big stars doing it today, but in most cases, we already knew they were gay. With me, most people don't have a clue. Since my dad has retired, I am out of the limelight for the most part, and I just go about my business. I am just a councilwoman now, nothing big, nothing major, not in the state political ring. So what good would it do me to come out now?"

Me: "I have to say, for a while, I thought, *Why in the world have I done this? All my so-called friends had left me.* I was so alone and scared, and when I walked away from any conversation, I knew they were saying, 'Look at the fag.' I stayed in, and I worked even harder. I got in better shape than anyone else, and I pushed myself to the point where I thought I could not go further. But I did. There are still days when I am at the grocery store and run into people I grew up with. I see them with their kids in their happy lives. I mean, don't get me wrong, I am completely happy, but at the same time, I hate that I couldn't have that too. But it's not a choice. If it was, why in the hell would I chose to go through this living hell?"

Kelly: "Yeah, agreed. But in the end, when all is said and done, you're glad you came out?"

Me: "I am glad it is over with. I am much more self-confident. You have to be, because other cops feed off of any weakness you show. Plus, I got to the point where I was having to lie about who my friends were and why they were all single. At one point, my mom tried to set up a buddy of mine with her best friend's daughter. It gets really hard explaining to your gay friends that your mom is trying to set them up. In the end, life is much simpler. I'm not looking over my shoulder to see who is at the restaurant and who might see me with my gay friends. I feel freedom for the first time in my life. Freedom is a good thing."

Kelly: "Yeah, I know what you mean. In the end, we live our lives for ourselves. At the end of the day, you have to live with your choices and your decisions. Even though this isn't a choice that most people would have, it is something you do have to live with."

Me: "Well, the sad part is that conservative right-wing American Family Association, or whatever you want to call them, says that being gay is a choice, that you are bound for hell, and that you are wrong. How do they know how I feel? Have they been gay for a day? Why can't they read their own words? The Bible says, 'For God so loved the world.' It doesn't say that God so loved the straight world. Their beliefs undermine everything I was ever taught about God's love. They say we have an agenda, Kelly, but I disagree. I believe they are the ones with the agenda and they use us as a part of their agenda to take control of our country. I believe if our founding fathers could see how one form of Christianity has taken hold of our government and how they discriminate and show hate, they would be appalled. History repeats itself. Look at the '60s. The heads of the church were the ones trying to get rid of African Americans. Now it's us; who's next? Who are they going to pick on next?"

Kelly: "In the end, what are we left with? I mean, can you be gay, be normal, and be accepted? Can you just live your life as normally as possible? I want that and my partner wants that."

Me: "I want that too. You know, when I see my friends who I grew up with, I get depressed. When I am with my parents and someone asks them if they have grandkids, I get depressed. All I would like is to meet some great guy, adopt a few kids, buy a house, settle down, and grow old together, like my parents have done. But our society today says no. So we, as a gay community, have to outsmart our strongest opponents. Many gay couples today are going overseas. Adoption rates in countries like Guatemala are going through the roof thanks to gay men and women. We turn around neighborhoods in which most straight people would never want to live. After we fix them up, they run us out; we make this country a better place. Meanwhile, we are attacked daily, and until we become more mainstream, it will continue. But, Kelly, being gay isn't something you can change; hiding it is."

Kelly: "Yeah, well, if it were only that easy."

Me: "I am lucky now. I work for a department that not only supports me, it encourages diversity—not only in the police department, but in the whole town. I have seen guys who ten years ago would have stood up and confessed they would never work with a gay man. Today, they embrace me. In fact, my old sergeant, during a first line supervisor's class, stood up and confessed there was no room in law enforcement for gay men. Today, he would tell you he would rather have a gay officer working for him than a straight one. He knows that I will not back down, I work hard, and I know that if I screw up, I have more to lose than the rest of the guys because I would lose respect. But it takes time, education, and a willingness to be open-minded. I ultimately had to prove myself. You want to know why I spend three hours a day in the gym? It's so I can be the strongest, fastest, and most athletic officer on our force. When you're gay, you need to be the best at what you do. That way, it gives them less to talk about and shows your place in your workforce. Nothing is easy, everything requires work, and life is a journey. Just remember, in the end, when the days are growing to a close, you and your partner are together sitting in the rocking chair reflecting on your life, your accomplishments, and your success, don't regret what you have done. Rather, you should rejoice in it, for you have taken the road less traveled. Never forget my motto."

Kelly: "What is that?"

Me: "I have taken the road less traveled, the road only taken by a few, hated by many, but admired by most. In the end, believe in yourself."

When I first knew I was gay, I was around 14, and the lack of gay role models forced me into a closet filled with deep depression, a lack of self-confidence, and a life of misery. In 2007, we in the gay community still lack good gay role models. We still have far to go for equality and recognition, but it only takes one to change the minds of millions. You could be that person. Working together, we can stop hate, build trust, and form a stronger bond with our straight allies.

It is hard to believe I faced my fears over five years ago. Today I am the happiest I have ever been, meeting great gay men and women, like Kelly, who change my life daily and who continue to influence me and encourage me to strive for my life goals. Sometimes, life seems to be at its worst, and the only way out is through death. But, remember, there will always be someone for you to lean on. Rely on your friends for support. Hundreds of men and women, both in law enforcement and the military, put on that uniform daily to do one thing: protect the lives and property of the American people and the freedoms we enjoy daily. The worst part of it is we protect everyone equally, but we never get the same equal treatment back. Military men and women live their lives in the closet because they love their country and the job they do. They sacrifice any hope for a personal life and are unable to share their true life with anyone. The same is true in law enforcement, where many officers have to hide their own sexuality out of fear of retribution from their co-workers. The time has come, in both the military and law enforcement, to change the attitudes of the administrations. We have to be more accepting and educate the ones we work with. One person can make a difference in society. My advice to anyone is this: read stories from others who have been in similar shoes; talk to them and learn from their mistakes. Don't fear the unknown, because in the end, fear will consume your life, and happiness will never be achieved.

SWEET HOME ALABAMA

My Maw Maw (that's grandmother for all you non-Southern folk) said that I used to dress up like a lawman when I was little. She said that I holstered my cap guns and pinned on my grandfather's badge just to go with her to Otasco. I don't remember these things, but she shows me pictures of it as evidence to corroborate her stories. I guess I was always drawn to it. Aside from a short period in the third grade when I wanted to be an astronaut, the only thing I ever wanted to do was be a police officer. As with all of us who wear a badge, I dodge the question of why I put one on. I usually tell a story of great pay and benefits for someone who dropped out of college, or the whole, "If ya can't beat 'em, join 'em" ruse. Everyone sees these statements for what they are, complete lies, and moves the conversation to safer ground. Usually, it's discussing my boyfriend.

I have absolutely no idea why I am gay. But I do know how the idea of policing crept into my brain. The reason I avoid telling people will be obvious after this story, but the simplest answer would be to say that I am a public servant so that a little redheaded boy on Sanders Street can go to sleep at night.

When I was younger (before I knew what pubic hair was), I saw my aunt fall off of a swing and break her arm. Don't worry, I'm not about to tell you some crybaby story of how seeing that traumatized me. This is more of a ghost story. As I said, she fell from a swing and struck a magnolia tree. The fall broke her arm, and she was screaming for help. My dad and I went to her. Another aunt got to her at about the same time we did. I should have been paying attention to my injured kin, but the arrival of the stranger caught my attention. He came from between the two houses and seemed as out of place as snow in Gulf Shores. He did not break eye contact with me until he knelt next to my aunt. He was dressed in black from his brimmed hat to his shoes, and he carried a bag. Dad was telling someone to call for an ambulance since his brother's wife had a broken arm. I said that there was no need; a doctor was already here (it was his bag that made me think that). I thought that Dad should have known this since the stranger was in whispering distance from him. The look on everyone's face told me told me that I was the only one seeing the man in black. And he smiled at me. He stood and walked away as other relatives ran to the scene (it was a Sunday tradition for the entire family to be together). He returned to the place from whence he had come, and I never saw the stranger again, except for in a few nightmares.

I suffered night terrors as a child. I dreaded sleep because of the unusual amount of nightmares I had. After the incident with the stranger, I had a new fear. My overactive imagination had concocted the notion that the stranger would return for me when everyone else was asleep. I thought that if I was the only one awake, then he would somehow fit me into his bag and take me back with him to wherever it was that he went. There was only one solution to this: my parents had to stay awake until I went to sleep.

This went on for some time until my overworked mother, in bad need of sleep, came in, asking me what I was so afraid of. I told her of the man in black and his plans to steal me as she sat on the foot of the bed that my little brother and I shared. She yawned and pulled back the quilt that we used for a window curtain. She asked me if this stranger was inside the house or out there somewhere. I thought that he must be out there somewhere. She motioned for me to come to the foot of the bed and look out of the window. As I did, she said, "Do you see that police car across the street?" I nodded yes. "Well, he may be asleep, but he has friends who are awake. There are other police cars out there right now. His friends will keep watch over the town until he wakes up and takes their place. The police are always out there, looking out for the monsters. They are always a few of them awake, and they will keep you safe."

I don't have to tell you who became my heroes overnight. I'm sure the midnight tour had no idea of the service that they were providing to a small child and his tired young parents by just being around. Kind of gives new meaning to that phrase we hear every once in a while of "being able to sleep at night."

Mom knew about police. Her father was an Alabama beverage control agent during the days of white lightning. He died when she was eight years old, but she remembered him well and passed on several stories. She also gave me his badge. I plan to pass it to my son when he is old enough. To my knowledge, no one in Dad's family was ever in law enforcement. But he also had respect for the police. I remember a time when an officer passed us and someone made a rude comment about him. My father told me (loud enough for the guy to hear), "Son, only criminals hate the police."

I am proud of the family I came from. My parents married as teenagers a few months after I was already growing in Momma's belly. We were poor, but it seems like everyone was back then. Or maybe we didn't know any rich folks. Momma worked in a store in the bad part of town, until she was robbed at gunpoint. Not long after that, she began working for a television manufacturing plant over in Huntsville, or Huntsvegas, as we like to call it. She worked hard and fulfilled her dreams of being a nurse. She later became the charge nurse of a surgery center. She is a loving, caring woman who has always been devoted to her family. She took to it since her childhood family was cut short by the death of her parents. As I said before, her father passed when she was eight. Her mother died of a brain tumor when she was 18. There were several reversed similarities between her family and Dad's family. Mom's immediate family was three sisters and one brother. Dad was one of three brothers who had one sister. Dad's mom had one sister, who she was close to, and had the same number of children (matching sex and almost age) in a different state. Mom's dad had one brother who lived in another state and had the same amount of children. Confusing? Yes, but I felt the need to share it.

My biggest hero has always been Dad. My dad whipped me more times than I can remember. I needed every one of them. And the one time when I really needed it, he hugged me. But I'll get to that later. Dad taught me the importance of hard work. I remember he worked as a minimum-wage helper for a commercial heating and cooling construction company. He worked during the day and went to school at night. He moved up. It wasn't long before he was a foreman. He told me never to be a yes-man. Hard work was the way to get noticed. My dad left that company as the president (with a six-figure income) to start his own HVAC business. Before he left his old employers, I went to work for him one summer. It was hard work with little respect from the community. I remember stopping at a convenience store on the way home, and a woman wouldn't let me hold the door open for her. I stank and looked like I had been run over by a Mack truck, but dang, she was rude. Knowing that my dad went through all of this every day, for the purpose of providing for his family, made me admire him that much more.

I wanted to make both of my parents happy. So I went to the Baptist church for my mom. It seemed important to her. I actually enjoyed it before hormones started kicking in. God is love. That's what they teach you as a child. Then you start stirring in your pants and God is wrath. And when they told us that the thought was just as bad as the act, I thought, *Well, I'm screwed.*

High school was hard for me. I was noticing the guys and not the girls. I would get so mad at myself for it. I was taught that it wasn't natural to be attracted to guys. I knew better than to try to play football. It would have been way too hard to try to conceal my attraction in the locker room. Nope, couldn't handle that much. My mental state was already a mess; I would go home and fantasize about some hot guy in school and then pray for forgiveness right afterwards. Sunday school taught me to believe that the devil was responsible for this. So I figured I must be possessed by a demon. Thank God I got myself a hobby.

I became a Civil War re-enactor. I grew up with the stories from my great-grandmother of how the Yankees made war with us once. The notion of our country at war with itself seemed strange to me, and it held my interest. Skirmishes had been fought all over town. In fact, it was one of the first cities to be sacked by, as General Lee called them, "those people." I was far from being the only War for Southern Independence nut-job in town. There were several of us. I fit right in.

So I took to this hobby. It became a huge part of me. It helped me avoid my feelings and focus on studying a different time, a time I romanticized. Family legend and the school's history books made it seem like the world made sense back then. I was put under the impression that all Confederate soldiers were riding horses and throwing rocks (you know, an agricultural society didn't have armories) at the invading blue horde. Then I began studying.

I mention all this because I have applied what I have learned to almost every facet of my life. After five years of detailed study of a four-year period in American history, I discovered something. The books that the school provided were full of crap. When the war began, slavery was hardly an issue. The citizens were treated poorly by both governments and the armies were run by drunks or folks addicted to painkillers (excluding a few, of course). A total of 650,000 people died over bad politics. Thanks to Gen. Josiah Gorgas, the C. S. Armies had more weapons than they had people because squabbling leaders rarely sent the weapons where they needed to be, out of spite. Official war reports never matched the descriptions in diaries or the letters home. Knowing that the schoolbooks lied about all that got me wondering what else I might have been lied to about. This caused me to rarely study anything at school. I don't remember ever studying at home either. Somehow I managed to escape high school with an advanced diploma. But before I left school, I met someone.

She had long brown hair and her smile matched her eyes. She was in the lunchroom, and I was in the waiting area for the principal's office. A sheet of glass separated us but we made eye contact, and she smiled at me. Of course, saying that we met is a stretch since it was a small class of 250 seniors. We already knew of each other. We started talking to each other that day. Before I knew it, we were dating and I was falling for her. I had never really been attracted to a girl before. Granted, this was not a physical attraction so much as it was an emotional one, but I thought that was a start. Bringing a girlfriend home, especially a pretty one, would make my parents happy, and I could feel normal.

And life went on. A few months after graduating high school, I was sworn in as a reserve deputy sheriff. I began wearing a badge at the ripe old age of 18. It was a proud day for me, to say the least. My girlfriend had supported me through this, as did my parents. Things had gotten serious between me and my girlfriend, and by the winter of my nineteenth year, we were engaged. She had become my best friend and my lover. We decided to hold off on marriage until we were both finished with college. She was going to school to be an X-ray technician, and I was going for, you guessed it, criminal justice. That same year, I went to work as a county jailer. I was told that it was a necessary evil to becoming a deputy. It was an old jail, built in 1961. Three stories of two hundred cigarette-smoking, foul-mouthed, violent, feet-and-ass-smelling inmates. If I was lucky, there was at least one other jailer on duty with me.

But most of the time, I was by myself. In the two years I worked there, I learned more than the community college could have ever taught me. I learned how to earn the respect of criminals. I learned to be firm but fair and never to be afraid to stomp someone's ass when necessary. It is a fairly small town (about 25,000 souls) so I became familiar with most of our criminal element. I learned their nicknames, knew their families from visitation, knew their enemies, and knew the type of crimes they preferred to commit. I know that the other jailers who read this will understand what I mean.

In the meantime, I was struggling with school. I was in my second year at community college on an academic scholarship. Having the attention span of a gnat, I knew there was no way I would ever finish school. Plus, the shift work at the jail was cutting into class time. One day I left and never came back (except to work part-time as a campus police officer). Do I regret it? No, not really. Maybe someday I will go back, but the thought of sitting through class all day never brightens my spirits.

My wife-to-be kept going to college. She was almost finished when I turned 21. I had decided to leave the sheriff's office and try my luck with the city police force. I was hired the first time I applied. We scheduled the wedding date for a couple of weeks after the completion of the police academy. She was already a practicing X-ray technician. I bought a house in a tiny town just a few miles north of the town we grew up in. For the most part, we were happy.

Four important things happened when I was 21: I got married to the only person I had ever been intimate with; I became a city police officer, working the midnight shift on the side of town where I grew up; I was initiated into the local Mason lodge; and I started watching gay porn. A couple of days after I was of legal age to rent porn, I made the 45-minute drive at least once a week to get it. I found out the place existed by accident. I was working undercover (on loan) for that city's vice unit, attempting to buy all kinds of things while underage. Porn was one of those things. I had picked out the movie to attempt to rent, and I passed the gay section. Blood started flowing, and I didn't need that kind of attention. I averted my eyes and made a mental note to never forget that the place was there. When I got to the counter, the guy looked at me and said, "You ain't 21, are ya, kid?" I answered that I was not and he told me to come back when I was. I did. A lot.

How did I explain to myself that I wasn't gay despite jacking off to gay porn once a week? I told myself that I was bored with straight porn since I did that in real life every day. It was either that or lose the life that

I had built. So I stayed in denial. In the meantime, I was going crazy. And I had developed something of an addiction. I had never met a normal gay person. The only contact I had with homosexuals was in the jail. And I had no desire to be anything like those people. Plus, it interfered with my family plans. The wife and I were trying to get pregnant.

After three years of being together as husband and wife (and mother-in-law), she relented to my constant begging and allowed me to get her fat. Nine months later, our son came home with us. I have a vague notion of what life was like before the little man came around and I can't say that I miss those times. Our son is definitely the best thing that has ever happened to me. But it didn't change me like I thought it would. For some reason, I had it in my head that my demons would go away when I was a father. Looking back now, I know I was slowly losing my mind. And things really didn't get better for a couple of years. Things would get worse before they got better.

My secret was killing me. I let it control me. It seemed to be omnipresent. I knew that if I didn't talk to someone soon, it would devour me completely. Sounds dramatic, I know, but that's how I remember it. So who could I confide in? Not my parents. Dad's opinion of gays was obviously negative. My brother and I rarely got along in those days. Mom raised us as Baptists. The preacher used up at least an hour of sermon time every few months on the evils of homosexuals.

My co-workers were my friends, and they gossiped like women. So my choice had only ever been one person: my best friend, the mother of my child.

We were sitting in my truck, parked in the movie theater parking lot. We had about 20 minutes to kill before the movie started. It was our first outing by ourselves after the little man joined our family. She was making conversation, but my attention, as usual, was drifting. Then she brought up one of her co-workers. She thought he was straight but I thought different. There was a playful argument that ended with her asking, "Well how do you know he's gay?" I replied, "Because I am." Needless to say, we didn't see the movie.

I had fought to continue my existence as a jailer numerous times. A plot on my life had been foiled by a snitch. There were many times I had been a little (or a lot) nervous as a police officer. I had been in numerous armed confrontations and life-or-death struggles. But I can't describe how terrified I was waiting on my wife's response to me telling her that I might be gay.

She didn't run away screaming. She didn't do any screaming, at least not at that time. She was very supportive. Later she would say that she got to meet me again for the first time. She said that she loved the real me, not the fake me. That's not to say that it didn't hurt her. It did. And I will carry that guilt (even with her forgiveness) for the rest of my days.

We tried to stay married. Remember, we had been together since we were 17. Our only sexual experiences had been with each other. So when I was 24, she asked me if I was about to leave her. I told her that I didn't want to cheat on her so that was my only option. She asked me not to leave and gave me permission to try it before I did something rash (her words) like leave before really knowing.

I tried it. I knew right away. I had a huge dilemma after that. I was gay, but I loved my wife. I wanted my family. She did too. We never sought counseling, even though we probably should have. We did things our own way. She allowed me to go do the "gay thing" on the side and then come back home. The conditions that we made changed with our moods, save for one. I was never to develop feelings for a guy. But that happened anyway.

It was after I had decided to stop having gay sex and just have some gay friends. So the idea worked about as well as solar power did. I met a guy and, for once, kept it a secret from my wife. I loved his voice. He didn't dance like a white boy. He played ball, cooked, and the sex was … well, let's just say I was hooked.

I couldn't lie to save my life. My wife found out, and that's when things changed. I had cheated. I betrayed her trust and could never get it back. I saw my family slipping away. What would happen to my son? Where would my wife go? I needed help. I turned to Momma. They said that a momma always knows even if she doesn't say anything. I found out the hard way that they don't know what the hell they are talking about.

Mom didn't have a clue. She cried. She told me that I was going to hell. She made me promise not to tell Dad. She told me that I should pretend to be straight and lie to myself again. I died on the inside when she left that night. That was the day I became suicidal. I had it all planned out. It would look like an accident. No one at work knew that I was depressed. My son would go to college for free and not have to worry about getting teased at school for having a faggot as a father. My wife would live comfortably from my insurance, and my family would never know of my horrible secret. But when the time came, I couldn't do it. There was a picture of my son on my dashboard, and I changed my mind

Time passed along, with the desire to end things. I decided that was pretty damn weak of me. We decided to give our marriage another shot and it failed miserably. Divorce was inevitable. We had been together for so long. To say that it was a painful divorce would be a bit of an understatement. No, I'm not talking about mediations, lawyer fees, and constant squabbling. We had none of that. We used the same lawyer, who put our requests in writing, and a judge stamped it. It was painful in that it was the end of our life together.

During the divorce, I went to talk to my dad. Word of our divorce (and the reason behind it) had started to spread. I knew I'd better get to him before the rumors did. I went there on my lunch break. He was eating supper by himself. Mom was in the kitchen, crying, because she knew what I was there to do. We started with small talk. I don't remember what it was about. He shifted to my son. He asked how he was doing. I said that he was fine but things had changed drastically at home. I couldn't look at him when I spoke. I asked him if he had remembered how I always used to lock myself up in my room and rarely came out after puberty. He said yes, and I could tell he had tensed up. I told him that I was always depressed back then because I was fighting something. With my lips trembling, I said, "I can't fight it anymore. I'm gay."

Before going over there, I had all these preconceived notions of what would happen. I was prepared to take a punch from Dad (but only one). I figured it would be the last time we talked. So when Dad stood up, I braced for impact. I was sitting on the hearth in the living room. He walked over to me and hugged me and told me that he loved me. I cried like a baby.

What followed was a two-hour conversation of Dad asking questions and me answering them to the best of my ability. He wanted to know if I was dating anyone and if he would be able to meet him. He never said one negative thing about it. In fact, he apologized for everything he had ever said about it in the past. He said that he never knew he was poking fun at me or talking bad about me since he had no idea I was gay. He asked if my friends knew, and I said that I hadn't told them yet. His next six words always hang in my head: "Son, I didn't raise no liar." Dad might not have hit me, but he sure did knock some sense in me. And I felt so bad for underestimating him. Turns out, I had underestimated all of my friends.

One by one, I told them. And after the initial shock wore off, they were all pretty accepting. Did I mention that all my friends were cops? I can tell you for a fact that the old saying is true: "Telephone, telegraph, tell-a-cop." The message gets around just as fast. Mom had come around. Her circle of friends thought it was trendy to have a gay son. And she had changed her mind on a few issues. She too accepted it, as did my brother. We have never gotten along better.

My captain called me into his office in about a week's time. I was pretty nervous about it. There are no laws protecting my job in Alabama, so I figured I was going to have to leave law enforcement. He said that he had been defending me against some rumors for a couple of weeks and figured it was time he told me about them. I told him that they weren't rumors; they were the truth. My captain, whose wife helped bring my son into the world, said, "Jason, I've known you since you were a baby. Your family lived across the street from my family. I'm going to keep defending you. It will just be in a different way. Let me know if anyone starts treating you badly because of this." And that was it. I was out of the closet.

Did I keep every friend that I had? No. But the ones I lost were never really my friends to begin with. Were there still bad days? Of course. But the good ones started to outnumber the bad ones. And as for work, nothing really changed. My boyfriend got invitations to the shift parties, and he went with me to eat with other officers and their families. I got promoted to sergeant at the old age of 27. My son is treated like the other children in school and neighborhood kids. My ex-wife and I are still close. We still end our phone calls with, "I love you."

I know there are a ton of horror stories out there. Mine might have gone that way if I had given in to the desire to just give up. But the end of my old life (before coming out) was a happy one. The best way for me to describe it is to say that it is as if a cloud has been lifted and I can now see. It is as if I battled my biggest fear and destroyed my darkest secret. I was finally free from that demon that haunted my youth.

I asked for health

That I might do greater things,

I was given infirmity

That I might do better things.

I asked for riches

That I might be happy,

I was given poverty

That I might be wise.

I asked for power

That I might have praise of men,

127

I was given weakness

That I might feel the need of God.

I asked for all things

That I might enjoy life,

I was given life

That I might enjoy all things.

I got nothing that I asked for

But everything that I hoped for.

Almost despite myself,

My unspoken prayers were answered.

I am, among all men,

Most richly blessed.

--An unknown Confederate soldier

FROM OFFICER JON HENDERSON, MUNCIE, INDIANA

My name is Jon Henderson, and I'm a police officer in Muncie, Indiana. I was not always on the right side of the law, though. I was very selfish as a kid and only really cared about whether or not I would get caught doing something. When I was 19 years old, on the first weekend of the school year at Ball State University in Muncie, I was drinking with some friends at one friend's house. I had drunk a bit kind of quickly and started feeling sick. I felt it coming and didn't think I had time to make it across the house to the bathroom. So I went just outside the living room door and puked in the bushes off the front porch. Well, "po-po" happened to be rolling by as I did this. Needless to say, my three friends and I got arrested (cited and released) for minor consumption of alcohol. At that point, if you had tried to tell me I would want to become a cop, let alone actually be one, I'd have punched you in the mouth. But I think, in a weird way, the experience was one of the better things to happen to me in my life. It forced me to start maturing real quickly. I couldn't afford to get in trouble again. One of the great ironies of the arrest is that after I got out of the academy, my sergeant was the officer who had arrested me. He did not remember it, because we make so many alcohol arrests here.

I first realized I was gay when I was 20 years old. One day, I was riding my bicycle around campus and decided to ride more around town. I ended up riding to this park we had gone to visit for an architecture project. I was an architecture major, and we had a project to design some structures for the area by this park. The architecture program was the reason I went to Ball State. Well, this park has a big soap box derby hill in the middle. I rode my bike up to the top of this hill. At this point, I'd been riding around for two to three hours, so I was getting tired. I decided to rest on a picnic table at the shelter on top of the hill. Next thing I know, some guy pulls up to the shelter, right in front of me. The guy starts trying to make small talk. I was more scared that he might be some homicidal kind of guy than I was concerned he was homosexual. So I tried to play him off without getting him mad. The small talk finally got old for him, and he asked if I was gay. I said, "No." He asked if I was bisexual, and I again replied that I was not. He went on his way at that point, and I saw another car driving up toward the shelter. I wasn't going through that again, so I pedaled back to my dorm as fast as I could. Then I was telling the guys on my floor, "You won't believe it, some gay guy just tried to hit on me!" But after that, on some level, something must have clicked inside my head. Shortly after, I ended up meeting a guy and experimented with him. It was a cheap one-time deal, but at least at that point I realized that being with a man felt right. So, in my mind, that meant I was bisexual at that point. It took another six months before I realized that I was just plain gay.

Kind of like how figuring out I liked men came to me like flipping on a light switch, the same thing happened with my major. I had figured out that architecture wasn't quite what I wanted for a career anymore, but I had no idea what to switch to. I looked through the course book of majors, and when it hit the page that said "criminal justice," it was like someone had just turned on the lights and I saw so clearly. When I was younger, I saw and understood the importance of police work to society, but I thought it was something for someone else to do. Why would I want to deal with the crap they have to deal with? But by this point, I had grown and matured enough that I could finally see myself in that role. While growing up, I was just way too selfish. Once I switched majors to criminal justice, I finally felt like I had a direction in life, and I felt confident about how my future would pan out.

Shortly after figuring out I was gay, I got a campus job as a parking enforcement officer (a.k.a. ticket Nazi). We worked out of the campus police department station. Now, while I was working there, I was not out, but I did take a big chance by wearing this bead necklace that had the rainbow colors in it. I actually wore it to work, which to this days surprises me, because I *really* did not want anyone there to find out I was gay. I guess it was that conflict within myself between wanting to be proud of who I am and wanting to protect myself. I aspired to get onto a police department after graduation and figured if I got found out, I'd never get hired. I didn't really have any problems while working there, for the most part.

At one point, I started hanging out with a couple of the other guys I worked with. They eventually suspected I might be gay. I found this out because of a little set-up stunt they pulled. I was checking my campus email account and saw a message from one of the guys, Jim. In the email he wrote about how he and his girlfriend were having problems and that part of it was that he had these *feelings* and wondered if I understood. Basically, he was setting it up like he was curious about being with a guy. So the next day that I went to work, I was riding with Jim in a van we used while working, and I (kind of taking the bait since I didn't know if he, in the email, was being legit or not) asked him what was up with that email that he sent me. He then tried to play it off. Later in the day, I found out that one of the other guys I had been hanging out with, Shawn, was hiding in the back of the van just to hear what I would say or if I would come out. Well, I did not come out to Jim in the van because he basically blew off the email, and I was smelling a set-up at that point. If he had gone to the point of claiming he really was serious (even if just to get me to say something), I probably would have told him about myself.

On a different day, I was at our office in the police station with the girl, Jennifer, who worked my same hours. She brought up to me that one of the other guys, who worked a later shift, after ours, was telling her that he thought that I must be gay because of my necklace. But what she said after that kind of made me laugh on the inside. Jen told me that after this guy said that, she told him that she did not think I was gay because I didn't act girly at all and that she thought I just wore the necklace because I had a friend who was gay. Jen told him that if he really thought I was gay and really wanted to know if I was, he should just ask me straight up. Jen then asked me if I had any friends who were gay, and I told her I did, which was the truth. So in her mind, that was the answer to the necklace mystery, that I was just wearing it to be supportive of my friends. I was very happy to let her believe that. And the other guy never asked me about it, so maybe that satisfied him too. Perhaps he just did not have the balls or did not care enough about it to ask. He never acted weird around me either, and I was happy with that. So I was able to play off that situation without having to tell any lies. I did not want to have to lie, and I wondered what I would do if I got cornered; would I lie or not? So any time that I could deflect any inquiry by telling a partial truth or by saying something that, while true, was misleading, I was all over it.

The third incident I had while working as a ticket Nazi was one day when I was getting ready to leave at the end of my shift. Shawn was standing by the dispatch room, where I had to turn in my radio for the day. Another parking officer was standing by him. Just as I get to the door to the room they were standing in, I heard the sound of Shawn saying something, though I couldn't hear the words he was saying. Then I heard the other guy (I can't remember his name but he was a Marine) kind of chuckle as he said, "He's queer." And just as quickly, I could see Shawn make a gesture toward the guy as if to say, "Shut up. He's standing right there!" I turned in my radio, and they acted like nothing was wrong, like nothing was up. I went home and I started getting very upset. The next day at work, I went about business as normal for the first half of the shift. I worked from three to seven p.m., and Shawn and Jim worked from five to nine. Normally at five o'clock I would come back to the station to greet Shawn and Jim, and we'd grab a bite to eat at the student center before heading out to ticket cars. Well, this day, I did not come back to the station at five like normal. Shawn got on the radio and asked if I was coming back to the station, and I told him I was just going to stay out there. Shawn then got on the radio and asked me again if I could please return to the station, so I did. Shawn asked me if something was wrong because he could tell I was upset about something. I told him that I was pissed off because he was talking smack about me behind my back to this other parking officer. I told Shawn that I heard him talking to the other guy and that whatever Shawn said to him made him reply that I was queer. Then I told Shawn that I saw him gesture to the other guy to shut up, and that I'd seen Shawn use the same gesture in other situations when he was talking about other people behind their backs. Shawn wouldn't admit to anything, though, and told me that he really did not think I was gay or anything. He tried to say I was totally misconstruing the situation. What makes all of this so funny is that before, he had gone with me and his girlfriend to a mall in Fort Wayne, Indiana (about an hour to the north), and while walking down the hallway, he walked between me and his girlfriend. Shawn was holding his girlfriend's hand and then reached over and grabbed my hand as well. I think he was just trying to see if I would get all "weirded out" or something, or maybe he wanted to see if I liked it, to try to figure out if I was really gay or not. Needless to say, Shawn had a lot of growing up to do. I hear he is now a cop with a nearby police department, but I have not bothered to try to contact him since I became a cop.

I had been living off campus, in a house with four other guys. The following year, I was to room with only one of the guys, Darren. This was around the time when I really wanted to get out and start meeting some guys. So the possibility of me wanting to bring a guy home was growing. I figured that I did not want Darren to find out that I was gay by noticing that I kept having these male friends of mine spend the night. So I figured I had better tell him that I was gay before we moved in. That way, if he had a problem, he could just not sign a lease with me, and I would get a place by myself. He was shocked when I told him, but he was very cool about it and supportive from the get-go. I remember when I told him, I was still kind of scared of doing it. I actually told him, "I *think* I'm gay," instead of, "I'm gay." Even though I knew it for sure, I was still kind of scared to actually say it.

But he really took it well. That is probably the biggest reason why we are best friends to this day.

In the middle of my time as a parking officer, I went back to my parents' house up in South Bend, Indiana, for the weekend. For some reason, my being closeted to my parents was just eating away at me. I wanted to tell them so badly, but I was scared to. I was especially afraid of how my dad would take it. When I had heard stories from others about bad reactions from families, it seemed like it was always the dad who reacted the worst. I feared that my dad might cut me off financially if he found out, which could have forced me to drop out, or at least drop to being a part-time student, and I would have to get a full-time job. But this night it was really grinding on me and stressing me out.

Late at night, I was sitting at the computer desk in the dining room. My dad was in the living room, asleep in his easy chair, and my mom was in the kitchen, doing odd tasks. From the television in the living room, I could hear that *Ricki Lake* was on. Her topic happened to be parents who reacted badly when their kids came out. For some reason, all of a sudden, I took that as some kind of sign and decided that was going to be the night I told them. My dad started getting up to go upstairs to bed, but I asked him to come back into the living room. I called my mom in from the kitchen. Then I told them that I was gay. I swear, I could have said the sky was blue and gotten more of a reaction out of my dad. He pretty much was like, "Okay, well I'm off to bed." My mom was different, though. I think she thought that me telling them meant that I was just figuring it out, when really, at that point, I'd been dealing with it for a year and a half. She thought I should go see a counselor. Eventually, she came around, though. Each time I'd visit, I'd push the envelope a little with her, telling her about a couple of guys I'd met. I can talk with her about anything to do with it now. I got really lucky with my parents.

I figured that with my parents having such a close relationship with my sister, Karin, that I could not expect them to keep it secret from her. I just told them to give me a few days to tell her. At the time, I had no means of telling her other than email, so I wrote her a message telling her that I was gay. The response she sent back just floored me. She said the devil was talking to me and that I needed to stop listening to my liberal friends. She told me I needed to come back to Jesus, because being gay is just as much a sin as murder. The next summer, I visited her in Illinois, and we went for a walk to talk about things. After talking a while, I told her, "You have your beliefs, and I have my beliefs. They are obviously not the same things. It would be foolish of me to think you would change your beliefs for me, and it would be foolish of you to think I'm going to change my beliefs for you. So maybe we can just agree to disagree on this subject?" That just did not seem like an adequate enough solution to her. The following Christmas, she left a gift for me at my parents' place. It was a book titled *Pursuing Sexual Wholeness: How Jesus Heals the Homosexual*. It's a good thing she wasn't there, because there would have been a fight. I was so angry.

While I was still in college, I met a gay guy who worked as a security officer for a private firm in the Indianapolis area. He talked me into doing some part-time work for the company while I was still in school. The company's owner was rumored to be bisexual, and the number two guy in command was gay. At any given time, probably at least 25 percent of the employees were either gay or bi. So I saw the company as a cool place where I could work and not have to worry about being out. Well, since this guy introduced me to the company, they all knew I was gay even before I actually applied. On the whole, while I worked there, I'd say the gay aspects were cool in that I never worried about negative issues of my sexuality. Now there were a few guys who did get under my skin because of their comments. These guys would say that they did not have a problem working with or being around anyone who was gay and said that they accepted gays. But the flip side to this apparent acceptance is that they kind of felt like getting that out of the way meant they could get away with saying things that would be considered offensive. I remember the one guy would constantly refer to anyone that was gay as a "rammer," a reference to anal sex.

Now, around the time that I was graduating college, I had met a guy, J.B., on the internet. We both aspired to be full-time law enforcement officers. At the time, he was a part-time dispatcher and a full-time special deputy assigned to working the paddy wagon for a department in Indianapolis. I think I met him either in a gay cop chat room online or in a gay Indiana or Indianapolis chat room online. We met up and became friends. When we first met to ride bikes on the Monon Trail (a rails-to-trails pathway in Indianapolis), he told me that he had a boyfriend, so I instantly went into friend mode. I could very quickly tell that this was the type of guy who I could see myself being friends with for the rest of our lives. I could tell he was that quality of a person, and we seemed to have a lot in common. We were both gay and both absolutely dead set on becoming cops.

One night, J.B. invited me over to his apartment by the Eagle Creek Reservoir. We decided that we were going to catch the major from the security firm in his lies about supposedly being a trooper. This major was going the full nine yards to make J.B. believe he was a state trooper. J.B. had also invited the major over, and we were going to just watch the look on his face when he saw me there and realized that the jig was up. But when the major called J.B., J.B. slipped up and accidentally mentioned that someone else was over at his apartment. The major got spooked and said he could not make it there that night. Needless to say, it was just me and J.B. there. So we just continued to hang out by ourselves and shoot the shit. J.B. started making some mixed drinks, and we both were feeling pretty good, alcohol-wise. We started doing this macho tough guy stuff with each other, getting into each other's face and saying one of us could whoop the other one, etc. Well, the second time we started doing this, it broke down into a friendly wrestling match. After a short while, I, having some background in wrestling, gained the upper hand. I finally had J.B. pinned down on the kitchen floor, and he looked up at me and raised his eyebrows a few times. At that point, I realized that maybe we were not in that position because I was such a great wrestler. I could not believe it was about to happen, but we started to make out on the kitchen floor. We then figured it would be more comfortable to move to J.B.'s bedroom. After the fact, we both enjoyed what had happened, but both knew that it was not right because J.B. still had a boyfriend. So things were kind of weird between us. But to this day, I still say that on that night, J.B. gave me the most passionate experience of my life. And I must admit, even though J.B. was weirded out enough to kind of back off from me for a while, right or wrong, I fell for him big time after what had happened. Shortly after our experience, J.B. broke up with his boyfriend. I thought that was going to be my chance, but the guilty feelings J.B. appeared to be feeling seemed to get in the way, and he told me he did not think it would be a good idea for us to try to start dating. But he did say he still was okay with being friends. That was very hard for me to take because I had quickly developed such strong feelings for him.

I started applying to police departments while I was still in my last year of college and continued to do so after graduation. Not having a police job lined up after I graduated, I decided to move on as a full-time security guard for the firm. I figured I would get onto a police department within six months of graduation, so I figured it would be a decent job just to get me by until I became a cop. I guess I was a little naïve back then about that. It seemed like as much as I tried to apply to departments, I could never get all the way through the hiring process. Many times, I got to the background investigations, and then all of a sudden was told that I was not selected to get hired.

Later on, I was told by the guy who introduced me to the firm that the major of the firm, who was gay, and who I thought was a friend, was actually giving a bad reference about me to the Indiana State Police when they were doing background investigations for the hiring process. But there is no way to prove anything like that, so I just had to deal with it and move on. I surmised that if the major was badmouthing me to I.S.P., that he probably was doing the same with other departments I was applying to as well. Before I became a full-time security guard, the major had come over to my apartment, just off campus, for dinner. Apparently he thought it was going to be more than just dinner, because he seemed upset afterward.

I did not know if I had done something wrong or if he had expected that I would try get intimate with him that night. so I don't know if his bad references were merely revenge for that night or if it was jealousy. As I mentioned earlier, for a while the major was impersonating an I.S.P. state trooper to my good friend J.B. At the time, J.B. was not a cop yet, so he could not just arrest the guy for impersonating an officer. But if this major would impersonate a trooper, maybe he just could not stand a guy like me getting to be what he secretly wished that he was. I do not know to this day if he just badmouthed me or if he told them that I was gay so that they would not want to hire me.

Luckily for me, I was finally able to use a connection to get hired away from that firm. I got hired as a corrections officer in Noblesville, Indiana. Now, unsure if they knew I was gay, I knew that I would have to go back into the closet at work if I wanted things to be smooth. And also, as I was still hoping to move up to a police department, I figured that getting hired may have been contingent upon them not knowing that I was gay. Since no one at work knew I was gay, I never had any direct problems. I would hear anti-gay comments from other officers and from the inmates, but I knew I could not say anything for fear of being found out.

After 9-11 happened, it was a very emotional time for all of us Americans. I had almost gone into work that day without knowing what had happened that morning. In the next couple days, J.B., who at this point had been a full-time cop for a little over two years, was talking with school children and telling them to have faith, support the government at the local level, be vigilant, pray for our national leaders, reflect on what happens to us as a nation, and say thanks to public safety, fire, and police personnel.

A couple days later, J.B. made the ultimate sacrifice in the line of duty. J.B. was shot and killed at the end of a pursuit. The suspects had opened fire on him with AK-47s during the pursuit. When the suspects finally bailed out of the car, spraying bullets, J.B. was fatally hit in the face. Medics tried to rush him to the hospital, but J.B. did not make it. Since I was at work that day, I did not hear about it on the news. That night, I got home from work after midnight and had voice mails left on my phone. The first was from a friend of mine who worked with J.B.'s department and also knew of J.B. The message told me that a cop from that department had been shot and killed, and that it was so sad. The next message was this friend again, saying that from the way they said it on the late news, it sounded like it might have been J.B. who was killed. At that point, I half lost it and was half in disbelief. Another message from this same friend then said that after talking to other officers, it sounded like it was indeed J.B. who had just died. I still did not want to believe it. So I kept checking the news updates online, and they had not released the name yet. So for the next couple of hours, I sat at my computer, crying and praying that somehow it was all a mistake and it really was someone else who had been killed. But finally they released the name; it was J.B. who had been murdered. That was probably the lowest point in my life.

About three weeks before this happened, I had been talking to J.B. online. We had not really talked or seen each other for a while, and I told him that we really needed to get together sometime soon and talk. I wanted to talk to him about what had happened between us a couple years earlier, and I wanted to talk to him about another matter that is too personal to delve into in this forum. J.B. told me that he agreed we should get together and talk sometime soon. Alas, we never ended up getting to do that. So in addition to the sorrow of losing someone I really cared about, I was left with so many unanswered questions about things. It still kind of eats at me from time to time.

After J.B. was killed, I started talking online with several people who knew J.B. These were all friends of J.B.'s who I had never met or talked to before. With things getting weird between me and J.B. after what happened between us, we kind of moved into just being internet friends and seeing each other only very occasionally. I was not in any of the other circles of friends he had. From the way J.B. talked to me, it seemed that no one other than friends knew he was gay. He told me of how he was afraid of people at work finding out about him. He also told me how he was just about deathly scared of his father finding out and disowning him. But after talking with more of these people, I found out that more people knew about him than I had ever imagined. And I then heard even his dad knew. His boyfriend (well, I heard they had just broken up before J.B. was killed) would go over to the family household and still stays in close contact with J.B.'s family, from what I hear. I remember talking to J.B. online once after I had heard a rumor that he had been outed at the academy. He strongly denied that anything like that had happened. I don't know if that was true or not. But I guess the rumor had gone around the department. After J.B. was killed, I heard of cops not really caring too much about it because he was "just a fag." Hearing that saddened me so much. But many others actually respected J.B. very much for a cop with only two years on.

But even though I knew J.B.'s dad knew he was gay, I was still just too intimidated by him to talk to him the first few chances I had. I just felt like I couldn't talk to him without eventually touching on the gay issue. Well, I finally did talk to J.B.'s dad when I saw him at National Police Week in Washington, DC, in 2005. Though I did tense up a bit when he asked me how I knew J.B., I just told him that I had met him online when we were both trying to get onto a department full-time. I am not sure if he was savvy enough to figure out that meeting J.B. online meant that I knew J.B. because I was gay just like he was. Who knows? I just felt good to have finally said something to him. But at the same time, I felt bad that I felt I couldn't talk about the gay subject. I just don't know where he stands on it. Maybe it might be that he's totally okay and comfortable with the subject, but maybe he's only okay with it in a private setting and not a public setting. Maybe someday I'll find that out.

I remember after J.B. was killed and I went back to work at the facility, I told my co-workers that J.B. was a friend of mine. But I could not tell anyone why exactly it was affecting me so much and what kind of connection I had with him. At least at work, I had to bottle that part up.

At one point, toward the end of my tenure there, I was talking with another officer, J.M., about how much I wanted to get out of there. The management treated us young guns like crap and catered to the old guard that was going to stay there until retirement. So I was ready for a change. I told J.M. that I was looking for more varied departments to apply for since I was so ready to get out of there, and that I was not going to be as picky anymore about where I applied to. Another co-worker had already gotten hired by a nearby town as a deputy marshal. J.M. was telling me that I should apply there, and that they would probably hire me.

Now for a brief background on this town. Many of the people, or the heterosexual ones at least, who worked for the security firm had a close connection to this town, and some of the town reserves would work security details for the firm for spare money. Now the firm had a reputation for its gay connections and employees. Some officers from another police department in the area even referred to it as "Gay & Co." So needless to say, I figured that if I applied to that town, the secret would be out again, and I may not even get hired.

So when J.M. was telling me I should apply to that town, I told him that I did not think I wanted to apply there. J.M., being a very inquisitive officer, kept grilling me, asking why I did not want to apply. He kept thinking up different reasons why I might not want to apply there, to try to get me to slip a little clue. At one point he asked, "Well, are you afraid to apply there because you're gay?" Man, my heart skipped about three beats. I do not know how he did not pick up on some kind of physical reaction. But the truth is that it was not my being gay that made me not want to apply, but rather that they would surely know about it. So technically, the answer to his question was no. Then, to try to deflect, I asked him if he thought I was gay. Of course, very quickly, he exclaimed, "No! I'm just trying to think of possible reasons." So I very nearly averted a huge one there. That scared the crap out of me. J.M. ended up getting hired by another local police department, and I soon finally got my lucky shot.

I got hired by my police department in the late spring of 2002. I was finally getting to live out my dream. Now, granted, I did not have a clue that I wanted to be a cop until halfway through college, but once I figured it out, much like figuring out I was gay, I knew that it was what I was meant to be when I was put on this earth. It just took me a while to realize it. Of course the name of the game at this time was that I had to stay in the closet at work. This was especially stressful for me, because during my first year as a cop, my probationary year, I could be fired for any reason at all and would not have recourse. I'm not sure if that is just an Indiana thing or if it is the deal in other departments around the country as well. If you looked at the chief funny, they could fire you, etc. So I had to very much stay on my toes.

One time, while I was with my field training officer, we went on a call for an attempted suicide. The guy had tried to cut his wrists but really did not do that good of a job of it. We took him out to the hospital to do what we call an "immediate detention" on him. It's basically where we can make him go to the hospital to be seen by a psychiatrist, to be evaluated. While we were at the hospital, my training officer left the room to talk to someone else, and I was talking to the guy by myself, getting more information for my paperwork for the incident. I was asking the guy why he wanted to kill himself. He must have felt relatively comfortable with me being there alone, so he told me why. His family had recently found out that he was gay, and they did not take it well. They started treating him like crap. He did not have many friends, so his family was about all he had. He tried to kill himself because he could not take the pain of the treatment from the family, and he couldn't live with the shame that they claimed he was bringing upon them. I so badly wanted to be able to tell him that I was gay too, and that it was okay. But I was afraid to, because I had no idea who this guy might tell about this gay officer in Muncie. So instead, I just tried to be as re-assuring to him as possible without telling him about me. But maybe, in a way, that was almost as good as telling him, because if he could see me as a straight cop who had such supportive viewpoints and insights, that maybe gave him a little hope that not everyone who was straight was going to degrade him for who he was.

Of course I heard plenty of "faggot" comments or degrading jokes from other officers. And all those comments hurt, but being a cop was so important to me that I had to just try to ignore it. I realized if I let it get to me, that I would not last very long at all. But for the most part, things went smoothly on the gay front and I was able to stay in the closet. I did some time on the road with my field training officer, and then, after a while, I finally got to go to the academy.

Going to the academy was very intimidating at first. I had an image in my head that it was going to be like Marine boot camp. So I arrived at the academy already on edge and *very* nervous. Then, all of a sudden, I saw something that I was just not prepared to see: the guy from the security firm who called gays "rammers." He was also in my academy class. He got hired by some township school police department or something like that. I started freaking out inside my head because I was sure that he would remember who I was and would spread it all around the academy that I was a "rammer." So I figured my only chance to avert disaster would be to ask him to *please* not tell anyone that I was gay. So I got a chance to say something to him. As I approached him, it became apparent to me that he did not remember who I was. So before I stuck my foot in my mouth and re-outed myself to him, I just brushed it off and went on about my business. Another near-disaster averted. But I knew I would have to stay on my toes during the academy in case any other incidents cropped up and posed a threat to my closeted status.

I had two pretty cool roommates during the academy. The Indiana Law Enforcement Academy is a live-in academy during the week. We were released on the weekends. I would always bring my dirty clothes home on the weekends to wash them. We also had something called "liberty," which was one night during the week that we could leave the academy grounds from seven to ten. Well, one weekend was especially busy, and I was unable to do laundry. So when liberty came on Tuesday night, I asked my roommate, Mike, if I could tag along with him and go to his house to do a load of laundry that I desperately needed to do. Mike said that was cool, so I loaded my laundry into his truck and left with him. That night, when I was back in my academy dorm room and trying to go to sleep, I heard the guys in the next room talking. The walls were paper thin, so you could easily hear conversations next to you, and my bed was on the wall of this other room. I could hear one of the other guys from my department, Owen, seemingly freaking out about how odd it was that I was loading up some of my stuff into Mike's truck and that I left with him for liberty. Owen basically made every implication he could about the situation, short of saying that he thought me and Mike were having sex. Later, once out of the academy, I confronted Owen about it. I told Owen what the deal really was that night and that he was overreacting and being a drama king about it. I told Owen that I could not believe that he thought I was having a sexual relationship with Mike. Owen backed off, saying that he never thought I was gay but thought that Mike might be gay. Owen apologized, saying he did not mean to offend me by implying that I was gay. Well, I guess I was able to get out of another close call again without telling a lie.

The academy had a library in it, and on one of the shelves, sure enough, was a book titled *Gay Cops*. I heard plenty of snickers and derogatory comments from the other guys about the book. Many asked why the hell they would even put a book like that in there. Now I had heard about this book online beforehand but had never read it or seen it before. So my curiosity wouldn't let me be with that book being so close by. I would try to sneak to the library when I thought no one else would be in there to take a look at it. But I would inevitably have to abandon my plan after reading a few words, as someone would walk into the library, and I could not be seen reading that book. Though it was a very interesting thing that, for a period of a week or two, the book was no longer up on the shelf and was not in any of the book racks where we were to put any books that we were reading but did not check out of the library. So that was telling me that someone actually checked out the book. I'm curious to this day if that was indeed the case, and if so, who checked out the book?

After the academy, it was kind of life as usual. I kept my personal life and my professional life totally separate. I was kind of an outsider in the department, even without the gay issue. I'm the only non-local who was hired in the last five years. So I did not have to work too hard to socially distance myself from other officers a little bit. I felt that I had to do this to protect myself from the possibility of being found out.

Then, around the late summer of 2003, with me having been in the department for about a year and a half, I came into work before the start of my shift, and my former field training officer was walking out to his car at the end of his shift. He called out to me, "Hey, Squid!" (My nickname at work is Squid, which is short for Squidward from *Spongebob Squarepants*; that's a whole other story.) He stopped me and had a serious look on his face. He said, "I have something I need to ask you, and I'm just going to come out and say it. Do you have an ad on Yahoo Personals?" As soon as he asked that, my heart sank because I instantly knew what he was getting at and what he was really asking. I had always wondered how I would handle it if I was ever directly asked if I was gay. I knew that even though he was not directly asking me, he essentially was. So I told him, "Yeah … that's my ad." He responded by saying that was fine and he did not care if it was, but that he just wanted to make sure that someone was not trying to mess with me by putting my picture on a gay ad.

At the time, I had put my picture on the gay personals ad online, figuring that someone would have to be gay to be searching through ads and come across it. Then they would have to recognize my photo, because there was nothing in the ad that said I was a cop. I figured it was safe to put my picture on there. I asked my former field training officer where he heard about the ad, and he told me that word about it had been spreading around the department for about a week. So I have no idea of who outed me, but it is probably best that I do not know, because I would be tempted to do something to that person that would get me in big trouble. It is just really bad that someone who is, at a minimum, bi-curious felt a need to out me and put my career in jeopardy. Whoever it was could have merely said something to me first instead of this behind-the-back BS.

Needless to say, my former training officer may have taken it okay, but as I set out on the road for my shift, I felt sick to my stomach. I could see my entire career passing before my eyes. I was out of my probationary year, but in Indiana, there still is no protection from discrimination based on sexual orientation, in employment or in anything. It is a Red state, after all. I could see myself basically getting run out of town, or maybe keeping my job but never getting backup. I felt so sick I about called the lieutenant to see if I could go home sick. But I toughed it out. Luckily, nothing serious happened that day, because I know my head was not in the game. In the days that followed, I did not see any kind of negative reaction to the rumor.

A week later a friend of mine who was a gay cop in the Washington, DC, area came to visit me. We had decided (long before word got out about me) that he would ride along with me one day, to see how similar or different it was in my department. Also, it was a chance for him to see how well I did my job. At one point, my sergeant drove by a call I was on, and I stopped him to introduce him to my buddy. I did not think about it at the time, but I wonder if the sergeant instantly assumed that my friend had to be gay since he was my friend from out of state. The sergeant did seem a bit like he wanted to get out of there, so I took it as a bad sign. Much, much later I found out that the sergeant was merely in a hurry, and it had nothing to do with being uncomfortable with gayness.

Later that night, toward the end of the shift, I had to turn in some paperwork to the midnight shift office because of how late it was in the shift. One of the midnight supervisors was in the office. As I turned in my paperwork, with my buddy standing outside the office, the sergeant said, "Squid, can you close the door for a second?" Again, I instantly knew what was up before he even said anything. Sure enough, he asked me if that was really my ad on the Yahoo Personals. It's funny how even though they had the balls to ask about the subject, neither the sergeant nor my training officer could actually just ask me if I was gay. So I told the sergeant that it really was my ad. He told me that he did not care about that, and that the chief's office had heard the rumor about it, and they did not care if it was true or not. The sergeant then asked me if anyone had given me any trouble yet because of it. I told him that nothing bad had happened yet that I knew of. He then told me that if any of his midnight officers ever gave me any problems I was to come to him and he would put an end to it right then and there. So that made me feel good, and that I did not have to worry so much.

A couple of weeks later, this one veteran officer was sent as backup for me on an alarm call. I had pretty much cleared the call when he arrived, since he was coming from farther away and I was practically on top of the call when it came out. It was a false alarm. But as I was walking back to my car, the other officer pulled up next to me. Like the others before him, he wanted to inquire if I really was gay or if it was just rumor. I told him that the rumor was true. He told me he did not have a problem with me or with working with me or backing me up. He did tell me that he was a very religious man, and that my "lifestyle" (I *hate* that term) went against his religious beliefs, but that I would never have to worry about any problems from him. That actually made me feel really good, since he was still willing to accept me in spite of his religious beliefs about homosexuality. That really gave me hope, especially when viewing that in contrast to how my sister reacted.

As I told more people, the word that I admitted I was gay started to spread. But it's funny—I still think that some officers do not believe it. At least, that's the impression I get from the way they act and talk. Maybe it is just denial. But I'm the kind of guy who no one would really suspect of being gay anyway, so maybe that is why. Like Jen from back when I was a parking officer, maybe some of the officers now think I can't be gay because I do not behave or present myself in a stereotypical manner. But it seems that the more time that passes, the more it becomes something that does not seem to make a difference to many people on the department. And at least if someone does have a problem with it, they try to keep it to themselves.

One night, in the wintertime, I was in the roll call room before the start of the shift. We had these uniform sweaters that we were allowed to wear during the winter. On midnight shift, only Rick and I ever wore them. It was more an afternoon thing for some reason. Well, that night, Rick wore the regular uniform shirt instead of the sweater, but I wore the sweater. The one sergeant, who is a supreme joker, came into the room to start roll call and said something to the effect of, "Hey, Rick, did you leave your sweater over at Squid's place?" (With the unsaid implication that something was going on between us.) Everybody in the room just started busting out laughing, me included. Roll call then proceeded as normal from there. About ten minutes after, we all got to our cars and headed out on the road. The sergeant sent me a message on the M.D.T. in my car asking to meet him somewhere. I got there, and he asked me if that was too much or over the line, referring to the joke at roll call. I told him I thought it was hilarious, but that if anything, I thought that Rick might not have liked the implication that he'd be slightly associated with any kind of gay activity. The sergeant said he just rolled with the joke but afterward felt bad about it because he did not know how I felt about that kind of thing. He told me that he does not have the slightest problem with me being gay. I told him that as long as I know where a person stands on the issue, and I know that there are no ill-intentions, I'm all for joking around.

I think, as long as it's not derogatory, it can be a way for others to gradually see being gay as not really a big deal. Normally, you can tell if someone means to insult with a joke or if it is just playful ribbing, which most police officers do with each other constantly. If a joke is questionable then all you have to do is say so. This had happened right before Valentine's Day, and I came up with an idea that I would have tried, if it was for anyone else other than this sergeant. He is such a master of jokes that I knew I couldn't hang with him in a joke battle. But what I was going to do was buy

148

a pair of Valentine's boxers from the store, red with some sappy love message on them, and then ball them up in my hand and bring them into roll call. I was going to hold them under the table so that the sergeant couldn't see them as he walked in to conduct roll call. Then, at the end, when he'd ask if anyone had anything, I was going to take my hand from under the table and throw the boxers at him. Then I was going to say, "Yeah, sergeant, you left these at my place last night!" I know that would have become department legend if I had done that. But I also knew his joke back at me would have been three times worse than mine. I later even told him of my plan, and he did think it would have been funny as hell.

Some of the other guys had some fun with this one very short foot pursuit I got into during the winter. This drunk kid had been in a fight and had tried to run from me. I caught him, and he started resisting me. I used a sweet takedown to get him on the ground. It was a very quick and short distance chase, and I hadn't had a chance to get on the radio to say what was going on because everyone else was on the radio at the time. But once I had him in custody, I got on the radio. "Thirty-one, I'm out on a subject that tried to run from me, and *I've got him in the rear* of the Sig Ep house on Riverside." Everyone told me they were dying of laughter at hearing me say that over the radio.

At this point, I think I am even ready to bring a date to the Christmas party. I suppose I would first have to find a guy to date in order to do that. I do not know if the others on the department are ready for that, but I think that I am. To this point, none of the other officers have had to deal with my being gay other than to know that I am. No one has had to see me "being gay." For them to see me hold another man's hand, kiss, hug, or slow dance with a man may be a whole new ball game. I don't like being the kind of guy who tries to throw my sexuality in everyone's face. And I do not think that bringing a date would be doing that, but I'm betting that some officers may take it that way. At least they did not seem to care the few times that I've worn my University of South Carolina hat, which says "Cocks," to department functions or training sessions. I guess there's one way to find out. Hopefully, I'll find a date for the party this year.

One problem, though, is that I feel this pressure to bring someone who will blow their minds as far as being a masculine kind of guy no one would normally think was gay. I have this image in my head of other officers thinking that since I'm masculine, any guy I would date is going to be more feminine (to play the female role). If I can bring a date who is completely masculine, it would force others to redefine their image of what a gay man is and how they perceive a gay relationship. Now I know that I should just bring someone who I'd want to date and not worry about how they appear, but I still feel that internalized pressure to use my date to try to show something. But heck, I have a hard enough time finding anyone local to date, so I may not have much choice in the matter.

Recently, one of my best friends on the department went through a divorce. Another officer who used to be on our shift decided to try to start spreading rumors to anyone who would listen (cop or civilian) that the reason my friend got divorced was because he and I were having sex. The ironic thing is that this rumor-starting officer was really a major precipitating factor in the divorce. In the long run, I think the rumor spreading was more meant as an attack on my friend, but it upset me as well. What upset me about it is that many people he was telling the bogus rumor to were the people who have never really interacted with me and are more likely to believe what this officer said. It goes against what I stand for. I am all about breaking stereotypes about gay men, and this rumor only goes to further the stereotype that gay men are predators and will try to convert straight men and ruin marriages. Not everything has been rosy with everyone knowing about me. But at least this incident is the worst thing that has happened yet, that I know of.

I just recently attended the 11th Annual LEGAL International Conference of Gay and Lesbian Criminal Justice Professionals in Providence, Rhode Island. I really enjoyed myself there, and it was very cool to get to meet some of the brave officers who fought to pave the way for those of us today. Some departments may well be scared to openly discriminate against gay officers because of lawsuits that have been won and are being fought currently. There were several great seminars on issues that gay officers have to deal with and ways for departments to be more responsive to the GLBT community. I got to meet officers from GOAL New England (Gay Officers Action League), GOAL New York, Mid-Atlantic GOAL (Washington, DC area), Florida LEGAL (Law Enforcement Gays and Lesbians), Protect and Defend (a new gay public safety/military group in California), and GSPOA (Golden State Peace Officers Association). A good friend of mine recently started a chapter of LEGAL in Alabama. Currently, Indiana has no such gay cop organization. Being at the conference a couple of weeks ago really got me juiced up, and I would like to see an organization for Indiana officers, perhaps a new chapter of LEGAL or GOAL, form in the future. I'm currently trying to gauge other local officers' opinions and interests in such a group forming. Hopefully, I will find enough officers willing to get a group off the ground. Wish us luck!

I guess I can say that, on the whole, I've been kind of lucky as far as the issue of being gay and being a cop goes. I know that every situation is different. There may be some things from my experience that other officers can use, and there may be parts that would be bad for other officers to use. As any good officer knows, you have to deal with every situation differently, and I think the issue of coming out of the closet, in general or at work, is very much the same. I do think that it is good in general for more and more GLBT officers to be role models by being out of the closet (or more important, by being themselves). But I cannot say when would be the right time for an officer to begin the process of coming out. Every officer will have to come to that decision himself. But having input from other people does help because it can give you a frame of reference, and it gives more options for you to consider. But for any gay, bi, or curious officer who reads this, I wish you the best of luck in however you decide to go about things. Even though I may not know you, you have my support and the support of many others like me and many who have gone before.

FROM AUXILIARY POLICE OFFICER DAVE LEWIS JR. NYPD CPP

I am a 34-year-old man who lives in New York City. I am a former deputy sheriff from Colorado, who served for a rural department outside Denver. I started my law enforcement career as a community corrections officer for a private halfway house. While working at the halfway house, I volunteered as a reserve police officer for a small country department of 35 for two years. While working at the sheriff's office, I worked in the detention, patrol, community relations, and investigations divisions. I left law enforcement to pursue a career in the private sector, but I still have the passion to work with my community. I am currently volunteering as an auxiliary police officer with the NYPD.

I have always been interested in law enforcement. I come from a family that has served in the military and the police forces. My father was a patrol, motor, and aviation law enforcement officer in Long Beach, California. When I was five, my father gave me a rechargeable police car that reached a maximum speed of five miles per hour. I would drive up and down the sidewalk, pretending to give the neighbors parking and speeding tickets. Since my childhood, I have had the blue blood.

I realized at a young age that I had feelings toward other men. I didn't come out to myself until I was 19. I came out to my family and friends shortly after I came to terms with my sexuality. I did not pursue the law enforcement career path once leaving high school. I didn't believe that law enforcement was an option for me because I was gay. During the time I was coming out, the debate over gays in the military was really heating up. I was under the impression that law enforcement mirrored the military and I would not be welcome.

When I was 21, I met a man who was a gay police officer. I had a relationship with him for three years. During my relationship, I realized that my law enforcement dream could come true. Meeting him was the biggest motivation to start my career. However, he was not open at his department and was very closeted. I decided I was going to apply to several departments and a private academy. My boyfriend at the time did not encourage my decision. I was even told that if I became a police officer, he would leave me. He feared for my safety and the possibility of hazing. I secretly applied to several departments and academies. Like most states, Colorado required a state certification. I was accepted to a private police academy sponsored by the Colorado State Patrol. I was so excited that I was accepted to an academy. I was overjoyed with the excitement, and I showed the acceptance letter to my boyfriend. He was very disappointed and angry about my decision. He did not understand and was not supportive of my career choice. We ended our three-year relationship as I was graduating the academy.

I was not out at the academy. I went back into the closet. It was a very difficult decision, but on the advice of a couple of cops and my father, I pretended to be something I was not. I never shared my secret life with anyone at the academy for fear I may be hurt or rejected. I created an elaborate life with a fake girlfriend. When asked what I did in my time off from class, I always said I was studying or hanging out with friends. I was not able to tell my classmates that I was out on a date with an incredibly hot and amazing man. I was not only dealing with the stress of the academy; additional pressure was added by this elaborate façade of being a heterosexual man.

I was not out at my departments. I worked in a very Republican and rural area of Colorado. I would hear words like "fag" and "queer" tossed around on a daily basis. Amendment 2 was a heated topic on the Colorado ballet. This was a law that would make it illegal for local jurisdictions to create legislation protecting GLBT citizens and would abolish existing legislation. I was terrorized daily with the thought that my colleagues would find out my secret and kick the crap out of me. This was probably something I created in my own mind, as my colleagues never expressed a desire to do so. It was just typical heterosexual locker talk, but I was still scared. The only reference materials I had about being gay were a few books about military men who came out. I equated the military stories of physical harm and dishonorable discharges to the law enforcement world. I continued to create an elaborate pretend life for myself for several years.

The most difficult situation for me was living such an elaborate lie. Pretending to be something I was not took a huge emotional toll on me. I was always worrying about what people thought. It really wore me down and made me feel hollow. It was very depressing that I could not be myself. I consistently overcompensated on the job and over-exceeded in everything I did. I was obsessed with making my paperwork perfect, working every extra shift as asked, volunteering for special assignments, and always striving to be the most reliable deputy, to keep attention off my personal life.

Eventually, my secret life caught up with me. I resided in the same jurisdiction I patrolled. I had a man named Richard living with me for six months, in a home I purchased. I believed I was in love. Richard was increasingly demonstrating odd behaviors and acting suspicious. I overlooked some of the behaviors, as someone in love typically does. Richard would easily lose his temper. Richard was increasingly yelling and throwing objects or punching walls. One day, while working in the garden together, we got in an argument about something minor. Richard lost his temper and threw the weed eater he was using at me. Richard stormed out of the house and left for several hours. When Richard returned, he apologized and said it would never happen again. Richard's attitude and temper started to change, and he started to use hurtful words toward me. Richard would always apologize after his blow-ups, and I would forgive him. After one argument over the type of toothpaste I purchased, he accused me of not loving him and having an affair. Richard cornered me and grabbed me. Richard pushed me up against the wall and threw me onto a bed. I tried to leave the home, but Richard took my keys and would not allow me to leave. I did everything I could with my professional training to not escalate the situation. A flashing warning signal went off in my head, and I realized I was in a bad situation. I realized I was the victim of domestic violence. I did not know what to do. I knew that if I called 911, an officer I knew would respond. I was terrified of the thought. I was stuck in a corner, and I didn't know how to get myself out. When I went to work the next day, I sought the advice of one of the department's victims' advocates, Patty. I did the most difficult thing I could imagine, and that was coming out to one of my colleagues. I explained what had taken place the night before. Patty was extremely concerned for my safety and was very respectful of my private life. Patty empathized with my situation and the fear of the department discovering my secret. Patty had me speak with our judge in private to get a temporary civil restraining order served on Richard. The restraining order required Richard to vacate the home and have no contact with me. This was somewhat extreme, and in a typical situation, most adults talk about breaking up.

The day Richard received the order, he came to my home. Richard knew I was inside from the lights that were on. Richard was yelling things outside the home, throwing rocks and breaking the windows. Richard threatened to call my department and tell them I was gay and I was molesting little kids. Richard said he would call my department and tell them I threatened him with my duty weapon and that I was stealing evidence. I realized the situation had now escalated, and I had no choice but to call 911. In that few minutes it took to make a call, I realized my entire life was about to unravel and forever change.

The local police in my county arrived. I explained the situation to the officer and provided him with a copy of the protection order. I had to tell the officer I was a deputy sheriff and that I would contact the on-call commander in my office about the situation. The officer was very supportive and didn't show any obvious changes in body language or discomfort in dealing with me as a gay officer. Richard was arrested for violation of a restraining order and domestic violence. The officer contacted my commanding officer on my behalf. I was ordered into the office the next day to meet with my commanding officer, the sheriff, and Internal Affairs. After the officer left and I was alone, I closed the door and cried uncontrollably for hours. I didn't know what to expect or what was going to happen. I thought I was going to lose my job. Worse, how would my team members treat me now that my secret was out?

I met with the command staff and gave my statement. I was very shocked at the way I was treated. My commanding officer asked if I was okay and if he could help me with anything. The sheriff told me he was very proud of the way I handled myself by not escalating the situation. The sheriff said that other officers had been in similar situations and they didn't show the type of professional restraint I demonstrated. The sheriff also said that he did not care that I was gay. The sheriff told me I was one of his best deputies and he wouldn't have it any other way. The sheriff encouraged me to be myself, and he wanted to hear if anyone hurt or mistreated me at the department.

In less than 24 hours the weight I had been carrying around with me for years was finally lifted by the permission to be myself. One dramatic and embarrassing situation was now my salvation. I was finally going to be myself. For weeks I was still paranoid about what took place and how I was going to be treated by my co-workers. I didn't receive any negative feedback. In fact, I received a lot of positive encouragement.

My advice for young gay or lesbian people: do not hesitate to pursue your career. Do not listen to what others say about being a GLBT law enforcement official. Above all else, be true and honest with yourself. Find a mentor who is in the law enforcement field that you wish to pursue. Seek advice from others and always strive to make yourself happy.

After being forced out of the closet, I started to seek out other gay and lesbian law enforcement officers. I found several social and support groups nationally. I started communicating online with several other officers. These officers would give me encouragement and support. I discovered that I was not alone in my experiences.

I found that on a consistent basis, several of the GLBT law enforcement groups would meet for a national professional conference. The conference was an educational forum on how to cope with being a GLBT law enforcement officer and how to improve relations within the departments. Reaching out for peer support was the most beneficial thing I did. First, it made me realize I was not alone, and second, I was provided with tools to give me additional confidence. After the conference, I was approached by my department to become a diversity instructor. The sheriff encouraged me to teach about all types of diversity subjects, and I created a unique curriculum in Colorado, which was later adopted by other departments. This encouragement led me to create several other unique law enforcement training programs that I later shared with other agencies nationally. Close to two years after I came out, I was named Deputy Sheriff of the Year for my department. I received this award for working to promote diversity within the community and within law enforcement.

The biggest thing I can suggest for someone who is supportive of gay and lesbian officers is to educate your department. Include GLBT issues in all aspect of training. Education is the most important tool we have in the law enforcement community. Discourage condemning remarks about the GLBT community and slang words that can be hurtful.

AN INTERVIEW WITH DANIELLE JONAS

Briefly describe yourself, including age, law enforcement, fire, and or EMS experience, what part of the country you are from and anything else you feel is important to know about you.

I am a five and a half year veteran of the Baltimore County Police Department in Maryland. I am 28 years old and started transitioning about two years ago, but have just recently come out to the department.

1. How did you become interested in law enforcement, firefighting, or the EMS profession?

My uncle was a police officer and I have always had a slight interest. I had a few other interests, but I was terrible at chemistry in college so that narrowed it down for me.

2. When did you discover you were gay, lesbian, or bisexual and what did you think about relative to your interest in law enforcement, firefighting or EMS?

When I was eight or nine years old, I remember feeling different. I wasn't sure what I was feeling, but I knew something wasn't exactly normal for me. I lived my life like a normal heterosexual male until I couldn't stop fighting the feelings any longer. I was about three or four years into my police career at that time. I know that the job is a very macho place and even some of the women are more masculine than feminine at times. I figured it would be a difficult jump, but it was one that I needed to do.

3. Describe your experience getting hired and going through your training academy. Were you out? Did you come out during the academy?

I applied in October 2008 to become a police officer and got hired in June of 2009. I was slated to go into the December 2008 academy, but I had developed Hodgkin's lymphoma in June of 2008 and was still going through radiation therapy. It was a rough time. In June of 2009, I was in Myrtle Beach, South Carolina enjoying a family vacation with my then fiancée. I received the call about a week and a half before the academy started. I ran up and down the hotel hallways just ecstatic. This was for a couple of reasons: 1) I had been waiting for quite a long time during a time that included a bout and victory over cancer and 2) I was running out of money and the academy is a paid academy! I was not out at the time and did not come out until several years after the academy.

4. What was it like starting off in your department? Did you come out? If not, what kept you, or is currently keeping you from coming out at work?

Starting out in the department, I, like every officer before me, was very nervous and made a few errors. I am now much more comfortable in the job and while I am still learning every day, I am frequently able to be an acting supervisor. I came out in August of 2014, but I had started hormone therapy in March of 2013. I was starting to develop small breasts.

I usually go on a small trip with two of my male friends. One is my co-worker and one is an officer in a nearby police department. I did not want to out myself just yet so I stopped taking the medications until December of 2013. Ironically, later I found out that my friend wondered how my pecs were so flabby when I am overall relatively thin. I continued my therapy and eventually came out to most of my immediate family. In March of 2014, I had an attorney from FreeState Legal draw up a letter to the chief, county human resources director, and county attorney advising that a nameless police officer was seeking to change genders. We received a positive response from the HR director who spoke for the other two. I had been wary that I would be fired or treated poorly as I had seen other transwomen suffer from coming out at their jobs.

After receiving the positive response, I spoke to the "fair practices liaison" sergeant at my work and basically spilled the beans. He kept my name private until I was ready to go further with my transition. I had been planning on waiting until the FAMA14 Bill came into law in October to reveal my plans to the rest of the department, but my plans did not matter to a few employees. I scheduled two surgeries, one to reduce my trachea size and a slight rhinoplasty and put in the required paperwork for them. The paperwork was vague and simply stated that I needed to use sick time for two scheduled surgeries and that was all. I had come out to a few of my close friends on the job and my direct supervisors were aware of the situation. My appearance had changed slightly over the course of 2014 and I appeared a tiny bit more feminine at work. A lieutenant on one of the other two shifts saw the paperwork and began to ask other people on his shift if I was having a sex change. I had heard of rumors going around the precinct, but a lieutenant asking?! He even asked my corporal who in turn notified me that people were talking about it even more. The very next day after roll call, I came out to the rest of my shift. I cried. I cried a lot. It was very emotional, but I got through it and life has been better since.

5. Describe your most difficult situation being gay in your public safety profession.

The most difficult situation I am presented with due to being transgender is when people call me faggot or something negative. I just want to lash out sometimes, but as a law enforcement officer, I need to keep my composure. The other slightly difficult issue is when I am at another call with transgender "customers." It irks me when I am having to deal with unsavory persons that are trans and give trans-people a bad name. It's already an uphill battle, but seeing my counterparts as prostitutes and thieves just gets my blood boiling.

6. What specific event or general experience surprised you most about being gay in your profession?

FAMA14, sponsored by Sen. Rich Madaleno, becoming law impacted me greatly by providing protections for trans-people in the workplace mostly. It just took a weight off of my shoulders. A person that impacted me the most is one of my best friends who is also a police officer. She was the third person I ever came out to and the first on the job. She has stuck by me and has been my confidant. She boosts me up when I feel bad and when I get on her nerves (and I know I do) she doesn't hold a grudge. When I came out, another female officer who is a lesbian ran right up to me. I was crying ... somewhat uncontrollably. She just wrapped her arms around me and told me how brave I was. It was probably one of the most touching moments in my life and I will forever appreciate it.

7. What, if anything, would you have done differently relative to being gay in your profession?

I'm not sure what I could have done differently other than come out sooner. I thought I was very calculated and careful in outing myself.

8. One of the important goals of this book is to help fellow gay law enforcement officers, firefighters, and EMS professionals and their allies. What advice can you provide to the following people?

Have a support system inside and outside of work. It helped me greatly to have someone to talk to at work about home and work issues. Check the laws of your state and counties to make sure there are protections and have a lawyer in mind in case something goes awry.

9. What else would you like to say that you feel is most important for readers to know about you or your ideas?

Don't close yourself off to people. If they have questions (not super personal stuff) educate them. It will only help in the long run.

FROM OFFICER JOHN SANDERS

I first met Greg Miraglia at an LGBT Law Enforcement conference in Palm Springs, CA, just after his first book came out. I was inspired by the class at the conference he taught and by the book that he had written. Up to this point I had read nothing addressing the topic of police officers coming out on the job. I had recently come out and realized the importance of the book. All my life I thought I was alone in my feelings and had tremendous fears and paranoia about being gay. I was wrong: I was never alone, and I just needed to look in the right locations for guidance and mentorship. After reading his book I wanted to share my story because I have not read of other officers who were married to a female and had kids. Unfortunately I was not comfortable enough at this point in my life to contribute my story.

In December 2014 I met with Greg a second time. I wanted to introduce him to my husband Cesar who I had recently married after Proposition 8 was overturned in California. Greg informed me that he was giving his class a tour of the Castro District of San Francisco and invited me to accompany the class. I gladly accepted. After the tour of the Castro District and seeing Harvey Milk's house, we hung out in the Castro District and had dinner with our spouses. He told me how he wanted to write a third book and was looking for stories. I had already come out in my personal and professional lives and was ready to share my story. I felt my story was important, not to put the spotlight on me, but to let others know that they are not alone. In fact, since coming out, I have met many in my age group that had been married and had kids and who have since come out of the closest. Some of their stories are very sad and some very inspirational. I think a big reason for this age group getting married is that we did not have the support of family and friends, the laws that would protect us from discrimination, the freedom to be equal and get married like anyone else, or the social networking ability that would help us understand that we were normal in our feelings. Instead many of us, like me, were bombarded with the conservative views of the church and society that being gay was wrong. Today I realize that being gay is not a choice, just like being Latino is not a choice. It's me.

Growing up I think I always knew I was gay. I was always attracted to the same sex and never really understood why. I thought I was the only one who felt this way. It was not something I would ever discuss with any of my friends. I was a kid like any other kid that just wanted to be accepted for who he or she was, but learned at an early age that things were not so simple. I loved to do all the boy things but at an early age remember viewing boys differently than girls.

As a child in 1978, after my father came home from work, I remember watching the nightly news with my parents when the news reported that some crazy guy shot some guy named Harvey Milk in San Francisco. I had no understanding at the time how important Harvey Milk was to the LGBT community.

I have two siblings, a younger sister and an older brother. My brother who is also gay was outed when he was a senior in high school in 1984. This really caused some drama in our household, as neither of my parents supported his "lifestyle choices." I remember they sent him to counseling to change him. Now I realize that being gay is not a choice. Since I am five years younger than my brother I really did not understand all the dynamics. Shortly after my brother graduated from high school, he was out of the house. I am not sure if this was his choice or something imposed on him. Whatever the reason, once my brother left the house I did not see him or talk to him for five years. At the time I understood that he was gay, but it is not something that my parents talked to me about. One thing I understood though is how he felt he was not accepted or deemed to be normal in society's standards.

I do not think that I can write this without explaining why I and many other men my age did not come out of the closest until a very late period in their lives. A lot of it had to do with the stereotypes placed upon me and the fear that society created about gays. As I have previously mentioned I think a big reason for this age group getting married is that we did not have the support of family and friends, the laws that would protect us from discrimination, the freedom to be equal and get married like anyone else, or the social networking ability that would help us understand that we were normal in our feelings. Being in law enforcement adds a whole new dynamic to this, because being a police officer typically means that you work with very conservative and religious people where the gay community is looked upon in a negative light.

In 1981 a strange virus started to appear across the country. Doctors did not know what it was or how it was spread, but knew something was certain: if you got it, death was inevitable. At the time the virus was identified as HTLV-III/LAV. This name of this virus would later be changed to the Human Immunodeficiency Virus (HIV). The cluster of symptoms associated with the contraction of the virus was termed Acquired Immune Deficiency Syndrome (AIDS). When the virus started to spread it appeared that only gay men were getting the virus. Society associated the virus exclusively with the gay community. At least that was the information the media was spreading at the time. This created a huge stigma against the gay community that I found myself falling into. There was so much fear placed against HIV/AIDS in society that people honestly believed that all gay men had the virus, as many today still believe. There was so much negativity placed on the gay community because of HIV/AIDS that I found myself trying to suppress my feelings throughout my high school years, in fear of being lumped into a group of society that was viewed as weaker, lesser, mentally ill, perverted and not normal. As the years went on thousands of men and women would lose their lives to HIV/AIDS.

I grew up in a small town 25 miles east of Los Angeles. While growing up I attended Baldwin Park High School (BPHS), a predominantly Latino campus. While in high school I found it awkward to be friends with others. The straight guys would always talk about girls and sports. I really could not relate to the straight guys because I was not into girls, but I could relate to sports. I loved swimming and was on the swimming team and water polo team. I hated to lie and say that girls were hot or that I was having sex with them. I really did not know any out gay teens in high school, but I wish I did. I surely suspected a few, but never found the courage to ask them.

In high school there was a tremendous feeling that I was alone in my situation and this made it difficult to get close to anyone, because I felt like I could not express my true feelings to anyone in fear of rejection by my peers. After graduating from high school I would learn that there were many of the guys in high school were gay, but didn't come out until they graduated. This is something that would take me years to find the courage to do.

While in high school I joined the local Fire Department Explorer program, because I always wanted to be a paramedic. I learned a lot in the Fire Department Explorer program, but also learned that it was a part of the Boy Scouts of America, an organization that until 2014 prohibited any gay scouts from being members. It seemed to me that everywhere I went there was a huge movement to keep gays in the closet. After graduating from high school I was able to obtain a position working as a Student Worker for the Los Angeles County Fire Department. Ironically it was in this position that I would meet another student worker that had the same feelings as me. He was a six-foot-tall, very muscular 21-year-old Latino. We both aspired to be firefighters and would go run and work out together after work. It was through this relationship that I began to realize that he was attracted to me and did not just want to exercise.

When we were together he made it clear to me that no one was to know about us and that we were only good friends. I was infatuated with him: his smell, his look, his friendship. The relationship would never take off. I was only a friend to him and nothing else. I later found out that he only called me when his girlfriend was away.

After my relationship with the other student worker failed to take off, I was confused and came to the realization that I could not be or act gay. I needed to conform to society's standards if I was going to become a paramedic or firefighter. At the time it was "common knowledge" that there were no gay paramedics, firefighters, or cops. It was through this employment with the fire department that I was eventually able to find the connections and encouragement to go back to school and become a paramedic.

While working for the ambulance company I met a female co-worker who I seemed to really click with. We became best friends, married, and eventually had two kids. I always questioned whether I should have gotten married, but did it anyway. Don't get me wrong, I truly loved my wife and thought I had suppressed my feelings after meeting her. I worked as a paramedic for several years until the Rodney King incident happened within the Los Angeles Police Department, Foothill Division. When the officers involved in the incident were acquitted of criminal actions, the riots started. Eventually the city burned down on live TV and there was a mass exodus of police officers who found themselves hated by the community. LAPD could not find enough cops to fill all the vacancies. The mass exodus was so bad that LAPD started heavily recruiting officers. Gone were the days of height requirements and there was suddenly a huge push to hire minorities and females. LAPD had long been known for being a department that was not reflective of its community and they were now trying to change this.

I cannot really say that I ever wanted to be a cop, it kind of just happened. I talked to the recruiters, and they showed me all the retirement benefits, medical benefits and pay benefits. It was so much better than the seven dollars an hour I was making as a paramedic. LAPD was still in the midst of numerous controversies. OJ Simpson had just been acquitted of murdering his wife and the community was still skeptical of the police. I applied for LAPD and several other departments. About a year later I was hired with the LAPD and started the academy in January of 1996. When I received the notice that I was hired, I have to admit I was scared. Being that I am only five foot six inches tall and weighed 125 pounds at the time, I was concerned for my safety. Los Angeles was known for being a violent city with numerous gangs.

After being hired I was never questioned about my sexuality, because I was married. I think most suspected I was gay though, because I was not overly masculine. It was very clear to me from the time I was hired that the culture of the department would most likely not be very accepting of gays and that I could never reveal my secret to anyone. I still caught myself being attracted to men from time to time. When I began the academy, I was placed in class 1-96. It was the academy class that started January 1996.

I remember the first couple of days in the academy. One of the instructors in the class was from the elite Metro Division. He told the class to look around the room and said, "Within five years of being hired one of you in this room will be killed on the job, don't let it be you"! These comments really took me back. What was I getting myself into? Little did I know that what he said was the truth. The first months of the academy had a college setting with physical fitness courses. When we weren't studying we were running. I hated running and still do. Man, we ran so much. I have never been so skinny in my life. While I was in the academy I really clicked with some of the other guys. There was this one guy that was so damn funny! I'll never forget his name, Robert Mata. There was another guy that looked a lot like me, but at the time I hated his arrogance. I remember the instructors asking who the fastest runner in the class was in the first days of the academy. He boldly raised his hand and said, "Sir me"! He was right through, he was the fastest runner in the class of 120. He was an ex-Marine, a trained warrior. Today he is one of my closest straight friends who is totally supportive of Cesar and me.

I should have known from day one how dangerous being a cop was. While on the shooting range at the old academy, I saw the recruit standing next to me go down and heard officers yelling, "Cease fire." The recruit had holstered a loaded, caulked weapon and it discharged a 9mm round right into his leg. The recruit never made it through the academy due to his injuries.

During the last part of the academy I was sent to Emergency Vehicle Operation Course (EVOC), in Ontario, CA, at the Ontario Airport. Little did I know this airport is owned by the City of Los Angeles. During this class we learned how to drive at high speeds and maintain control of the vehicle. We also learned how so many officers lose their lives in vehicle accidents. My partner through a majority of this class was Robert Mata. Damn! We had so much fun spinning the vehicles out of control and doing the practice pursuits.

Just prior to graduating from the LAPD academy I was assigned to West Los Angeles Station, a community that was much like Irvine, California. It is a predominantly wealthy community with many very prominent people. When I learned of this assignment, I was kind of relieved in a way, not that it was any safer, but I had heard so many horror stories about the southern divisions. That was short lived though: about a week before graduating I was called into the office. As I banged on the door and yelled, "Officer Sanders sir," I was terrified. When I was called into the office, I was informed that there was a change in assignments and that I would be going to Rampart Division and not West Los Angeles Division. This was one of the most violent areas in the city. It was a 5.4 square mile area just west of downtown Los Angeles the population of which was primarily composed of Guatemalans, El Salvadorians, and Mexicans. It had an extremely high crime rate.

When I started at Rampart, one of the first things I noticed in the briefing room was the homicide rate that they kept track of on the chalk board. 150+ was the number. 150 people murdered in a 5.4 square mile area in one year. On the other side of the board was the officer involved shooting they had. I do not recall the exact number but it was between 20 and 30.

I had various field training officers (FTOs). The one that taught me the most was a six-foot 5-inch-tall stalky female. Her presentation was amazing and you didn't dare cross her because she would kick your ass. It was clear to me while I was with her that I didn't have what it took to be an officer and needed to step it up. In an attempt to get me up to par, she went over the most important aspects of the job. On morning watch she would scream through the streets and alleys, then slam the breaks on. "John, you have just been shot. Put out over the radio what you are going to say." Of course I got it all wrong and had no idea where I was. "John if you don't know where the fuck you are, how is anyone else going to help you? Get the fuck out of the car and run to the nearest corner and figure out where you are!" After running to the corner and running back to the police car, I pretended I was putting out the emergency broadcast. "2A47, Officers need help West 5th St and South Park View Street, I need a perimeter…!" I never asked, but I think she was family (gay). She got this queen up to par and to this day I appreciate all she did for me. In an effort to get my confidence up she would seek out the most hardened criminals. I remember one day she stopped this hot 20-something-year-old Latino gangster. I guess I saw the good in people and tried to look past the tattoo above his right eyebrow that said "Fuck LAPD" and the tattoo on his chin that said "18." If there was no good inside him, he sure looked good on the outside. Following this contact she stressed the importance of not letting my guard down: these kids had no problem killing a cop. The uniform alone was offensive to these kids.

I was on the job only a few months when Officer Mario Navidad was killed. He had just left Rampart Division, where he also trained, to go to Wilshire Division. While on patrol he and his partner were flagged down by a citizen reporting a beer run. When Officer Navidad and his partner confronted the suspect in an alley, the suspect pulled a gun and shot Officer Navidad. Officer Navidad had only been on the job a year and was 27 years old. What a senseless loss of life. His death left two children fatherless. The suspect who killed Officer Navidad was a teenager. My FTO was right: they have no problem killing us. Officer Navidad was buried on December 31, 1996.

After completing field training, I was placed with other PII (pronounced "P2") officers. They were the real workers. The FTOs were too busy making sure the trainees didn't get themselves killed. It was ten minutes before the end of watch and the PII I was working with would work until the very end. My partner would drive around the worst areas of town and read off plates to me. As I ran the last plate of the night I overheard, "2A47 Code 6 Charles indicated verify your location." At LAPD, "Code 6 Charles" meant that you had just run a felony warrant if it were a person or a vehicle involved in something serious like a murder. "John! You gonna answer the radio they are calling you." I could not even respond to dispatch quick enough. "2A47 we are in pursuit south bound on the 101 from Rampart!" This would be one of the craziest pursuits I have ever been in. Forty-five minutes later it ended in Glendale, CA. The next day I was complimented for being so calm on the radio. I remember thinking that I was in too deep at this point. I was married and starting to be respected as a police officer. I began to believe the gay phase was over and I was becoming straight.

After working many months on "graveyards," I was transferred to day watch. I was not thrilled about this. On February 28, 1997 I was working with this old crusty FTO. He had been weathered by the violence he had seen in his time. He was a good guy, but he was nearing his retirement and preferred to start off slow and taper off. After leaving roll call, we drove to the Elysian Park Police Academy. My partner wanted to shoot and take care of some business. We arrived at the academy at about 0900 hours.

When we got there I stayed in the car as most boots (new hires) do when they are on probation. The elite Metro Division Officers were running and shooting as they did on a daily basis. At about 0917 hour, unbeknownst to me, two men had entered the Bank of America, in North Hollywood. Since we were on different channels I did not hear the initial radio traffic. At about 0930 hours, I heard over the Rampart radio frequency, "Attention all units this is a Tactical Alert Broadcast, due to an unusual event in North Hollywood all units are on Tactical Alert." What this meant is that no one could go home. Immediately following this broadcast, I turned my radio to the North Hollywood frequency. What could possibly be going on at this time in the morning?

Once I was on the frequency this is what I heard. "Officers need help! Shots fired! Fully automatic weapons 15L40 is requesting HELP... All units officer requesting help Laurel Canyon north of Kittridge!" What I heard on the radio stills makes me cringe to this very day. As I looked down I saw I had a 9mm Berretta and a shotgun with double odd buck. These suspects had fully automatic weapons. I got out of the car and ran to get my partner who probably didn't hear the radio traffic because he was on the range. As I ran up the hill, Metro Division was running down the hill in their tennis shoes, shorts and t-shirts. When they got to their police vehicles they threw on their tactical vest and sped toward North Hollywood. That is how dire the situation was, no time to put on the full uniform. After finding my partner I turned back to the Rampart frequency.

I then heard the Rampart dispatcher say, "All Rampart units Code Alpha at the station." Dispatch was requesting every Rampart unit to return to the station to get a group of volunteers to go to North Hollywood Division to assist in the shootout. When we arrived at the station, I immediately raised my hand and volunteered: this is what I had signed up for, to "protect and serve." My partner, who outranked me and was near retirement, immediately overrode my decision and advised the watch commander that we would stay behind. I was pissed! How could this straight male police officer choose to stay behind? Needless to say I was stuck in

Rampart shagging the few radio calls there were, because the entire nation was watching the shootout on live TV. Today I have a better understanding of why partner choose to stay behind, though I don't agree with it. In total 11 officers had been injured, seven civilians had been injured and two suspects were dead.

After being transferred out of Rampart to Southwest Division, I saw the bad side of LAPD. Officers who I had worked with were accused of criminal activity on and off duty. The officers were from Rampart Division and Southwest Division. The incident was labeled the Rampart Scandal. It really hurt me that I was trying to make a difference in society and other officers took advantage of their power. In addition to this I came to a division that was still very racially divided both in the community and in the police station. Despite all the bad things that were occurring at the time, a majority of officers were trying to protect the community. I don't ever recall the community protesting the tremendous amount of youth that lost their lives to gun violence but there were protests over the three or four officers that were corrupt, and I thought that was outrageous. When you have a 9,000 member police department, three or four officers was a very small percentage of crooked cops.

Not everything was bad, though. I met another great officer who shared my values and today is still one of my best friends. He is straight. It was also in this division that I would meet two other officers. Both also were married, so I never questioned their sexuality. Years later we would all cross paths at a gay cop party. They too had kids and had been divorced. None of us were out at the time and had no knowledge of the other until this party.

While working in Southwest, another Officer was killed in the line of duty, but this time it was at my station. He was shot in the head in a senseless attack on LAPD. His name was Officer Filberto Henry Cuesta Jr. Once again I attended a funeral for a fallen officer who died way too soon. He had only been on the job four years. He left behind a wife and two daughters.

At the first opportunity I left Southwest Division and transferred to Hollenbeck Division, also referred to as East Los Angeles. I think my spirit had been broken in Southwest. I felt like I made no positive change in this Division or this community.

I feel like Hollenbeck is where I belonged. I fit into this community and could relate to them and their struggles. A majority of the community was trying to make an honest living. There was a small percent of the community that was committing all the violence and crimes in the community. This small percentage of gang members ruled the community. People were scared to cross them. This area had several housing projects and it was well known that the Mexican mafia was heavily involved in the gang activity. They were dealing drugs, taxing the vendors and stores, and taking out those who crossed them faster than we could identify them.

With the Rampart Scandal still winding down, LAPD started to do integrity checks. One of my partners had a connection with the Rampart Scandal and I found myself being followed by helicopters anywhere we went. My partner was straight up with me and explained the situation. An officer (Rafael Perez) had checked out several kilos of cocaine in his name and it was never returned. He told me to go to the north end of the division. The helicopter followed at a very high altitude. He then told me to go to the south end of the division. The helicopter followed. I wanted no part of it, we literally did nothing the entire time he was my partner.

Though I can never prove it, I think I had many integrity checks done on me. Twice I was summoned to abandoned vehicles. One vehicle had eight kilos of cocaine in the back seat, the other vehicle had several thousand dollars on the floorboard. I truly believe that it was not coincidence. I believe that they were doing a sting operation on us, due to my partner's connections to Rampart. It was important that Internal Affairs did this, though. Despite the integrity checks, officers continued to cross the line and violate the trust of the community. While all this was occurring, I was still lying to myself and everyone around me.

While at Hollenbeck, an FTO would drop off his trainee and go make traffic stops on citizens. While contacting the citizens the FTO would steal their money. Needless to say he was arrested also.

I did well in Hollenbeck and was quickly assigned to Community Resources against Street Hoodlums (CRASH). They did not receive any radio calls and were to focus and gang issues. We were assigned to one street to enforce gang activity. Needless to say the second we left our area a shooting would occur. While working in CRASH, we would be sent to break up gang parties. One of things I came across working Hollenbeck was the gay gang parties in this division. As I stood like a military figure in front of these parties I could not question how these gang members had the courage to be openly gay gang members. These gang members were tough and they had no problem killing me in a heartbeat. This really struck a chord with me. Not that I had any respect for them, but I did question how they had more courage than I did. I was not honest with myself, my friends, my family, or my wife. I was lying to everyone! I was hiding behind the badge, behind my own fears, behind my paranoia.

Shortly after the fallout from the Rampart Scandal, CRASH would be disbanded. Our next assignment would be working Sunset Junction Street Fair, basically a Gay Pride. When we were assigned to this, I remember a lot of the officers complaining about the fags, the gays and such. One officer mentioned that he wanted to cite anyone he saw kissing. Despite all the grumbling, I was excited to take the assignment. Once again I questioned my own courage. How could all these men have the courage to be out in their personal lives, but I was hiding behind my marriage and my badge.

The disbandment of CRASH would be short lived. It was renamed the GANG unit and put back in action. The only change was, under the direction of the new chief, we were to take little to no enforcement action unless forced to. The writing was on the wall: I was not going to make a difference at this department and started looking elsewhere.

After responding to a shooting call in one of the projects, I came to a crossroads in my career at LAPD. As I looked at the crime scene and the innocent children who had been shot in the head with an AK-47 assault rifle, I was appalled. This was senseless, no suspects were in custody and several victims lay dead in the street. It would be over a week before LAPD took any action on this senseless act. I began to apply elsewhere and learned how much other agencies were earning in salary and saw that police were actually appreciated in those communities.

As I lay in bed with my wife I woke up in a cold sweat and panic. Something told me something was wrong; instinct, maybe, told me to turn on the television. "Breaking News"; I do not even recall what was said at first. I saw LAPD officers frantically pushing a gurney to an ambulance with an officer on the gurney. Paramedics were attempting CPR. It appeared that the officer had been thrown on the gurney. His right leg was hanging off the side of the gurney, dangling, limp, and lifeless. All I heard was that an LAPD Harbor Division officer had been involved in a traffic collision while responding to the call and taken to the hospital. I called my contact in Harbor Division, a fellow classmate, immediately. "Smith," I said, "who was involved in the accident?"

"John you need to come to the hospital immediately. Mata was involved in an accident and they do not think he is going to make it, he is at...."

As I woke my wife and informed her of the news, she also panicked as she was friends with Robert Mata's wife. I had not even gotten out the door before I received a call that he had died in surgery. I cried for days, didn't eat for days and went into depression. What the metro officer told me on the first days of the academy had come true. Someone in class 1-96 would die in the line of duty within five years of being on the job. In the time that I was at LAPD, seven officers would lose their lives in the line of duty.

Following this incident Peter Jennings did a documentary on LAPD. Jennings said in the documentary, "There is no more dangerous place in America to be a police officer, and there is no more dangerous place to be a young man." This was so true. I had seen so much violence and so many officers lose their lives trying to "protect and serve" their communities.

In Memorial
Mario Navidad Jr.

Van Derick Johnson

Steven Gerald Gajda

Filberto Henry Cuesta Jr.

Brian Ernest Fenimore Brown

Louis Villalobos Jr.

Robert Joe Mata

Shortly after Robert Mata was killed in the line of duty, I was hired by the Irvine Police Department along with three other LAPD officers who had had enough of the politics and the senseless loss of life of both officers and citizens. It was the complete opposite of LAPD, very professional, very conservative, and a very wealth community.

I managed to do well at Irvine PD. I was able to obtain a position as a K-9 officer. I guess I had no fear after working at LAPD. Though I was at LAPD for five years, I was never involved in an officer involved shooting (OIS) until I came to Irvine. At LAPD I had come close to shooting a suspect, but never pulled the trigger. On June 28, 2004 at 0156 hours that would all change. While working as a K-9 officer, I overheard another officer say that she was in pursuit of a vehicle. I joined in as the third unit in the pursuit—that's what K-9 officers are supposed to do. During the course of the pursuit the suspect vehicle was "spike stripped." This meant that we placed a strip in the roadway, ahead of the suspect vehicle, that was intended to puncture the suspect vehicle's tires when it crossed. Despite this, the vehicle continued to flee. When the vehicle finally crashed it still did not stop him. The suspect attempted to run my partners and me over with his vehicle. In fear for my life I fired one round striking the suspect in the "ten ring" (center mass of the chest). I had no issues shooting the suspect, and I had no second thoughts about what I did: it wasn't excessive, it was justified, and I had to go home to my two kids and wife alive, not in a body bag. I never had nightmares, depression or any other issues with this incident. I know I did what I had to do. Like any OIS, I was put on administrative leave for three days.

Following my OIS, I returned to K-9 training in Jurupa Valley. While I was at K-9 training I received a call from my wife. She wanted me to come home because we "needed to talk." I knew what that meant, something was wrong. When I came home she took me into the enormous living room in the house we lived in and told me she wanted a divorce. I didn't say anything: no argument, no discussion, no anything, I just said okay.

I think deep inside I thought that this was my way out of all the lies; I was actually relieved. We lived together for six months following her advisement, cordial to each other until she asked me to move out of the house. She confronted me and wanted to know why I was just willing to walk away from the marriage with no counseling, no discussion, no anything. I couldn't tell her the truth. This was what was best for us. I didn't tell her my feelings had grown deeper, and I found that I was having a hard time suppressing them. After thinking about our situation for several months I felt I needed to be honest for once in my life.

After a long drive home with her one night, returning home from a doctor's appointment in Orange County, I felt that I could lie no more. I told her, "The reason I am not trying to make this work out is because I think I am gay."

She said nothing for about ten minutes. "What do you mean you think you are gay?"

I should have prepared myself for this moment. It was a spontaneous statement. From this time on, things were not good. It is one thing to have a marriage fail because of another woman, but when your husband is attracted to another guy, how could she compete? The biggest fear I had is what would happen with my kids: would they be taken away from me for my disclosure?

Several months later I filed for divorce. I really wanted us to be cordial for the kids' sake, but unfortunately this would not be the case. The gay issue would be thrown in my face by everyone involved in the court process. While in court-ordered mediation, I caught the mediator making an issue about me being gay. She implied that I was less of a parent because I was gay and would expose my children to things that they should not see in society. The fact that I was a cop and had shift duty made it even worse. I was asked how I could possibly manage caring for my children when I am on shift work. The fact that my wife worked shift work didn't seem to matter. Immediately following this meeting, I filed a complaint against this employee for the comments made. It was the only time in my life that I truly felt that I was being discriminated against. After many months of court battles, the failure to compromise was prevalent. It was also taking its toll on our kids, who would show physical symptoms of the court process. Once the battle was over, we had accomplished nothing except to max-out all of our credit cards. The standard court order would be issued. I would have the kids every weekend except the second weekend of the month. This process took its toll on me. I became short tempered and fearful that my co-workers would find out what was going on in my personal life.

In the months to come I thought the worst part of my life was over. I outed myself to my wife, I outed myself to my friends, I outed myself to my family. I discovered two things: one, those who were my true friends supported me and stood by my side regardless of their views; two, those who claimed they were my friends but had their own prejudices against gays did not support me and immediately cut me off. They were those of strong religious views, those whose stereotypes overrode their ability to see all the good I have done, and those who viewed me as weak and a lesser human being.

Following this turmoil in my life, I understood why teenagers who were gay took their own lives when they had no support. The feeling of being alone on a remote island was incredible. Thankfully I recognized the need to maintain my mental health. I sought counseling and was reassured I was not alone. After searching the internet I found a support group. The group was called the Golden State Police Officers Association (GSPOA). It was a social group for gay police officers. At first I thought I was being set up, but on a leap of faith, I joined. This group would later be renamed the Gay Police Officers Association (GPOA). It was through this group that I met another LAPD cop who had been married and had kids. He shared his story with me and asked me to read a book called *The Other Side of the Closet*. This book helped me understand that I was not alone, and for the first time, I started to find comfort in myself. This book was written before any of Greg's books and was not anyone related to law enforcement. At the time it was the best I had.

Though I was out to my friends and family, I was not out in my professional life. As I walked through the back doors of the Irvine Police Department, I saw the poster displayed on the wall: "Integrity, Respect, Accountability, Quality of Service." How could I live by these values when I had no integrity? I lied to my co-workers on a daily basis. How could I be accountable when I was not accountable to myself? How could I provide Quality of Service to those I serve when I myself was lying in my daily life? I had an awakening when I read this, following my outing in my personal life. I could lie no more, in my personal life or my professional life. If I was to be fired for this, it was something I was willing to accept. I no longer cared what anyone thought of me, I needed to find my own happiness. In my decision to be out in my personal and professional lives a ton of bricks was taken off my back.

In January 2007 I would be faced with critical decisions again. "1A15 possible homicide in progress, respond code three." The comments of the call indicated that a subject had assaulted another person with a shovel. Well, Irvine is known for strange calls, so this did not surprise me. When I arrived on scene, what I saw was horrific. A worker high on methamphetamine had beaten his boss with a pick and shovel, bashing his head into the ground. Like the pursuit I was in, I would once again be confronted with shooting another human being, except this time it was a murder suspect. I could have easily justified shooting this subject as I faced off with him and ordered him to drop the shovel that he now held over his head, but I didn't. He was in an attack position about 50 feet from me. It's something that society never sees, that officers truly only use lethal for only when no other options exist. Was I scared? Hell yes. Was it the time to show it? Hell no. Thankfully Irvine PD had equipped me with options other than just taking a life. The suspect would eventually be apprehended with a 40mm less than lethal rubber bullet.

Though I now worked in the City of Irvine, I realized that there is a reason that I had a job: to protect and serve the community. Regardless of where geographically I worked, being a police officer was a very dangerous job, and being in Irvine was no different.

Following this I would work as a field training officer (FTO), and later go on to obtain a position as a detective. It was the highlight of my career. I was no longer on the street. I was now searching for those who escaped apprehension in the field. I worked property crimes and then was selected for a CRIMES AGAINST PERSON (CAP) Detective. CAP detectives investigated rapes, domestic violence, child abuse and homicides.

In this time I met my husband, Cesar. He never knew any gays cops and was introduced to the difficulties of dating a cop real fast. The shift work, the coming home late, the missing important family events, the uncertainty of the job. I met Cesar online through an online dating service. Once we met I knew it was a match. He put my children first, he was not selfish, he had a heart of gold, and, most important, he wanted a relation-ship and not just a hook up. These are qualities that can be hard to find in today's society. After dating for three years I asked him to enter a domestic partnership with me, since gay marriage was not allowed in the State of California. We had set a date of July 6, 2013 for a commitment ceremony. As the date neared, I already had the support of my friends and family and I could not wait for the date to come. I told those close to me about my decision. I also told my co-workers who all supported me.

I was finally comfortable in my skin and no longer worried about proving myself as an officer, because I had proven to myself over and over that I would back my fellow officers even if that involved placing my life on the line. The fact that I was gay was not an issue. The fears that I had about coming out in the workplace were fears that I created in my head, the paranoia was something I created. What mattered is how I performed as a police officer, not who I loved or slept with.

On February 7, 2013 I was on-call for the Irvine Police Department. My sergeant had called me late that night, the night of the Super Bowl. "John, I need you to come into work immediately, we had a double homicide."

I thought my sergeant was joking, and said, "Oh come on, what really happened?"

"John I am not kidding around, respond to…!"

As I ran to get my gear, I responded to the location. It was located in a wealthy apartment complex parking structure. When I got to the top of the parking structure, I walked up to the white vehicle and saw the two deceased victims in their vehicle. Both had been shot numerous times. My LAPD training and experience had kicked in. This was not a random mur-der; this was an execution, with a token left behind. I would later learn that the female victim was the daughter of a retired LAPD Captain and the male was an officer at USC. I wrote the initial search warrants for this case and woke the judge up to present the case to him. He could not believe what he was reading as the location was right across from his office. Once the search warrant was signed, little did I know that I was opening a Pandora's Box.

Though I was not the lead detective, I consulted with the co-case Detective in the 20th hour of work. We had both surmised that the homicide involved someone who was ex-military or cop. No one else had the skill to be that precise. A day or two later the leads would come. I came to work and told my supervisor of what I had learned from a friend at Gardena PD. He had informed me that the female victim's father was an ex-LAPD captain who represented police officers who were facing termination. My supervisor had shared that someone had called the watch commander and notified him that she suspected a former trainee of hers was suspect. His uniform and belongings had been found in a National City trashcan across from the police department. It was reported to us that he had been terminated in a board of rights hearing, at LAPD. I was immediately sent to National City to follow up on this lead. National City is a city far south of Irvine and near the Mexican Border. My partner and I then headed south to follow up on this lead.

When I arrived in National City I collected the video evidence that would later be seen on CNN. Other officers in Irvine were also collecting evidence from the Irvine crime scene. During the time I was in National City, Irvine Intel officers discovered the manifesto posted on Facebook and the pieces started to fall into place. Within an hour, a whole team of officers had arrived at my location to assist me in the search. Later that night my chief would go on national TV and announce that Christopher Jordan Dorner was the suspect in these murders. Within a few hours I found myself at the Otay Mesa border crossing. Since I stood out like a sore thumb in my business suit, I went to a local store and purchased street clothes. Intel had indicated he may be heading for Mexico.

I couldn't find Christopher Dorner that night, nor could my partner who had an AR-15 at his side. We looked until exhaustion. When I returned to the station after being unable to locate Dorner, I walked up to the Emergency Operations Center (EOC) to check out and go home. While in the EOC, word had come in that Dorner, had attempted to "boat-jack" a boat in San Diego. Detectives were again sent to San Diego with the FBI. As those detectives were returning from that investigation, word came into the EOC that Dorner had been spotted in Corona by LAPD, and an officer involved shooting occurred. The information was poor at best. Shortly thereafter word came in that two officers from Riverside had been shot. One had died from his injuries. Then the trail went cold.

Since I had been in the middle of the investigation, I knew things were going to get bad. At this point Dorner had shot three officers and a daughter of an LAPD Captain. One of the Riverside officers lost his life to Dorner. Since I completed the original search warrant I was concerned that my personal information would be obtained by the media and I had legitimate concerns about my personal safety and the safety of my kids, Cesar and my family. I remember telling Cesar that I could not tell him everything I knew, because much of the information was still confidential. But I told him to trust me in what I said, that he needed to protect himself. I informed him to take the gun out of the safe and warned him that all law enforcement and their families were in danger. I also spoke with my ex-wife who I had become cordial with and requested that in the best interests of our children she keep them at her undisclosed living location. She agreed. I also explained to our children that it was in their best interests to stay with their mother until this was resolved. When the leads went cold a decision was made to have a centralized command post where information could be shared with all the involved agencies. I was then re-assigned to Joint Regional Intelligence Center (JRIC). As I drove to and from this location I continually checked my six.

About a week later Dorner was located in Big Bear, California, but not before he could severely injure a San Bernardino County sheriff's deputy and kill another San Bernardino sheriff's deputy. This was the lowest point of my life. I, like others involved in this investigation, felt that all the loss of life could have prevented if we could have identified the suspect earlier. Like others in my department, we felt great guilt at the loss of life and the innocent victims who were affected by this mad man. In the following days I would attend two funerals with my co-workers and Cesar. There is a joke among the cops that it is important to take mental health days (MHD) if you are a police officer. Following this incident I realized that this was not a joke but a reality.

I don't tell these stories to be war stories, but because gay men and women protect and serve their communities on a daily basis. We place our lives in the same risk that any straight officer does, and no one really sees that. Prior to the overturning of Proposition 8, if I was killed in the line of duty my partner would receive no death benefits. I think have finally realized the inequality in that.

On June 26, 2013, Proposition 8 (the ban against gay marriage) was overturned just days prior to our commitment ceremony. Cesar and I scrambled to get the paperwork together and ran down to the courthouse so we could be legally married. We were one of the first gay couples to be at the courthouse. The local newspaper interviewed us and took our photo as we obtained our marriage license. I knew I was risking having my photo taken because it would be the paper that all of Orange County reads. Co-workers would later show me the photos. I received nothing but support.

On July 6, 2013 Cesar and I got married in our home, among those who stood by my side through thick and thin. This included many of my straight partners from LAPD and Irvine PD. It was one of the greatest moments of my life. Both my parents attended and supported me, though I know it was a long road to get to this point.

Today I am thankful that I have moved from where I was at to where I am at now. I am confident in my skin, and no longer shameful for anything. I am proud to be gay and proud to be a cop. When people say I am a gay cop, I correct them and say "No, I am a cop that happens to be gay." I am out in my personal and professional lives now and have found comfort in knowing that I am not alone. Others that I know have also found the courage to be out after seeing that I had no issues in the workplace.

No one really cares that I am gay and if they do they most likely are not my friend. I still hear grumblings about the LGBT community from time to time in public, such as, "Look at those fags holding hands." I think everyone will experience the inappropriate comments said in society at some point: you can ignore them or confront them about it.

As for my workplace environment, I don't think anyone cares. If they do have an issue with me they have not mentioned anything to me. Because when it comes down to it, your partners want to know that you are going to be there when that help call goes out. We all know that there are two types of people: those who run toward danger and those who run from it. As long as you're running toward the danger your partners will respect you, at least that has been my experience. Hopefully by telling my story others will find the same courage to come out in their personal and professional lives and come out of the closest, because it can be a very dark lonely place.

I do not think that I could have ever become the man I am today without all the love and support of my parents, and I cannot write my story without acknowledging both of them. Unfortunately, prior to the writing of my story, my father lost his life to kidney cancer in November 2014. I dedicate my story to him. You will be forever missed, Dad.

A LETTER TO LGBT YOUTH
FROM DEPUTY ANTHONY MORGADO

All my life I have followed my dream of becoming a peace officer. I have worked hard to reach my goals in life. I have struggled and I have cried. There was always part of me growing up that made me feel hindered about reaching my goals. I've known I am gay since I was a little boy. I can remember as far back as elementary school having this strange feeling in my stomach about a fellow classmate; freaked out because I'd never had this strange feeling before. At the age of 13, I became the youngest police cadet. I was held to the same standards and had to pass the same test as everyone else did to become a police cadet. But once I became a Police Cadet I quickly learned how being gay was not okay in law enforcement by my peer's and that most of Solano County was very homophobic! This experience truly made me feel like I was going to be the only gay peace officer in the world. I thought I would have to be closeted my whole life. I finally reached the age of 21 and went through the Napa Police Academy. Going through the academy changed my life forever! Something happened that I would have never thought of happening in a million years: I finally came out as a gay man! The warmth and support I received from my family and friends was absolutely amazing (to say the least), and I owe this major life-changing event to Greg Miraglia, who helped me and showed me it's ok to be who you are!

I went to my first Gay Pride parade in 2012 in San Francisco and marched with the San Francisco Police Officer Pride Alliance, a truly amazing feeling! Later on that year I was hired by the Solano County Sheriff's Office as the first openly Gay Deputy Sheriff, something I would have never seen in a millions years! The overwhelming support I've received from my co-workers has been inspiring and amazing. Now, for the first time in my life, I will be marching in the SF Gay Pride parade in my Solano County Deputy Sheriff's uniform with my amazing boyfriend Devin Kasper and the San Francisco Police Department.

The reason why I write all this today, is because just a few short years ago I would have never thought I would have ever been writing something like this, let alone marching in a Gay Pride parade in my uniform. The reason why I march in the Gay Pride Parade is not to rub in people's faces that I am gay, but to show people to stand up for what you believe in and follow your dreams. Take the risk, jump through the hoops, and see where life takes you. March in the Gay Pride parade to show other people that it's ok to be gay, that they can be loved, have a family and friends, to marry the one you love, and you can be who you want to be. It truly is an amazing feeling that's hard to describe when you're marching down Market St in SF and there are over a million people there supporting you and saying its okay to be who you are! I march because I hope that one day no one person has to feel or go through the struggle I went through. Thank you all for making a difference in my life!

AN INTERVIEW WITH OFFICER PATRICIA FITZPATRICK

Briefly describe yourself, including age, law enforcement, fire, and or EMS experience, what part of the country you are from and anything else you feel is important to know about you.

I am retired from the FDNY. I was hired with the first group of women firefighters in 1982. I was a New York City Transit Police officer from October of 1981 until I transferred to the fire department. I may have not articulated the fact I was a lesbian, however I have been out about my sexuality from the age of 16. As a firefighter I was instrumental is the early stages of FireFlag. I stepped down from working with Eugene Walsh because he outed active firefighters against their wishes to gain departmental recognition. I felt poorly, however I had other issues at the time that I needed to address. I was proud that Thomas Ryan stepped up and spearheaded the formal recognition of gays, lesbians and transgender firefighters. I did not march in the first Pride Parade, which included the FDNY, because that morning my dog was hit by a car and tragically died. I have marched in uniform since 1999 and had the honor of driving the first department vehicle in the parade after I retired. I was injured in the line of duty in a building collapse in 1997 and retired in 1998. I reported to my firehouse on September 11, 2001, although I had been retired, and served at the site for a few weeks.

1. How did you become interested in law enforcement, firefighting, or the EMS profession?

I took the tests for the police and fire department because of the benefits. I felt that I could perform the physical aspects of either job because I was an athlete my whole life. When thinking about possible careers, the idea of working in an office at a desk was unappealing to me.

2. When did you discover you were gay, lesbian, or bisexual and what did you think about relative to your interest in law enforcement, firefighting or EMS?

I knew I liked girls, the way boys liked girls, at the age of six, and had no idea what that meant. I often felt that a mistake was made because I was a girl who liked girls. I played softball and as a teenager began to play with older woman who were also lesbian. I do not think my sexuality played a role in my decision to take the civil service exams for these non-traditional occupations. My fears about financial insecurity because of the way I grew up was a greater influence. The fact that I am a physical person was another factor in my decision to take these tests.

3. Describe your experience getting hired and going through your training academy. Were you out? Did you come out during the academy?

My cousin was president of the UFOA when I was preparing to enter the fire service. I was already a transit police officer and was living with my lover on west 72nd street in Manhattan. We met for dinner and he basically told me that being a woman in the fire service was going to be harder than Jackie Robinson breaking into baseball. Vincent Bollon told me point blank to move out and not live with my lover. He knew of only one "fag" in the department and it was not a pleasant experience for that firefighter. I didn't take that suggestion, however I did do the things he said a probationary firefighter ought to do around the firehouse. The hiring process was difficult for the first group of women hired by the FDNY. I think that being a lesbian increased my levels of anxiety and fear. I may not have been a radical out lesbian, however I did not hide the fact that I was gay and eventually became more comfortable in time. I had trepidation being verbally open about who I was in the firehouse but did disclose my sexuality to some individuals. I felt uncomfortable taking my lover to the first company dance I attended. I asked my brother's lover Richie to escort me because these functions are important. At the dance, a co-worker, Tony, upon being introduced to Richie asked, "So how long have you been gay?" I realized that they knew on some level that I was a lesbian although I did not have the courage to be verbally open about it.

4. What was it like starting off in your department? Did you come out? If not, what kept you, or is currently keeping you from coming out at work?

I have the unique experience of being in one of the first groups of women to become a New York City firefighter. My sexuality increased my fear of acceptance. I was prodded at times during meals for information about myself, however I did not indulge them specifically. It took me some time to feel comfortable enough with them as a group to be open about my life. I was open with individuals who I worked with at the firehouse. My alcoholism advanced enough under the stress of these variables and I sought treatment in 1989, seven years after being appointed.

Recovery from this addiction and subsequent treatment gave me the inner fortitude to be inclusively authentic. In the early 1990s I worked with Eugene Walsh to get departmental recognition for FireFlag. I was co-president until a letter was sent to the department without my knowledge outing active firefighters to which I was opposed. As a result I was embarrassed and stepped down. I know today that I didn't handle it correctly, however I was pleased when Thomas Ryan stepped in and got the organization recognized by the department. In recovery I realized that my inability to discuss my personal life kept me from fully enjoying my relationships with all my co-workers. In 1996 I had a commitment ceremony and invited members of my house to attend. Of course I knew that some would decline. One firefighter thanked me for inviting him and said he was not going because he didn't believe it was right. I thanked him for his honesty, told him he was entitled to his feelings and that I was sorry he wouldn't attend because he was going to miss a great party.

5. Describe your most difficult situation being gay in your public safety profession.

I think that my own attitudes were the most difficult to overcome. I am grateful that I was able to get sober and deal with the issues that underlay my alcoholism.

6. What specific event or general experience surprised you most about being gay in your profession?

My cousin's remark put some fear in me however it didn't stop me from living my life, it only kept me from being out. That changed with my recovery from alcoholism. I began to be open and talk about myself, causing my relationships to deepen. I was fortunate to have friends and family who accepted me without question.

7. What, if anything, would you have done differently relative to being gay in your profession?

I think it all happened just the way it was supposed to and would not change a thing.

8. One of the important goals of this book is to help fellow gay law enforcement officers, firefighters, and EMS professionals and their allies. What advice can you provide to the following people?

Reach out for support. Be true to yourself.

9. What else would you like to say that you feel is most important for readers to know about you or your ideas?

The most important thing is to know is that my own fear and internalized homophobia kept me from being true to myself.

FROM OFFICER SCOTT GUNN

I guess we need to start with an introduction. My name is Scott Gunn and I am 47 years old. I started my law enforcement career at age 21 in April 1989 as a 911 operator with the Anne Arundel County Police Department in Maryland. The police department has over 800 sworn members and 200 civilian members and serves a population of 537,000 with over 588 square miles. I was hired because the police department had started to move from a punch card dispatching system to a computer aided dispatch one. When I was hired, I was trained on the punch card and computer dispatching systems. I moved quickly from being a call-taker to a dispatcher. At the same time as I applied for the dispatcher position, I also applied for the police officer position. In 1989 the waiting time for a police officer position was extensive. In March of 1990 I was told that I had been selected for the police academy class. On March 23, 1990 I started the academy. This is a time in my life that I was still trying to convince myself that I was straight. I was living in the straight world. The academy lasted a little over six months. I graduated third in my class and started my career in our Western District.

I absolutely loved my career and had a blast working with some amazing people. I was dating a female dispatcher early on in my career. We dated for a long time and then took the next step and moved in together. Things started to fall apart with the relationship and soon I discovered she was cheating with one of my co-workers. That relationship came to an abrupt end.

In 1992 I was still working patrol in our Western District. I became very close to my then side partner (female) and before I knew it we were dating. We eventually moved in together, bought a house, and—yes—got married. She was a few years older than me and already had children. That was good with me because I really had no desire to have children of my own. We had the happy life for a few years. We traveled, and had a great network of friends (mostly police.) I knew something was missing, but I was still not ready to admit that I was gay. I was always faithful to my wife, although she does not believe it. Our marriage lasted almost five years, but became very rocky due to financial issues.

It is funny to think back in my life at the time all of this was going on. I had great friends that I worked with every day. I became closest to several lesbian officers. It is a good thing because they sure got me through some rough days. I separated from my wife in 1998. I did a lot of soul searching and finally admitted to myself that I just might be gay. I was hanging out with my lesbian friends more and more. They dragged me out to one of their lesbian bars. I will never forget that first time stepping in the bar. I had a blast talking to everyone and got hit on by the doorman—yes, a man. I still had not admitted anything to my lesbian friends and they did not notice me being hit on. We left the bar and headed back home. After I parted ways with them I got in my own car and drove back to the bar. I stayed at the bar until closing and finally discovered that, yes, I was gay. I was over 30 years old at the time and was like a young schoolgirl. The next day I reached out to my friends and had them meet me at a local Starbucks. When I told them what happened, I think they were happier than I was. It was hilarious and something I will never forget.

I knew at that point that the marriage was over. I eventually made the biggest mistake of my life, which was being honest with my ex-wife. I thought it would be easier for her to know the truth, but I could not have been more wrong. She immediately started blackmailing me with what I had told her. She kept threatening to tell my colleagues, my friends and my family. I was terrified at the time, not knowing what would happen if she did what she was threatening. I would give in to whatever she was asking for just so she would not tell anyone. Finally, many months into the separation and months after I had been honest with her, she said something to me on the telephone that just set me off. She again threatened to tell everyone in my life. I had had enough and called her bluff. Well, she did exactly as she said she would. She called all of the mutual friends that we had and told them. She drove to my parents and told them and she told my co-workers and supervisors. I was completely outed to everyone before I was completely out to myself. I will never forget the call from my sister. She told me that my ex-wife had just left my parent's house and it would be a good idea for me to get over there.

I went to my parent's house immediately. I was not sure how things were going to go. I knew how racist my father could be so I kind of expected him to have issues. I was close to my mother, so I thought she would be ok. Things don't always go the way you expect them. My father was amazing, but my mother was distant. My ex-wife had been working sex-crimes and child abuse investigations at the time so not only did she tell my parents that I was gay; she accused my father of abusing me and causing me to be that way. The only thing my father was upset about was that he thought I had told her that I thought I had been abused. I had to assure him that I never told her that and knew that I had not been abused.

While I had been married I continued to move ahead with my department. I was the first officer assigned to a newly created Tactical Patrol Unit. It was the department's way of implementing a Community Policing Model. I was assigned to several communities within the Western District and became responsible for fixing their quality of life issues. I loved the one-on-one policing and made a lot of progress within the communities I was assigned to. I then moved to our Tactical Narcotics Team. We were an undercover street level narcotics unit assigned to the Western District. I had no idea what I was doing. The only drugs I had ever come in contact with were from the arrests that I had made. I had never even smoked marijuana before. It was the first time I was able to drive a covert vehicle and come to work in street clothes. I got really good at stealing people's garbage. I was always amazed at the items people throw away. We made so many great drug cases based off of stealing garbage.

My department got a new chief of police in 1996. He had a change in philosophy and decided to move all narcotic detectives to one centralized unit. I was still working at the Western District in the Tactical Narcotic's Team. I was then transferred to the Criminal Investigation Division's Narcotics Unit. I worked a variety of positions in the Narcotics Section. In 1998, just prior to my separation from my ex-wife, I was assigned to the Prescription Drug Fraud and Abuse Unit. It was one of my favorite times working. Once we separated and she outed me to everyone at work, it became a "don't ask, don't tell" working atmosphere. I am sure everyone talked about it behind my back, but no one ever gave me any problems or had the courage to ask me about it. I was okay with that environment because I preferred to keep my private life private. My separation and divorce from my wife became the topic of conversation at work and I really preferred that the people that I worked with stay out of my personal life.

The position I was working came at a great time. I was on-call all the time. My cases came from physicians and pharmacists, so if they were working, then there was a chance they would call me. I made a lot of contacts in that position and kept very busy. I could work as much as I wanted and was able to rack up a lot of comp time.

It was during this time that I also started going out to bars. It was the place where I knew to meet people. There were no gay bars in Anne Arundel County and there still are none there today. I had to travel to either Baltimore City or Washington, DC. I met a few people and dated a little, but never really knew what I was looking for or a type that I was attracted to. I still had the straight-guy attitude that most gay men were feminine and flamboyant, which was not for me. The only gay people I knew were the lesbians that I had started hanging around, and they were no help with finding me anyone, although they did try. I finally heard about this bar called the Baltimore Eagle. I was told that it was a leather bar where real men went. Well, I don't know about real men going, but it was certainly a breath of fresh air for me. There were finally gay men that looked like men and a place where I felt like I belonged.

This is where I met my first long-term partner. We hit it off right away and started dating. But what would a gay relationship be without drama? I found out he was already in a relationship with someone. That finally worked out and we continued to date and eventually moved in together. I continued my close friendship with a few of the lesbian officers. One in particular, Debbie Arduini, became my best friend. We got very close and did a lot of things together. She had been in some drama-filled relationships, but had finally found someone that seemed to fit her. She ended up moving in with her and starting a great relationship. They lived pretty far away so my time with Deb was dwindling.

I started looking for groups or organizations for gay cops. There was a small one that involved gay paramedics and police just outside of Baltimore that I found. Deb and I met a few of the members, but it did not stay as an organization for long. I did make one great friend out of that group, Dwight Polk, who I stay in contact with to this day. He teaches the paramedic program at a university in Maryland.

I also discovered a group in Washington, DC. It was the Gay Officers Action League of the District of Columbia. I met some fantastic people in the group and remain friends with a lot of them today. We gathered on a monthly basis, usually for brunch or dinner. It was such a relief to find other gay male police officers. I knew lesbian police but did not know another gay cop. This group became very important to me. I worked hard for that group and eventually became a board member. It is through this group that I found out about the Gay Officers Action League in New York and Law Enforcement Gays and Lesbians International (LEGAL Int)

I continued with GOAL DC in various roles. We would meet socially a few times a year, but really never gathered much traction. I think that many LGBT police from the Washington DC area did not feel the need to come together as a group. We would get some people joining us for a night out on the town, but no one seemed to want to get more involved.

On May 16, 2003 my life as I knew it changed forever. I was in court all morning working with a new grand jury that had just been seated. I was explaining all the various drug laws etc. When I was finished, I started driving to my office. My side partner at the time called me to tell me that we had just had one of our officers commit suicide. He said he had not been able to find out who. My best friend, Deb Arduini, had been assigned to homicide and I knew that if anyone would know the officer's name it would have been her. I had talked to her a few days before. She had been sick in bed with what she told me was possibly strep throat. I called her cell phone and her desk phone but received no answer. Since I knew she had not been feeling well a few days prior, I decided to call her significant other. She answered and I heard in her voice that something was wrong. I started to ask her how Deb was feeling and she immediately stopped me and said, "You have not heard?" She told me that Deb had just shot herself and was dead. I was driving at the time and had to pull over to fully understand what I had just heard. She told me that they had got into an argument in the morning and that it did not go well. She said she decided to remove herself from the situation and go to work. She told me that as soon as she walked out of the bedroom and started down the stairs she heard the gun go off.

I immediately started toward their house. While on the way I started getting phone calls from various people. My command staff knew how close Deb and I were and they were concerned. They were trying to convince me to come to the office because they had something to discuss with me. I had to tell them that I already knew and that I was on my way to the scene.

I arrived and was met by the jurisdiction that was handling the suicide. It was not my agency. I was also met by Deb's supervisor. They started questioning me like I was a suspect. I eventually made it to Deb's significant other and started talking. She was devastated and shocked that Deb even had her gun in the house. There was young children living in the home and

Deb had decided to keep her gun in the secured lock box in her department issued vehicle.

Once the supervisor from my department finished asking me questions, he came to me and told me that they were going to be leaving and that I could become the representative for my department. They cleared her uniforms out of her closet and put them in the department issued vehicle. They then took the vehicle and drove off, while Deb was still in the house.

The next few days were a blur. My department totally ignored Deb's significant other during this whole process. Deb's mother became the decision maker and decided to have the funeral way up near the PA and Ohio line. We traveled to the funeral and were in disbelief. The funeral had to be for someone else because all the things they were saying had nothing to do with Deb. It felt like two very distinct funerals going on at the same time. You had Deb's family and straight co-workers on one side of the room, and then you had Deb's extensive LGBT family, police and other friends on the other side. I will never forget that. Not two weeks later another co-worker of mine was killed in an automobile accident, and then shortly after that we had an officer kill himself and someone else in a murder suicide incident.

I thought I was handling it pretty good. I did what I always did: I put all my time and energy into work. One day my immediate supervisor came to me and asked me if I was okay. I told him no, I was not. He looked at me and said, "Okay, just let me know if you need anything." It was a good thing that I was still semi holding it together, because he certainly should have done more than he did.

I continued to work hard, trying to ignore the feelings I was having. I stumbled across a training seminar that was being held in the county next to mine. The class was Traumas in Law Enforcement being presented by a group called the Concerns of Police Survivors (COPS). Part of the training was dealing with Police Suicide. I did end up being able to attend the seminar. It was a life-changing event for me. I did well in the first part of the training. Once we got to the police suicide section, I had an emotional breakdown. The floodgates opened and I lost it. I met some amazing individuals that day and I was introduced to COPS. Because of that seminar I forced myself to get the help I desperately needed. This was also the first year that I heard of and attended National Police Week. I was living so close to Washington, DC, but I did not even know about this yearly event. I volunteered with COPS that year and attended my first candlelight vigil. It was an overwhelming experience. I knew that I wanted to expose as many LGBT police to National Police Week as I could.

I attended my first LEGAL International conference in Key West in 2005. I was overwhelmed at meeting so many LGBT police from around the country. I attended with a few members of GOAL DC. We went to a meeting during the conference that dealt with future conferences. I was the vice president of GOAL DC and our president, Robert Schoonover, was also with me. We had talked about it and knew that we needed to host the conference in Washington, DC during National Police Week. We were selected to host the conference in 2008.

On January 21, 2006, we had a tragedy hit GOAL DC. GOAL DC's President and my close friend, Robert Schoonover, committed suicide. For me, this brought back so many memories. It was such a difficult time, reliving so many memories of Deb and feeling helpless again. Since I was the vice president at the time, I immediately became the president of GOAL DC. We had to make a decision about the conference that was a little over two years away. We came together as a group and decided that we would continue with the conference in Robert's memory and we would change the name of the group to GOAL Mid Atlantic. It was something we had been discussing before Robert died. We thought that it may allow us to attract more members. I did attend the next two conferences. The 2006 conference was in West Hollywood during Pride. We actually marched in the Pride Parade. It was an amazing experience marching with hundreds of LGBT police being led by the chief of police from the LAPD. The following year the conference was in Providence Rhode Island. It was hosted by GOAL New England also during Pride. We again got to March with so many LGBT police officers from around the country. That year I met an amazing individual, Preston Horton. He was one of the founding members of GOAL New England. I have learnt so much from him and consider him a cherished friend. I received many pointers from everyone from GOAL New England. At that point we were about eight months away from our conference in Washington DC.

The planning of the 12ᵗʰ annual LEGAL International LGBT Criminal Justice Conference was overwhelmingly time consuming. We had very few members at the time but knew we had to get it done. I spent six to eight hours every evening for a year at my computer making sure the conference came together. I was very fortunate to have all my speakers in place very early on. That left me time to work on other parts of the conference.

One of the people I met from COPS at the Traumas in Law Enforcement Training was Shirley Gibson. Her son, Brian, was a DC police officer killed in the line of duty. She touched me so deeply when she spoke about Brian and about the importance of COPS. I knew that I wanted her to be part of our conference. I scheduled her to be our keynote speaker at the start of the conference. I wanted everyone in attendance to know what COPS and National Police Week was all about. She was amazing and had the room in tears.

The conference was an amazing experience. We had LGBT police officers from five different countries and 32 states in attendance. We were able to get all of them to the National Holocaust's Special Police Presentation, and we were able to bus all the officers to the National Law Enforcement Officer's Memorial Wall for the annual Candlelight Vigil.

I had been very fortunate to have met some amazing LGBT individuals working in the criminal justice field. One of them was Greg Miraglia. I had seen his first book and was supposed to write this story for the second book. Greg was able to put me in touch with David O'Malley, the former police chief of Laramie Wyoming. He had been involved in the Matthew Shephard murder investigation. Because of Greg, not only was I able to get Dave O'Malley as our closing ceremony keynote speaker, I was able to get Matthew's mother, Judy Shephard, to join us as well. We were more fortunate because Matthew's dad, Dennis, also joined us for the closing ceremony. I could not have been happier at the way the conference turned out. The one thing that people kept saying is that we had two powerful mothers, one at the opening ceremony, and one at the closing ceremony, who had both lost their sons. It is something they will never forget. I still have officers talk about how much they enjoyed the conference.

Once the conference ended I was exhausted and did not put together any further GOAL Mid Atlantic events. There were hardly any members left and the group just fizzled out. It was about that time that I had discovered Protect and Defend, an LGBT group for LGBT police, firefighters, the military, and other public safety members. It was refreshing to find an organization that had a lot of members from around the country. I started getting involved with them and eventually became the Maryland Representative. I continued to put together LGBT events for National Police Week. Protect and Defend was a big part of the events.

During Police Week 2010 I met an individual named Kelly Glossip. His husband of over 12 years, Dennis Engelhard, was a Missouri State Trooper killed in the line of duty Christmas Day 2009. I learned that Kelly was ignored and treated like the relationship that he had with Dennis did not even exist. He was not included in any of the services and lost his home and everything he and Dennis had worked for. It saddened me to know that he was treated so poorly. I knew at that moment that I wanted to try and do something about it.

In 2011, my personal life was not going well. I started having issues with my then 11-year long-term relationship. During Police Week 2011, I was coordinating the LGBT events for National Police Week. The events had grown from just a pure social gathering into a more support and fundraising events. I had started raising money for the Concerns of Police Survivors. I had heard about this large happy hour that occurred on Friday nights in Washington, DC. I reached out to the owner of the club and received permission to set up an information table for our events during National Police Week. Little did I know that is where and when I would meet my now amazing husband, Nicholas. I reached out to the owner of the club and got permission, but he had failed to let the person that ran that happy hour know that I was going to be setting up. When I arrived at the club to set up, someone else had just got there to set up as well. The owner of the club never told anyone that he was coming either. When I asked about a table, my now husband said, "Well, who are you and who told you to come and set up?" I originally thought he was not such a nice person. I noticed that all through the night he kept walking by the table staring. I even made the comment to a couple of people that he must really have a problem with us being there. Little did I know he was really interested in me. I had very little confidence in myself at that point and did not believe there was any way someone like him would be interested in someone like me. The job and the relationship and the quitting smoking all took its toll on me. I had gained a lot of weight and did not feel great about myself. Little did I realize I had become a Bear, which is exactly the type of person Nick, my now husband, had always been interested in.

I knew that my long-term relationship had been over for years. I think we both stayed because it was easier then leaving. We had grown apart and had not really been an intimate couple in a very long time. Before leaving the happy hour that night, I got a business card from Nick. I wanted to be able to reach out to him for future events. Well, that is what I told him. Anyway, we started talking back and forth about Police Week and my being a police officer and him being former military. We ended up really hitting it off. Things progressed over the summer and we decided to take a trip together. We traveled to New Orleans for Southern Decadence. We made it through our first trip so we decided that it was a good time to get into a relationship. Eventually I had to find a place to live. I had been trying to be roommates with my ex because I had four dogs, my work German shepherd and three Great Danes. Nick made a decision to move in with me. I managed to find a house close enough to Washington, DC for Nick and close enough to Anne Arundel County for me. We moved in with all four dogs and started our life together.

I continued to plan the LGBT events for National Police Week 2011. I had created a new event called CopCakes for a Cause. It was designed as a wine and dessert tasting fundraising event. We held it at Remington's, our now closed gay country bar, and it was a great success. We raised money for COPS. I was still working with Protect and Defend at the time. Meeting Dennis was still on my mind and I wanted to do something more. I started researching other LGBT police that had been killed in the line of duty. The plan was to hold a special service for them during National Police Week. I wanted to honor Dennis Engelhard and make sure that Kelly got the recognition he deserved, but he was unable to travel to Washington DC that year. I did find Officer Amanda Haworth, a Miami Dade officer killed in the line of duty in January 2011. I did research and made contact with those closest to Amanda. I told them that I wanted to have a special LGBT memorial service for Amanda. They were touched and in favor of having the special service.

We started the preparation. Originally we were looking at holding the service at the National Law Enforcement Officers Memorial Wall, but since it was National Police Week, it was not logistically possible. We decided to hold the service at DuPont Circle. It was the most appropriate LGBT site in Washington. It was an overwhelming experience putting the memorial service together. Since it was the first year, we had no idea how things would go. We ended up with a large turnout. We presented Amanda's family with a United States Flag that had been flown over the US Capitol in her honor, and a collage portrait that we had done by one of our LGBT police officers who is also an artist. We also had an all-female honor guard, at the US Park Police Mounted unit in attendance. The service turned out to be a wonderful event. I knew that this was something we would have to continue.

The LGBT Police Week seemed to grow larger. We held our then 2nd annual CopCakes for a Cause event and a couple other social events. It was a very positive experience.

Nicholas and I talked for a long time about our vision for Police Week and the memorial service. We decided that it was no longer appropriate to host these events with other organizations. We thought it would be better to create a non-profit organization just for the purpose of honoring our LGBT Fallen Police Officers.

The planning for the next National Police Week began pretty quickly. I started searching for other LGBT fallen police officers. I found Master Corporal Sandy Rogers from the Aiken Department of Public Safety. She had been shot and killed during a check vehicle in a park complaint. Little did she know the person in the vehicle had just committed another murder a short time prior. I discovered that Sandy had a significant other who was also a police officer. I finally was able to reach Frances Williams, Sandy's other half. They had been together over 20 years. I chatted with Frances and heard this heartbreaking story. Frances was treated so poorly after Sandy was killed, to the point where she was not welcome at a memorial service being held in Sandy's honor. She had been with Sandy for over 20 years and to be treated like this was unbelievable. I knew we had to bring Frances here for our memorial service.

We again scheduled the memorial service for May 13th at DuPont Circle. Frances was able to join us for the service. We had the all-female honor guard again and we presented Frances with the US Flag that had been flown over the capital in Sandy's honor and a collage portrait. Hearing France's story and seeing how much this special memorial service meant to her made me realize we had to keep going.

Nicholas and I made a trip to the Prince George's County Court House in the morning just prior to the memorial service. We had met one year before Police Week, we were engaged just after Police Week in another year, and we decided to get married during Police Week this year.

Since Nicholas spent eight years in the Marines, and I had been finding LGBT fire, EMS, and military members that had been killed in the line of duty, we decided to expand who we honor. We founded the LGBT Fallen Heroes Memorial Fund. We teamed up with the DC Center as an affiliate organization. This gave us our non-profit status, which opened more doors for us. Our goal was to honor our LGBT Fallen Heroes and to recognize their surviving significant other properly. A decision was made to concentrate on the special LGBT Fallen Heroes Memorial Service and two fundraising events. We would leave the planning of other social events to other organizations.

The most difficult part of what we do is actually finding our LGBT Fallen Heroes. There is no one place where we can look to find them. I find them by searching the internet, looking at obituaries, and by word of mouth.

In 2014 we started planning the 3rd annual LGBT Fallen Heroes Memorial Service. I was able to identify six fallen heroes. There were two police officers, two firefighters, and two members of the military. I was able to make contact with each of the surviving significant others. We again planned the special memorial service for May 13th at DuPont Circle. It was another incredible memorial service. Seeing the reaction from the surviving significant others tells me that we need to continue what we do. We also held our 4th annual CopCakes for a Cause fundraising event. It was our most successful year allowing us to donate over $5000.00 to the Concerns of Police Survivors (COPS).

I say every year that I am going to take a break for a couple months before I start working on the following year. That never seems to happen. I started my research again and was able to find nine LGBT Fallen Heroes for 2015. We decided to honor not only our LGBT Heroes that have been killed in the line of duty, but any LGBT Hero that had died. We found that regardless of how our heroes have died, their surviving significant others have been treated poorly and left out of any memorial or funeral service.

We will honor four police officers, one firefighter, one paramedic, and three members of the military. I am in the final planning of this year's service as I am writing this story.

One of my long-term goals has been to have an actual LGBT Fallen Heroes Memorial built. I knew that was a tall order, but we discovered a perfect location for the memorial. We met with the executive director of the Congressional Cemetery. This is an amazing place in Washington DC. They have a section in the cemetery that they lovingly call their "Gay Corner." There are several prominent LGBT people buried in this area. We managed to find the perfect spot in the cemetery for our actual LGBT Fallen Heroes Memorial. It is still a long way off but we have entered into an agreement with the cemetery to purchase the land. We had also applied for a grant from Brother Help Thyself. It was my first experience writing a grant request. We were thrilled when we found out that we had been selected to receive one of their grants. It will certainly go a long way in our memorial service planning and for the planning of the physical memorial.

Writing this story is bittersweet for me. I am in my 27th year as a sworn law enforcement officer. This is my last year with my agency. I will retire sometime prior to January 31, 2016. I have loved my career, and I have loved being part of the amazing LGBT police family. I am most proud of Nicholas and me founding the LGBT Fallen Heroes Fund.

AN INTERVIEW WITH OFFICER GREGORY ABBINK

Briefly describe yourself, including age, law enforcement, fire, and or EMS experience, what part of the country you are from and anything else you feel is important to know about you.

I am a Senior Police officer at the Austin, Texas, Police Department Training Academy. I have been a police officer with APD for nearly 11 years. I served in the US Army prior to that.

1. How did you become interested in law enforcement, firefighting, or the EMS profession?

I became interested in law enforcement toward the end of high school and received my Associate's Degree in Criminal Justice. What drew me to law enforcement was the idea of getting to help people and to protect people. I really enjoyed the various aspects of policing, from the uniform and equipment to the diversity of daily tasks.

2. When did you discover you were gay, lesbian, or bisexual and what did you think about relative to your interest in law enforcement, fire-fighting or EMS?

Although born anatomically female, I knew from as early of an age as I can remember that I was a boy. At the age of five, I would ask my parents why God didn't make me a boy and would pray at night that I would wake up as a boy. I wanted to be called by the name that my parents would have given me had I been anatomically male, which I can proudly say is my legal name today. Growing up, I was forced to think and act like the other little girls around me; all my mannerisms and interests were different from my female classmates and I knew I was different. I loathed having to wear dresses or anything that identified me as female, because on the inside, I was screaming for someone to hear me; that I was a boy. However, I didn't have any type of support group or individual that I could turn to to help me live as my authentic self. Therefore, I struggled with my identity and lived many years claiming to be a lesbian. Although I joined the police department as an anatomical female, I still didn't worry about the positive climate and diversity at the Austin Police Department.

3. Describe your experience getting hired and going through your training academy. Were you out? Did you come out during the academy?

While going through the police academy in the beginning of 2004, I identified as a lesbian. The department knew from the moment of my initial applicant interview that I was gay. However, it was in the beginning of 2014 that I came out to my department as a transgender male.

4. What was it like starting off in your department? Did you come out? If not, what kept you, or is currently keeping you from coming out at work?

I never felt any form of discrimination or harassment from my department. I have received so much support from my department since coming out as a transgender male in 2014. So many co-workers and supervisors have offered words of encouragement and for the most part I feel very comfortable at work.

5. Describe your most difficult situation being gay in your public safety profession.

There was no one person or incident that kept me from coming out as transgender, but I would say that the most difficult situation I have encountered as a trans-male police officer is the lack of information/education that people have about what "gender identity and gender expression" is. Any anxiety that I might have is due to my own apprehensions about how people will perceive me and accept me as a trans-male. I am very aware of other peoples' perceptions and always want to be considerate of their feelings. After all, so many people knew me as "Emily" before coming out as "Greg," so I take into consideration their adjustment period to new pronouns, etc. The other hurdle I have had to deal with is the decision of when to start using the appropriate restroom. Currently, I have chosen to use a stand-alone, gender-neutral restroom out of respect for my co-workers, but will eventually begin to solely use the men's restroom here at work.

6. What specific event or general experience surprised you most about being gay in your profession?

I was most inspired by my 18-year-old nephew who came out as transgender just months before I did. He inspired me to find the courage to reveal my life-long secret and to live the way I was always intended to. Growing up, I never had a support group or anyone who I felt I could trust to understand me and help me transition. In recent years, I was hearing more and more about individuals who were coming out as transgender and their courageous stories were inspiring to me. Since transitioning, I have met other amazingly brave and incredible individuals in this profession. Their stories have also inspired and encouraged me.

7. What, if anything, would you have done differently relative to being gay in your profession?

The one thing I wish I had done differently was to have been able to transition as a young person. I believe it would have been easier for everyone to have just known and accept me as a male.

8. One of the important goals of this book is to help fellow gay law enforcement officers, firefighters, and EMS professionals and their allies. What advice can you provide to the following people?

I have had such a positive experience within my department and from the LGBTQ community here in Austin. I was blown away by the sincere concern of my supervisors to assist me in my transition and all the paperwork that it entailed. I underestimated the men and women I work with and now realize what incredible people they are and how supportive (and protective) of me they are. It is a wonderful feeling knowing that you are supported for the person that you are!

9. A gay teenager who is thinking about the best way to get into your public safety profession.

The first step for anyone wanting to work in law enforcement would be to really think about the type of job this is and to research the profession. Doing a ride out with a patrol shift would also be a great idea for someone interested in law enforcement. Once you decide this is the career for you, inquire with the department's recruiting office in order to begin the application process. I can speak from personal experience that APD does not care if you are gay, bisexual or transgender. They simply want the best qualified individuals to become public servants.

10. A fellow public safety professional who is gay, but not out to anyone at work.

At the Austin Police Department, we have a Lesbian and Gay Peace Officers' Association, which is a valuable resource for anyone that may be worried about coming out. This Association offers support and guidance to anyone in the agency who may request it. There are probably more people than you know that are allies and would completely support your decision to come out.

11. An agency executive or manager who is an ally and wants to support gay public safety professionals.

It says so much about a department when the executive staff backs their officers, especially when it comes to equal and fair treatment and employment practices. Supporting the diversity of their employees builds so much credibility for that chain of command. Also, I think the reputation of a department with supportive leaders will also help attract a greater pool of diverse applicants.

12. What else would you like to say that you feel is most important for readers to know about you or your ideas?

I can't imagine working for any other agency! The Austin Police Department has been one of my biggest supporters since coming out as transgender. Our department is committed to the best training and employment practices and has allowed me to develop transgender training for our officers so that we can provide the best and most respectful service for the citizens of Austin.

FROM SERGEANT JERI MITCHELL

My story is different from most … it took a great tragedy to "officially come out," not that my life was ever "in hiding." Like most people I guess I just lived my life as a gay officer and it was never spoken about among my workplace peers. I met Amanda early in my police career around 1988. We met through work friends. She was a uniformed officer in the Miami Dade Police, Northside District, and I was assigned as a General Investigations Detective in the Intracoastal District. I had just broken off a seven-year relationship followed by a one-year relationship. I was definitely not looking for anyone, but it just kind of happened and we fell in love.

We planned to live our lives together. We purchased a house and planned a family as most couples do. In 1995, I became pregnant; it was wonderful. I was working in the Organized Crime Section of my department at the time. When I was three months pregnant I began to show so I explained my entire situation to my sergeant. We spoke of my relationship, my pregnancy and my career goals. He was very understanding, excited and happy for me, for us. When we spoke about my relationship with Amanda, he was not judgmental, but explained that I should keep it more to myself because he didn't want anything to change and people might not understand and treat me differently as I continued my career. In July of 1996, I gave birth to our first son Jordon. I was out of work for three months and had no issues with requesting the time off. My sergeant was very understanding of my relationship. In late 1996 I explained that my partner Amanda was pregnant with our second child.

In August 1997, Amanda gave birth to our second son Austin. The boys have the same father through insemination and are legal brothers.

We began raising the boys and they were wonderful. They shared the same room and at times the same bed. They liked to get out of their respective beds and cribs and climb in with the other.

Well, the best laid plans don't always come to fruition. We reached a point in our life that could not be overcome and we separated. Jordon was just shy of two and Austin just shy of one. It was a very difficult time for both of us and the boys. It was very difficult to discuss it with my sergeant. He was very understanding and gave me time off as needed. My sergeant and my work partner knew of my situation with Amanda, but it again was not spoken about openly as the department was concerned. It was sometimes very difficult to go in and do my job with my heart so broken and my life turned upside down and have to hide my feelings from my co-workers.

As with traditional marriages the divorce is handled by attorneys and a judge. But with our lifestyle at the time there was no help and we truly had to work together to figure things out and move forward. We decided to go forward with the sale of the house, but most importantly to remain friends for the sake of the two young men we had brought into the world together. Trying to remain friends and keeping the boys first in our lives was now the main focus. Really the best thing about our separation was that we insisted on the boys being shared between us. Even though Jordon remained living with me and Austin with Amanda we share their custody jointly. Every weekend Jordon stayed with Amanda and Austin and on Saturday Austin would stay with me and my new partner.

My new partner, Diane, was and is wonderful. I'm sure it was not fun at first having Amanda come to our house, but Diane is wonderful and understood that our lives were focused on the boys. We shared vacations and holidays together as well. Even with new relationships the one constant in both our lives was the boys. Amanda became my best friend and I still loved her greatly but was no longer in love with her. Over time our bond grew stronger as friends and the boys grew. They went to the same daycare, the same elementary school, and would be picked up by both of us, or sometimes Diane, when we were working late. Our system seemed to work and we were all very happy.

We continued our lives both as now an extended family with our new partners as well as in the workplace. We both worked in the same division in our police department. We often worked together on cases and details that required an abundance of manpower. Again, very few knew of our relationship.

On a horrible day on January 20, 2011 my life and that of the boys, my partner and family and friends drastically changed forever when beautiful Detective Amanda Haworth was shot and killed while trying to take a murder suspect into custody. In 19 seconds detectives Amanda Haworth and Roger Castillo were gone from our lives.

When news of an officer involved shooting hit the radios no one knew who was involved and information was very sketchy, so officers, detectives, the whole world started to go to the area of the shooting. While en route I received a telephone call from a major who requested that I respond to the hospital because he knew I was "friends" with Amanda and that she was shot and her work partner had been injured and were on their way to the hospital. He also told me that Roger had been killed on the scene. Again, no one knew of our true relationship and trying to drive in emergency mode and deal with the emotions was very difficult. I immediately tried to contact my partner as well as Amanda's partner to inform them both. When I finally made it to the hospital, which seemed like an eternity, I was able to see Amanda in the emergency room. There was a tremendous amount of blood and it was a horrifying scene. I spoke to a homicide detective, who again did not know of our relationship, informed me that the doctors were not sure that she would survive due to the fact that she had been shot twice including once in the head with a .40 caliber handgun. I wanted to lie down and cry. Trying to hold it together, I made contact with Diane and asked her to pray and to go get Jordon from school and I would take care of getting Austin. I made contact with Amanda's partner and waited for her at the hospital. I was also asked by homicide detectives to make contact with her immediate family. I reached her sisters who were able to call Amanda's mother and father, who are divorced. I also called members of my family who dearly loved Amanda.

I waited at the hospital until I was able to kiss her and tell her we all loved her and I would take care of things with Austin as they wheeled her into the operating room. That was the last time I saw her, as she did not make it through surgery. I then went to take Austin out of school and take him to my house. While taking him out I was notified that she has passed away from her injuries and, in excruciating pain myself, I had to tell her birth son, our 13-year-old boy, that she was gone and never coming home. We cried and spoke a little and came home, where the craziness began.

I guess this is really where the official "coming out" started. In a situation like a double police murder the news media is in a frenzy and everyone wants to interview "the family." Then the questions of one or two boys came up and everyone's lives were turned inside out, including our relationships. I was very direct with members of the police department in order to assist with the funeral arrangements and the inner workings of our lives were fully explained and we were officially out to not only friends, co-workers, department staff, news media, but the world. I always laugh at the fact that she always wanted to "keep things to ourselves" and now she outed everyone.

The remaining months were extremely difficult. There was the handling of the will, obtaining legal guardianship, and other legal paperwork, but the Miami Dade Police Department was outstanding. Amanda truly changed the hearts and minds of people within the department for the better. The department fully recognized Jordon as Amanda's son the same way she has always looked at him. There is an organization by the name of "Police Officers' Assistance Trust" that assists officers in need. Amanda's death caused the organization to change the bylaws to include same-sex relationships. There has never been a question as to the boys being both our sons in our minds and now by the Miami Dade Police Department.

Coming out within the Miami Dade Police Department should not be feared. It is a very caring department. I have since retired and remain in close contact with members of the department. Jordon has graduated high school and is currently in college to study computer engineering and is doing great. Austin just graduated high school and in his senior year won a state championship in baseball. He is going to college to study to be a police officer and is playing baseball at college level. These young men are truly and inspiration. They have struggled at times but have come through their loss and are going strong.

A LETTER FROM OFFICER KEVIN COLLINS

Hello fellow officers and juvenile department staff,

This is Detention Officer Kevin Collins and I would like a moment of your time.

I want to apologize for what you're about to read. I also want to apologize for the method of delivery. This can be a real sensitive subject and so I felt that by delivering my message via a written document you can read in private and at your own choosing would be easier and I wouldn't feel as if I'm putting anyone on the spot.

What I'm about to share with you comes at a huge personal cost to me as well as to those I love.

I need you to realize that I have fought long and hard with myself. I have denied and lied to myself.

What I'm about to share is what is best for me.

I'm sharing this with you not to offend you or to hurt you but as I am tired of living a lie. I'm tired of having to watch what I say or who I say it around. When you all ask me what I did last weekend I don't want to have to lie anymore. When I'm asked who I did it with I don't want to have to lie anymore. I'm tired of only being able to show one half of myself and hide the other.

I'm fully aware that some people will never accept me. While that is painful, I also fully understand their position and would never hold anything against any one.

I've been blessed by surrounding myself with very understanding people and so far no one that has heard my story has had a problem with my decision.

I told my neighbors a few days ago, my dad this past weekend, my son a few weeks ago, and ex-wife a few months ago, my younger and older brother, all my friends a few years ago, all my cousins, my Facebook family, most of my ex-girlfriends, and now I am telling all of you.

I realize that in my 16-plus years with the department I have developed close friendships and a great working relationship with a lot of you. I should have told you in a more individual and personalized manner, so for that I apologize.

It is my hope that we can get past what I'm about to share. It really is just a small part of myself, but when I'm forced to hide it, it becomes everything. And so I hope we can get past this. I hope that you can recognize this for the small thing that it is. But, I will also understand that if this is too much for you and you feel you need space.

I'm in no way trying to justify myself or trying to win people over, nor am I trying to change your perception of me or people like me. I simply want to explain what I've been hiding and what it will mean going forward.

For all the downsides of delivering such a personal message via a written document, there are a few good sides as well. I like this method as I have a lot I need to say. If I were to deliver this message face to face, I'm sure I would leave a lot out. Anyway, I wanted you to know that while you may not like my message or agree with my decision, I would like you to understand that this is the best thing for me.

Trust me, the decision I've made took many years and is not something that I take lightly. About three years ago I stopped lying to myself and finally admitted to myself who and what I am. And I have never been happier with myself.

The self-loathing is over, the doubt and shame and embarrassment is gone. I've accepted who I am and am proudly and eagerly working toward that end. I still have my tough days, days when I doubt my own strength or my own personal courage, but never once have I doubted that this isn't the best thing for me.

And I guess if you only take one thing from my message, I hope that it is that this is the best thing for me.

Looking back I can safely say that I have always felt this way. I recall playing dress up in my mom's clothes and playing with dolls and such. As I grew up my desire to play dress up didn't change, just my ability and desire to hide it. It was my security blanket, a way that I could express myself. What I am trying to say is that I am transgender.

I am almost a year into HRT (hormone replacement therapy). I'm in the beginning stages of my transition from living life as a male to living as a female. To tell you everything, we need to go back a while.

Like I said earlier, I have always felt this way. I have always felt more comfortable expressing myself as feminine than masculine. It's just that I never knew what transgender was or what that meant.

When I was married I would occasionally wear my wife's clothes whenever I had a discreet moment. It wasn't a sexual or a role-playing thing. It was my attempt to express myself in a feminine manner. Those moments were few and far between.

I didn't know what transgender was when I was married nor did I have the slightest clue then as to where my life would eventually lead. All I knew was that dressing up felt right. Anyway, after the divorce, I dated a lot. I had a few serious relationships where the girlfriend would almost be living with me.

One night as I was cleaning my house I found some of her clothes and for whatever reason I put them on. Once I put her clothes on, I think I wore them the entire evening. It really is hard to explain, but I had this "ah ha" moment. I mean, it wasn't like I felt "whole."

For how good I felt, I was also aware of how "sick" and "wrong" I was, so of course I kept this from everyone. I was afraid that my secret would get out so I stayed out of her clothes, but eventually I went back. I wore more and more of her clothes and loved the way I felt in them. Of course the girlfriend found out. She said she was fine with it, but it came out that she wasn't.

After this breakup I went out and bought my own feminine attire. I bought clothes, makeup, and wigs and dressed freely in my own home. I was becoming good at makeup (well, maybe not good, but I was definitely improving; makeup is definitely a learned skill) and I started to love both the way I felt and now the way I looked. I found myself dressing in women's clothing more and more often.

Despite all this happiness, I was still very aware of how "sick" and "wrong" I was. I had tons of sleepless nights worrying that my secret would get out. I hated myself for enjoying and loving myself so much. I threw everything away and swore to myself to live a "normal" life. I got another girlfriend and pretended to be a straight masculine heterosexual male. I wanted so badly to fit in and be normal and be someone that was worth respect.

Of course my life was a lie and it was painfully obvious. I wasn't interested in her as a romantic partner at all. I tried to feel something. I tried to want this.

This relationship didn't last long and I was single again. The first thing I did was go resupply my feminine attire. I think I even got my lower back tattoo at this point. I was dressing up even more often. One night my son came out of his room and caught me.

It was midnight, so I had thought he was fast asleep. As a loving dad, you can imagine how petrified I was at having my son catch me. At that time he was four years old. That morning I threw everything away.

The act of throwing everything away is very common among trans-gender people who haven't yet accepted who they are. It's called "the great purge." You throw everything away and promise to never dress again. I never talked about this with my son. He was four and so I assumed that he would forget about it anyway. As much as I wanted it to, the fright and embarrassment of my son catching me couldn't stop me from being me and I needed my security blanket again. It was time to go resupply. This time I wanted to be smart about it. I was questioning myself about why I needed this so much and why I was so at peace with myself, and so I took to the internet.

At this time I was still dating women. I took a year off of dating and really wanted to devote a full year to myself. I needed to get answers but I wanted them in a discreet way. I did a lot of soul searching and internet browsing. My time on the internet led me to a transgender support group. This really was the first time I had heard the word transgender. I started to read their website and find out what they were all about and I vowed to attend a meeting.

As you can imagine I didn't actually attend a meeting, I was so scared. What if one of my masculine male friends walked by and saw me head into a building with a rainbow flag on it? I really wanted to attend a meeting, but was just so scared. I think it took many months for me to just say "the hell with it." I attended my first meeting and instantly knew I had found a home. So many other people there had the same feelings, same desires, same fears and same experiences. This meeting excited me and showed me that I wasn't alone, nor were my feelings unique. I did a lot of research and eventually discovered that I was transgender. This label wasn't one I was quick to put on, but it was obvious to me that this is what I am. Once I figured this out life was a little easier, but not much.

I now knew what I was feeling and why I was so happy, but I was still very much in hiding. No one knew this about me, no one knew that I was very happy, but also very disgusted with myself. I was a man that dressed as a woman, how else but disgusted could I possibly feel? And so of course

I vowed again to be normal, even though being "normal" was to live a lie and deny who I was.

I got another girlfriend. The difference this time was that I knew it was a lie.

I got this girlfriend just for some attempt to prove to myself that I was a man. I entered into this relationship with no regard for her feelings. I knew I was lying to her and to myself.

This relationship ended quickly. After this breakup I swore that I was done pretending and that I would make a decision one way or the other. I took another year off of dating and devoted another year to myself. I knew if I was to try to continue living a "normal" life I had better be prepared to lie to more people and to myself. I knew that I could enter into regular male-female relationships, but I also knew that they would be based on deceit and that they wouldn't last long. One night I decided that enough was enough: I admitted to myself that I was transgender and asked myself what I was going to do about it.

It took me four-plus years to admit to myself that I was transgender and another three-plus years to tell my friends and to do something about it. And so here I am.

I told one of my best friends and she was very supportive. Through her strength I was able to tell the rest of my friends and they all treated me very warmly.

I then approached my doctor and told him that I identified as transgender and asked him about transitioning. He referred me to a counselor. I saw that counselor regularly for a little less than a year. By the end of that year the counselor determined that starting my transition was something that I felt that I needed to do and he gave my doctor authorization to start HRT. This has been a seven-plus year internal struggle with who I am.

My transition from male to female started in early March of 2014. I started HRT (hormone replacement therapy) and took my first Estradiol (Estrogen) pill as well as my first Spironlactone (testosterone blocker) pill.

Hormone replacement therapy is just one of many steps in that transition process. There is no guideline, no order of operations. For many transgender people HRT is the beginning. What HRT (male to female) will do is eliminate body hair, it will change male skin (which is thicker) and it will thin it. It will also give skin a shine. HRT will also change the way your body stores body fat. Males typically store body fat in the stomach. HRT will change the way my body stores body fat and will redistribute mine to more feminine areas like my hips, butt and thighs. HRT lowers your libido and makes you a lot more emotional. HRT will decrease your muscle mass and will eliminate most of your upper body strength. And HRT will also make you develop breasts. Everyone's body is unique and therefore everyone's results will be unique. I can say that I have already started to experience all these effects, some more than others.

They say that when you go through HRT your body essentially goes through a second puberty. Just like the first puberty your body went through, the second one will take a few years to achieve full effect. I am almost a year into HRT. Right now I am transitioning in stealth. I know that everyone knows, but I still live the majority of my life as male. I got my lower back tattoo, my ears pierced, traded my super masculine muscle car in for a more feminine car, have been through months of laser hair removal on my face as well as my chest. I've seen a counselor for a year, submitted to quarterly blood work and doctor's appointments, and taken seven pills a day. I have been on HRT and have started to develop breasts.

I don't have a timeline for when I will transition to a full-time female life. I understand that that may be hard to understand, but to be honest, until just a few days ago I didn't know that I would be sharing this with you right now.

Transgender, or the "T" in LGBT, is the least understood and also the least accepted in that group. I'm well aware of the challenges that I face and so I am trying to do this right.

The last thing I would want is to make my transition harder for me or my department.

I have a few personal things I need to take care of first before I transition. So while I have no set date for when I will go full-time, I need you to know that it is coming and that it will happen.

I am telling work and you all now so that when that day does arrive the process may be a little easier. What does this mean and where is this going? Well, this can mean as much or as little as you want it to. I'm still the same person that will bore you with stories of my son and still the same person that travels often and shares the vacation videos. I am still the same person that loves taking my son mountain-biking and still that same person that can't wait to get back under the water. I still have that same rigid view of right and wrong and I'll still have that same sarcastic humor and be that same person that loves playing jokes. I'm still the very same person. The only difference is the outward appearance of my body and the clothes I will wear while off duty.

I hope that you don't feel I am pushing any "lifestyle" and I hope you don't feel that I am trying to convert you or to make you accept me. I am who I am and I am proud to be a transgender woman. The reason I am sharing this with you is that for 16-plus years you all have known me as Kevin. I'm sure you had an idea of who I was and that my letter may change things. I realize that my transition really isn't just mine. I realize that while this is the best thing for me I understand that it affects you too and for that I hope you can forgive me.

I have fought myself on this every step of the way. I have lied to myself and hurt people I loved along the way to try to be "normal." I am at peace finally and I love myself and am very happy that my secret is now known and that I'm free to be me. I also realize that I have had years to come to grips with my transition and you are just now finding out.

I am an open book and I enjoy talking about myself. If you have any questions at all please feel free to contact me either directly or through a supervisor and I'd be more than happy to chat with you. If you have an honest curiosity about what brought me to this stage of my life or if you would like to know about my hopes, dreams and fears than please contact me.

I will never ever tell you how you should feel, but please understand that this is the best thing for me. I want you to know that there is no right or wrong way to handle this.

This news will affect us all differently. If you can't handle this please feel free to approach me and I will be more than happy to discuss this with you.

In my 16-plus years with this department I have come to think of this as my department. I also know that this is your department too. It is my wish, my desire and my mission to make my transition as easy on myself and on you. If you have any ideas on how that can be done I'm very open to suggestions, and so are the supervisors.

Snickering, jokes and laughter are all human reactions and I fully expect them. It would be foolish of me to think that rumors or jokes would not be told. I want you all to know that I will hold nothing against anyone who partakes in that. All those are natural reactions to something that makes us uncomfortable or when we don't fully understand things.

I have no interest at all in trying to change your perception of people like me. That is not why I come to work and is not why I have stayed for 16-plus years. I want to come to work, do my eight hours and stay for overtime when I can. I love my department, love my career and my profession and have a great respect for the people I call co-workers. I realize that everything I have in life, all that I have achieved, can be directly linked to Kitsap County Juvenile Department.

I am open and flexible and will do whatever you feel I need to do to make my transition work for all of us. I only ask that I can continue to call this department home.

Once I go full-time and start living and working as a female there may be some areas of concern.

1. Bathrooms: We have so many unisex, single stall restrooms and those are what I will use when I need to change or use the restroom. I will not make anyone uncomfortable by using the female restroom.

2. Pat downs: These are a foundation of day-to-day operations. Logic would suggest that I would pat down the gender in which I present as, but I also know that this is just one of many things that will need to be worked out (which is why I've decided to come out now ahead of my full-time, so that the department can research things and we all can be ready).

I contacted a non-profit called "Coming out from behind the Badge" and they have put me in contact with a lieutenant in the Los Angeles County Sheriff's office. The LA Sheriff's Office is the leader when it comes to agency policies. They recently published very comprehensive policies related to transgender personnel. I am waiting to hear back from that LT.

I will share whatever I learn with my supervisors.

I hope you know that I am here if you want to talk, and if you feel that you need time to process this, that is fine too.

FROM DARRAN MAZAIKA

As far back as I could remember, I always felt different, and that there was something within me that made me different than everyone else while growing up compared to all my other friends and family.

You could say I had a pretty unique childhood. I grew up on a family-run cattle ranch in the Town of Moraga, California, which is a small suburban town with a population of approximately 16,000 people nestled up in the hills of Country Costa County. The family ranch, known as Carr Ranch, consisted of my paternal grandparents, maternal grandmother, paternal great uncle, uncle, and my father's cousins and their children. No one on the ranch was religious, but everyone was VERY conservative.

As early as five years old, I knew I wanted to be a police officer. Between my father being a firefighter in our hometown, my family knowing all the local police officers, and my mother and grandmother addicted to murder mystery television programs, such as *Murder She Wrote*, *Perry Mason*, *Columbo*, and *Matlock*, law enforcement must have been ingrained in me or was my dynasty.

It was probably around fourth or fifth grade. I knew something was "different" about me. A lot of gay and bi guys say the same, about being "different," but literally there was something inside me that said, "You aren't like all the other kids." It was also the time when all the guys in school were starting to talk about the cute girls and getting girlfriends, my parents hiding the fact my mother's brother was gay even though I knew he was from an early age (they told my brother and I that his partner was his "roommate" but my gaydar knew otherwise), and society shaming gays and lesbians because of the HIV/AIDS epidemic in the 1980s. Being "different," looking back now, is that I was attracted to both the guys and girls in school. All through elementary, junior high school, and high school I had no problem talking to my friends and family about the girls I liked or dated, but there was no way I could say or tell anyone about the boys that I thought were cute.

Sports were also a huge part of my life growing up. In elementary school I did gymnastics and soccer. I didn't do gymnastics long, but played soccer until I started high school. In middle school, I played basketball and also started taking karate lessons with my best friend, Jay Lo. I only played basketball in middle school, but continued practicing and learning karate for the next 20 years. In high school, I played volleyball my freshman year, but had to stop due to a major knee injury. During my freshman year of college I did crew as a way to keep busy and meet new people. Doing sports was a way for me to fit in with everyone else even though I knew I was different from them.

During high school, I was sexually attracted to both guys and girls, but I was only able to verbalize and explore the "straight" side of me. I knew I was sexually attracted to both sexes, because I would fantasize about guys and girls depending on the day. The only way for me to explore the "gay" side of me during high school was through the internet. In my summer school government class in high school, I was required to do community service, so I decided to go to the local police department, Moraga Police Department, to see if I could do my community service with them. I scheduled a meeting with the chief of police and told him about my community service requirement for my high school government class, and he allowed me to volunteer for the police department. After my summer school community service project was completed, I was offered a volunteer police cadet position with the Moraga Police Department.

I decided to go the local college, St. Mary's College of California, in the Town of Moraga, so I could continue to work at the Moraga Police Department to build up my law enforcement experience. I picked the closest major to Criminal Justice that SMC offered, which was Sociology, as well as minoring in Religious Studies. It was my junior year of college when the United States was attacked on September 11, 2001. The 9/11 attacks made my desire to serve and protect grow even stronger, so I decided that if I did not get hired as a police officer I would join the US Military instead.

I graduated from St. Mary's College of California in May 2002 and started the Napa Valley Criminal Justice Training Center's Police Academy Class #50 in June 2002. While attending the police academy, the Moraga Police Department offered me a conditional full-time police officer job upon graduating from the police academy. The police academy was 22 weeks long and graduated in December 2002. A week following my police academy graduation, I officially became a police officer with the Moraga Police Department. My childhood dream had finally come true and I started the career that I had always wanted.

During my career as a police officer, I dated women and had sexual encounters with them but there was something emotionally missing during sex. It was if there was a missing puzzle piece in my life. In 2005, I sustained a back injury that led to me being medically retired from the Moraga Police Department in October 2006. I was 26 and forced to retire from the job that I had always wanted to do since the age of five. I was emotionally lost and became depressed due to it.

It was in December 2007 that I met my future wife at Starbucks in Walnut Creek, CA, when I went to meet and have coffee with my college friend, Heather, who was visiting from London, England. Christina Michelle came along with Heather to have coffee and I knew her because we were acquaintances in college since we hung out in the same social circles. While having coffee with Heather and Christina, there was something about Christina that instantly gave me butterflies and I was really attracted to her. After coffee, I contacted Christina and asked her out on a date. We instantly clicked and started dating right away after that coffee meeting. Of all people, she was the daughter of a preacher. I immediately connected with her father and stepmother as well as her mother and stepfather. After six months of dating, I proposed to Christina and we got engaged. We got married on August 22, 2008 at Garré Winery in Livermore, CA.

Throughout our marriage little issues started building up into bigger issues and after trying all options we mutually decided to separate in March 2010. It was in June 2010 when my ex-wife and I decided to start the divorce process. We both realized it was the best thing for both of us. When I tell people today that I was marred to a woman, they always ask me if I ever cheated on her with a guy since I'm now gay, but the answer is **NO,** I never cheated on my ex-wife because I loved her and was very dedicated and faithful to her.

Even though the divorce was a mutual decision, it was still emotionally draining on me, so I decided I needed to take a vacation to decompress and clear my head. In July of 2010, I went to Maui, Hawaii, for ten days with my brother and best friend, Justin. My brother and Justin left after a week and I stayed an extra three days to clear my head about the divorce. During those three days, I mostly went to different beaches and just chilled and relaxed.

While in Maui, I decided to email Greg Miraglia and asked him if he would like to meet up and chat because we hadn't spoken in a while and I wanted to talk to him. I was relaxing on Kihei Beach on Maui and just thinking about my life, when I finally told myself that I was 30 years old, single, still had attractions toward guys, and I just needed to be true to myself and "test" out those feelings. I didn't care anymore what people thought of me, so if my family or friends judged me then that was their problem, but I needed to start living my true life, which was dating guys. The next day, Greg emailed me back stating he would be happy to meet up with me and gave me three (3) options to meeting up: 1) Meet him and his friend, Ben, who was a San Francisco Police Officer, in Castro, San Francisco, for happy hour, 2) Meet for dinner in Napa, or 3) Meet for coffee in Walnut Creek. I was debating back and forth in my head about Castro

233

or dinner, when I just emailed Greg back and told him I would meet him and Ben in Castro. I told Greg I picked Castro because I had never been there before, but in reality I probably picked Castro for alternative motives.

It wasn't until October of 2010 that I took Greg up on his offer for happy hour in Castro. Greg picked Ben and I up from the Pleasant Hill BART Station and drove us to Castro. On the way to Castro, I started panicking about my decision to go to Castro and could feel my heart beat faster and armpits starting to sweat. The three of us were chatting during the ride, but I was also thinking to myself, "What have I gotten myself into?" I was questioning my decision about Castro because I thought all the gays in Castro would be flamboyant, feminine, and bitchy. I didn't see myself as the stereotypical gay guy and worried I wouldn't fit into the Castro crowd. Imagine a gay guy not fitting into Castro: it's sad, but even gays have stereotypes of other gays.

When we finally arrived in Castro Greg took us to his favorite bar, Badlands. I was so nervous when I stepped foot into Badlands, because I had never been to a gay bar before and didn't know what to expect. It was definitely a surreal experience. As we were walking up to the bar to order drinks, I felt someone grab my ass. I whipped my head around and saw this old drunk guy smiling at me. I was not a happy camper, but I just let it go. Greg ordered all of us drinks and handed Ben and I two drinks each because it was 2-4-1 for happy hour. We sat down in the back of the bar and to this day I remember exactly how and where the three of us sat—Greg and Ben were sitting against the wall and I was sitting in a chair across from them. After taking my first sip of my drink, it was more like four drinks because the drinks were so strong. I was still extremely nervous inside the bar and I gulped down those two drinks like they were water.

The bar wasn't packed and the three of us were just chit chatting so my nerves eventually calmed down. We were just chatting away when somehow the conversation turned to guys being bisexual. Ben stated he didn't believe guys could be bisexual. The drinks must have hit me because without thinking I blurted out, "Guys can be bisexual because I'm attracted to both men and women." After realizing what I just said, I thought to myself, "What did I just say?" Greg's mouth dropped practically to the bar floor and he looked as if he had seen a ghost. Ben on the other hand said, "I knew it!" I asked Ben how he knew and he explained that the first time he met me at the Napa Valley Criminal Justice Training Center to evaluate the cadet scenarios his "gaydar" went off and he thought I was gay. Ben said he even asked Greg that night if I was gay or not. I asked Ben what made his "gaydar" go off that night and he stated what I was wearing and the shoes I had on. The three of us started laughing about it. I went on to explain to them about my divorce and how I always felt something was missing when I dated women and was married to Christina. Ben, being the smart ass that he is, replied, "Yeah, about nine inches was missing!" We all busted out laughing from Ben's comment, but the funny thing is now, looking back on it that statement, he partially right. From that day on, Ben and I became really good friends and are still really good friends today.

Without going into detail, let's just say the sex during my first gay sexual experience was like nothing I had ever experienced before and I knew immediately that I was gay. There aren't words to describe or explain how that sexual encounter immediately made me know I was gay. The missing puzzle piece that I talked about earlier and that was missing all my life was finally found and completed my life's puzzle.

The first family member that I came out to was my Aunt Trudy, but it was not on purpose. I needed to have knee surgery on my knee for a torn meniscus and my aunt offered to bring me home afterwards, so I took her up on the offer. During the drive home, I was laying down in the back seat still very loopy from the anesthesia and in my own little world. My aunt was talking to me, when she asked me if I had started dating anyone yet since my divorce, and I told her that I had actually started dating again. She asked me what her name was, and without thinking I replied, "You mean **HIS** name?" I immediately realized what I had just and couldn't believe I said that. My aunt whipped her head around toward me and looked at me with the widest eyes. After a few seconds, she realized she was driving and turned her head back on the road; and said to me, "As long as you are happy, then I am happy." There wasn't much said after that, but when she dropped me off at my house, she told me she was loved me.

The most gut-wrenching person that I came out to was my best friend, Justin. He and I have been friends since first grade, and practiced martial arts together for over 20 years. I finally told myself that I just needed tell Justin that I was gay and get it over with. I had just finished some early morning "retail therapy" at Union Square in San Francisco, CA, when I randomly called Justin and asked him if he wanted to go to lunch at our favorite dim sum restaurant in Concord. He said he did and I told him I would meet him there in an hour. On the way to lunch, my stomach was twisting and churning and I seriously thought I was going to throw up in my car. A million different scenarios were running through my head as I drove to meet Justin. I didn't know how I was going to tell my best friend the one secret I had hidden from him all these years. I was so afraid of losing my best friend by telling him I was gay. Justin is a police officer, meat and potatoes, gun loving, and ladies' man type of guy.

We both arrived at Imperial Dim Sum around the same time and were seated at a table. While having small talk, I kept wondering how I was going to tell Jay that I was gay. After chatting for a while, I finally just told him that I needed to tell him something. I explained that I hadn't been completely honest with him over the course of our friendship and had started dating guys after my divorce from Christina. Justin replied, "And? I thought you were going to tell me something bad." My jaw dropped because I couldn't believe what came out of his mouth. I was blown away by his response, or was I really surprised? I guess I wasn't really surprised because had always been there for me during the good times and the bad times in my life. I had the biggest knot in my stomach that I had ever experienced in my life when I told him, but I didn't really have anything to worry about. It's funny now looking back at the scenario because I made it so much more of a big deal than it truly was.

I still chuckle to this day about my coming out story to my ex-wife Christina. I didn't plan on telling Christina I was gay when it happened, it just sort of happened. Christina had called me one day because she needed to pick something up from the house, so I told her she could come over. We were chit chatting in my kitchen when she stated that she had noticed on Facebook that I had been going out a lot since the divorce. She wondered why I was going out so much, since I never really went out before or during our marriage. I had to come up with some generic answer, so I told her that my new group of friends liked to go out. "Which bars?" she responded.

I just replied, "In the city."

"Come on, what bars?" she asked.

I finally said, "Why don't you seriously sit down for this."

"Are you serious?" she stated.

I told her, "Yes!"

Christina sat down on one of my kitchen table chairs and I told her that I had been going to the bars in Castro. She had a puzzled look on her face and asked me if I was trying to tell her something; and I responded, "Yes."

Christina's shoulders slumped and she said, "Wow, I'm not surprised at all. That explains a lot." Um, that was not the response I was expecting at all. Christina actually took it much better than I thought, but I thought to myself, "What does she mean she wasn't surprised at all?" I was dumbfounded by that response. Christina then told me, "As long as you are happy, that is all that really matters." Christina stood up gave me a hug and left. After Christina left, I just stood in my hallway thinking to myself, because I was expecting her to be upset, yell, cry, or ask me a lot of questions. Since our divorce and me coming out to Christina, there was a period of time where we gave each other our space and didn't talk to each other; but now I can say we have become really good friends and still care about each other dearly. We have even gotten to the point where we can talk about our current relationships and ask each other advice about them. I consider Christina one of my dearest and closest friends to this day.

The relationship with my parents was pretty ugly when I came out to them. It all started when I decided to take one of my best friends, Sean, to go see the ranch that I grew up on. I showed Sean the barn, the cattle, the gardens, and my parent's yard. I then brought Sean inside my parent's house and introduced him to my mother. We probably only talked for about ten minutes and then left. Later that night I was watching TV in bed when I received a phone call from my mother. After saying hello, the first thing she asked me, "Was that creampuff your boyfriend?"

"Excuse me?" I quickly responded back to my mom.

My mom asked me again, "Was your friend and creampuff that you had over today your boyfriend?"

I completely lost it and went off on my mother and yelled, "DO NOT EVER call any of my friends creampuffs, and NO he is not my boyfriend, he's just a really good friend and he's married." I then went on to call my mom a homophobe and one of the most disrespectful persons I had ever met. I then told her that she doesn't have to approve of me being gay, but she does need to at least respect me as a human being.

She then told me, "Why would I want a son who is going to get AIDS and die?"

She says she doesn't remember saying that to me, but I remember it word for word and as if it was just said yesterday. I had a few choice words for her that I now regret saying, but before hanging up with her I told my mom, "Until you respect me as human being, we don't need to talk and you don't need to be in my life."

The saddest thing about the situation was that my mom and I used to talk to each other at least once if not twice a day. It took over three years before my mother and I started talking again and that was only due to my uncle being diagnosed with Alzheimer's disease. My mom and I talked about our big blow up and decided we would put the past in the past and move only forward. She did tell me that she is proud of me and has never stopped loving me.

SECTION III

HOW TO "COME OUT"

While each of these professions has its own unique culture, the coming out journey really begins the same way no matter which badge or uniform you wear. The place to begin is in front of a mirror and by taking an honest and serious look at yourself. There is no perfect age to do this. For many young people these days, this look comes at 12 or 13 years old, but if you have been working as a police officer, firefighter, or EMS professional, for 10 or 20 years, you may have avoided this mirror until now. Just know that it is never too late to begin the journey of coming out.

You need to be honest with yourself first and foremost. More than likely, deep down inside, you know if you have had a same sex attraction in your life. Realize that it's not a matter of being only straight or gay, there are many variations in between. As Alfred Kinsey and others have proven through their extensive studies, sexuality is a continuum. How you identify depends on the label you decide best fits your sexual attractions. Be cautious though about becoming lost in denial. It's easy to rationalize away those feelings, fantasies, and longings in order to fit in with what your friends, family, and professional colleagues expect. The image of yourself that you create can easily be shaped by the expectations of others, but ultimately, when you take a close look at yourself in that mirror, you need to look honestly and without shame at the truth you see. You can try to deny all those attractions and feelings all you want, but they won't go away.

The image we create of ourselves is shaped by many outside influences. It begins with the approval of our parents, our siblings, friends at school, and what we see and learn about through the media and rest of society. Non-heterosexuality is probably not part of that image others have created for you. But, the reality is that your sexuality is not a matter of choice. You cannot consciously decided to "follow in your father's or mother's footsteps" like many of you did when you got into law enforcement, the fire service, or emergency medicine. Yes, it is true that you can cover it up and decide to live a heterosexual life, but living that life does not change your sexuality or make you straight—no matter how hard you try. And ultimately, you will be the one who loses the most in this lie.

Look in the mirror and don't be afraid of what you see. Even if you have denied seeing yourself and your true sexuality before, it is never too late to see your true self with 20/20 vision. It's never too late to start reversing the lie you have been living, but you must begin that journey by being truthful with yourself first. You cannot expect anyone else to accept the true you if you are not ready to accept yourself first. Now it may not be easy and you may be unsure, but you must begin your journey here, in front of the mirror, by coming out to yourself first. You cannot expect others to even consider accepting who you are if you are not able to accept yourself. I know so many people in my life who are struggling with just this very stage and I want badly to say, "It's ok, you can come out and be who you were created to be."

"How do you come out to yourself?" you ask. You step up in front of that mirror and say those words out loud. "I'm gay," or, "I'm bisexual." Say the words out loud and give yourself the credit of being honest with yourself for perhaps the first time in your life. Verbalizing your identity is the first step toward accepting this aspect of who you are. It is also the first step in ridding yourself of the shame and fear that has accumulated throughout your life. This is where the coming out journey begins.

Now that you've made it through the first and most scary phase of coming out to yourself, you are ready to move on about the business of living your life in the truth. For many people this also means beginning to unravel all of the lies, masks, and smoke screens that you have put in place to protect yourself from suspicion. For some, this means removing all of the "beards," those people of the opposite gender that you kept around to look the part at social events, family gatherings, and at work. For others, it might mean considering a divorce. In our second book, *American Heroes Coming out from behind the Badge*, Sergeant Pete Thoshinsky writes about having to make this same decision. At the age of 44 and after marrying a woman, Pete came out. His new-found partner was in a similar situation, but also had kids. Although the pain of a divorce is nothing to take lightly, it is certainly better than continuing to live a lie and to lead on those you still love. Think your decision through carefully, but know that every day you continue to lie is one more day of pain that you, your spouse, and your children will have to suffer through.

Living your life in the truth means that you will no longer lie about who you are. It means that you will stop making up stories about the dates you had, the "hot women" or "hot men" you are chasing, and that you start thinking about sharing who you really are with those in your life, including friends, family, and co-workers. It would be easy if you could just go to work and to be able to keep your private life totally separate. However, the reality is that, for almost every job, especially one in law enforcement, it just doesn't work that way. Think about it: what's the first question you or your co-workers ask on a Monday? "Hey, how was your weekend? What did you do?" Almost every workplace has some social activity at some level, so even if you never attend these events, at some point you are going to be asked or wondered about. Living an authentic life means not only being honest with yourself, but with others close to you. Of course, this leads to the next phase of the coming out process, which is to share your secret with others.

If you think that coming out is a once-in-a-lifetime event, let me tell you from experience that it is not. In fact, you will likely come out every day for the rest of your life. Now it certainly won't be as dramatic, scary, or emotional as it is the first few times you tell people, but the reality is that, straight or gay, people come out with their sexuality in the normal course of business. Whether it's in the pictures you put up on your locker or desk or who you talk about sharing your life with, we express our sexuality in the normal course of life's business. I've talked to several friends now who have told me that they don't ever "come out" to anyone. One friend told me, "if you talk to me for five or ten minutes about who I am, you will discover on your own that I'm gay. The most important people in my life are my partner and our son. I almost always have something to say about us." And this is so true. In today's age, gay and lesbian people are "out" everywhere, even in law enforcement. It is a huge event in your life, but in the big picture, it's probably a bigger issue for you than most others. The older you are and the more lies you have to unravel, the more individual conversations you might need to have. But, you don't have to throw a coming out party to share your secret.

Here are some thoughts about the first few people you tell. First of all, think about those people in your life you care most about. Who has earned the place in your life to be among the first to know your truth? Think next about who is most likely to support you. Don't set yourself up for the expectation that everyone will embrace your news, but do pick one person who is most likely to listen and accept you unconditionally. In our books, I recommend first building a network of gay friends, people you can talk to about coming out and how to do it. This network can also support you when you feel most alone. Once you do identify the person you want to tell first, set up a quiet and private place to talk. The Thanksgiving dinner table is not the place! A party is not the place. The locker room or police department briefing is not the place. Make sure you have enough time to really talk and to listen. Don't make a game out of it and be careful not to create such drama around the set-up that you create more anxiety for you and the recipient of your secret than is necessary. For me, the best place to talk is over a meal in a restaurant that is not crowded or too noisy. Don't get drunk before you begin sharing, and remember, you've known the truth about yourself for a long time. The person you are telling may just be finding out. Be ready for any reaction, but don't be disappointed when you hear, "Yeah, I know. What took you so long to tell me?" Go slowly and share your secret at a pace you feel comfortable with, but understand that once you do tell someone, you can't expect anyone else to keep it a secret. It's not fair to say, "I'm going to tell you something about me, but you can't tell anyone else" and then hold the person accountable if they slip—it's not fair.

I recommend making a list, in order, of who you want to tell, thinking about how the people on your list associate with each other. And don't be afraid of letting the word get out on its own. You don't have to make a formal announcement to everyone in your life. Reserve those special times and sharing for those people closest to you or who you need to unravel a lie with. Let nature take its course, but know that you can never again lie about or deny who you are. You must make a commitment to live your life in the truth from this point on.

Now that you have come out to yourself and have had some success telling other people close to you in your life, you are probably thinking about how to come out at work. Remember that once you begin to tell people in your personal life that you are gay, lesbian, bisexual, or transgender, you cannot reasonably expect that secret to be maintained. It's not fair for you to be able to come out, but then not allow anyone else in your life to "come out" as an ally or simply as your supportive friend. If there were rumors at work about your before, you can expect those rumors to increase or re-surface at work. Why is your life so interesting? Well, law enforcement folks, by their nature, are curious. In fact, I would say we are fascinated by each other's lives. Whether motivated by interest or caused by boredom, we like to talk about each other all the time. It's part of the culture everywhere I've ever been. It is the nature "of the beast." What I've found most curious though is that we aren't nearly as interested in facts or truth as we are in speculation and rumor. Once you do come out at work, you will find that the rumors stop because talking about what everyone knows isn't very interesting.

There are a few things to think about before coming out at work. First of all, as of today, only 21 states provide for employment protection based on sexual orientation and/or gender identity. This means that in the majority of states, you can still legally be fired simply for being a member of the LGBT community. I haven't heard of it happening often, but I have talked with officers within the last couple of years that suffered from this kind of "legalized" discrimination. You should know where you stand legally before making the decision to talk about who you are at work. You should also review your agency policies and procedures as well as any municipal or county personnel rules and regulations related to discrimination. Knowing exactly where you stand will give you confidence as you make the decision to come out at work.

As much as law enforcement work and culture is the same, no matter where you are in the country, every agency does have aspects of its culture unique to the people working there. If you work for a small department where everyone from the chief or sheriff down to the part-time volunteer knows everyone else, think about talking to your chief or sheriff first. Whether it's out of respect for the position or relationship, having support from the top helps. Now, of course, this assumes you do in fact know your agency executive well enough to know he or she will be supportive. I've talked to a lot of officers who told me that telling their chief was important and knowing of their support made the rest of the process easier. In larger agencies, as a line officer, you may not have any connection with the chief or sheriff at all, so coming out to them probably isn't an issue. Consider your assignment, the relationships you have with supervisors and peers, and your own comfort level. You also need to think about any "beards" or "cover stories" you've used to conceal your sexuality as these facts and stories need to be undone. If you work with a partner on the job, respect that relationship and consider telling your work partner first. I don't recommend doing it on duty or even around the workplace. You don't want to risk having someone overhear your conversation or, worse yet, have a hot call go down right in the middle of telling your story. Like in the last article, find a place to have lunch or dinner, set aside a good amount of time for conversation, and then go for it. Be ready for questions and don't set yourself up for any one particular reaction. If it doesn't go well, be prepared to let it go for the moment and give your work partner time to think about what you've said.

One of the common reactions I encountered as I came out to people at work and to friends in my life is, "why didn't you feel comfortable telling me before?" It's not that you didn't tell THEM, it's that you didn't tell anyone. Make it about you, not them. Coming out is a very personal decision that, in this profession, takes courage above and beyond. Explain yourself without making excuses or placing blame. That was then and this is now.

It took a good year for rumors and gossip to stop after I came out. No one ever said a negative thing to my face. While I'm sure there was a lot talked about behind my back, I never heard about it. People at your workplace will talk and there is nothing you can do about it. Encourage open dialogue, and remember: your co-workers will be as comfortable with you as you are with yourself.

So what happens if you take our advice and come out, but when you tell your parents or someone else close to you, it doesn't go well? Despite all of the success stories we know of, unfortunately there are many that end up being tragic. This was recently the case with a good friend of mine after he came out to his parents. For most of his life, he strived to please his parents by achieving in school and then finding a "good woman" to marry. In fact, he did find a woman who he truly fell in love with and married. He was destined to create a traditional family just as his mother dreamed of for him. But then, a few months later, his true self, that had always been there, began to emerge and his marriage ended. At the age of 31, he identified who he truly is and came out. It wasn't easy for him at all, but the courage was always there and he marched out with confidence and great enthusiasm all the while knowing that telling his parents might be the greatest challenge. When he did tell the two people who for most of his life he has tried to please, it didn't go well, at all. Tragically, they rejected him entirely and blamed him for "ruining the family." He heard all of the usual non-accepting responses, like, "There are plenty of good women out there for you. You just haven't found the right one." He was no longer invited to holiday family gatherings and when he would call with holiday greetings, the phone would go unanswered.

Is it all worth it? Well, that's a question you have to answer for yourself, but consider the sacrifice of living your life for your parents or anyone else. We spend the first 18 years of our lives growing, learning, and developing, much at the whim and desire of our parents. When we become adults, we begin making our own decisions. As an LGBT person, you can decide to live your life as someone else—someone you are not—to satisfy the dreams and desires of others, including your parents. Many people, especially men, do this by getting married, having children, raising a family, and then later in life destroying it all by coming out and admitting that it's all been unreal. The other option is to realize who you are, accept who you are, understand that you were created to be who you are and that being LGBT is not a choice or lifestyle you select. You can choose to live your life in the truth and then to share who you are with those you love. It is not, however, your responsibility to make sure others accept you.

In all that we've written about coming out to date, we've always said that finding the right time and place to share your very personal news is critical. Hopefully you didn't and won't choose a holiday or other family gathering. You know your parents and others who are closest to you the best. And if you don't know how they will react, plan for all possible outcomes. Remember that just because you get an emotional and seemingly negative response, it doesn't mean that things won't evolve and change. Parents, too, need time to "come out" about having an LGBT son or daughter. Allow them the time to process the idea and consider they really may not have known about you. But the point of this section is about what to do if it doesn't go well. The simple answer is that you can't do anything about it.

Aside from being aware and sensitive about how you share your sexual orientation or gender identity, you are not responsible for how your parents or anyone else accepts you. Rejecting you is not going to change one bit of who you are. Making you feel guilty about "destroying the family" or telling you that you are a sinner and that you are going to hell is not going to make you any less gay. You are who you are and no one, including your parents or even you, can change that. Part of your plan should be preparing to walk away from it all, and I mean actually leaving. It should include the idea that you may no longer be welcome at family gatherings, holiday celebrations, and that your calls may go unanswered. Your "best friend" could decide to walk away and dissolve your friendship. But, then again, how good of a friend were they really if they cannot accept you for who you really are. Have courage, have confidence, and if you are tossed away by your parents, walk away with confidence. Of course it might hurt you a great deal, so allow yourself some time to mourn. But once that mourning has come and gone, move forward with your life. If you have done what we suggested early on about forming a network of LGBT friends and supporters, you will never be alone. You will have a new family, a new place to gather for holidays, and a community that loves and supports you for who you are. You simply have to look at the important people in your life differently. Those who reject you are no longer as important as those who do support you. Let those who do not accept you go. Let the stress from all of those years of trying to please them slip away. Allow yourself to experience happiness independently from the approval of anyone else. If and when you find someone to love, to become your partner, husband, or wife, the only person's acceptance of that partner that is at all important is your own. If you get from your parents the old line, "Well that's fine if you are gay, just don't bring it around here," then don't. This is not acceptance and you are worth so much more than having to live your life under those limitations. Go out there and find the love you deserve and let go any consideration of how your parents will accept or not accept your partner.

Here's the bottom line: hope for the best, but prepare for the worst. But in all cases, be who you are. The acceptance of others won't change the reality of who you are. Be true to yourself always and leave the responsibility for others to accept you to them. Lean on your friends and those who support you for strength and confidence and know you will never be alone.

One of the questions I frequently get from LGBT law enforcement applicants is whether or not they should "come out" at any point during the hiring process. Most of the writers expressed concern about suffering from discrimination and worry about being disqualified by a homophobic background investigator or by an agency that simply doesn't want LGBT employees. These are legitimate concerns especially in states that do not have any type of employment protection from discrimination based on sexual orientation and/or gender identity. Here are my thoughts.

First of all, as an "out" LGBT person, you need to consider seriously where you want to work and if you are willing to go back into the closet in order to get and keep a job. This may at first seem like a sacrifice you are willing to make in order to get into law enforcement, but you need to really consider the risks and long-term implications of making such a sacrifice. Here is the important question: Are you willing to sacrifice happiness in your personal life for potential happiness in your professional life? Is it possible to realize happiness professionally, without happiness personally? I would say most likely it is not.

The reality today is that law enforcement is evolving, ever so slowly, in its acceptance of LGBT employees. As more law enforcement professionals come out at work, the law enforcement culture will evolve as it did when women entered the ranks of patrol officers some 40 years ago. Do your homework and do your best to fine a department that is likely to be accepting and even valuing of LGBT employees. Check out your state's employment protection laws, city ordinances, and department policies to see if any or all include protection based on sexual orientation and or gender identity. If they do not include such protections, there is, of course, a

252

greater risk of being disqualified or "legally" fired if your chief or sheriff doesn't accept your sexual orientation or gender identity.

Now to the real question. In states where employment protection exists, it would not be likely that you would be asked about your sexual orientation during the initial selection process. In fact, it might be unlikely that anyone would ask you directly at any point during the hiring process. It will, however, come up indirectly at several points during the background investigation, including the pre-investigation interview and during the psychological interview.

Every state has different regulations and different levels of detail that are considered during the background investigation. I'm most familiar with California's process and believe it to be fairly comprehensive, so I will provide advice based on the process I know. California has very inclusive employment protection that includes sexual orientation and gender identity. It is not permissible to ask about either aspect of identity during an initial interview, so there is no need to offer up anything you are not comfortable discussing.

The background investigation includes a comprehensive personal history questionnaire, an investigation that includes interviews with most people close in your life, such as family members, spouses, roommates, employers, and work colleagues. It also includes a psychological evaluation, medical exam, and could include a polygraph or voice stress analysis interview. The first point at which you will have a decision to make about disclosing your sexual orientation is likely the personal history questionnaire. You will be asked to identify everyone you have lived with over the last ten years, people you have had a close relationship with and who you have married (and that could include domestic partners). You will need to provide names, addresses, and telephone numbers. So why not just identify your same-sex partner as "a roommate"? You could do that and probably get away with it, unless you live in a one-room apartment. And yes, you can expect the background investigator to visit in person to see where and how you live. The risk here is being perceived as deceitful, evasive, and/or that you are hiding something, which in this example would be true.

Here is the more important consideration. Sexual orientation and gender identity are both protected classes in California, but an act of dishonesty is not. Being dishonest in any aspect of your background investigation is absolutely a legitimate reason to disqualify someone, even if the subject of that dishonesty is sexual orientation or gender identity. And once you document a lie in one background investigation, you will likely never recover from it because future background investigations will include looking at past personal history questionnaires. Law enforcement agencies have no tolerance for lies, so don't do it even if it means having to "out" yourself.

The background investigation usually starts with a meeting between the applicant and the background investigator. This interview involves going through the personal history questionnaire line by line. Be prepared to answer questions about personal relationships, who you have dated or are dating, and who you are living with. Background investigators consider a failure to disclose as an act of dishonesty, so it's not just about being accurate, it's about answering questions completely. Keep in mind that everything you include in the personal history questionnaire will be verified by the background investigator through interviews with the people closest in your life.

The next phase of the process where you will likely encounter questions that would lead to your sexual orientation would be the psychological exam. It's perfectly normal and expected that you would be asked about your dating relationships, marriages, and other related topics as this phase of the hiring process is designed to ensure you are mentally stable and prepared to be a law enforcement officer. Being even perceived as dishonest in the psychological exam will likely result in you not being recommended for hire.

I heard recently from a new officer who happens to be gay about how he handled his sexual orientation during a hiring process that I think is perhaps an ideal example. This applicant was "out" at the time he applied for a position as a deputy sheriff with an agency that has never before employed an "out" deputy. In fact, this applicant would become the first "out" male law enforcement officer in the county's history. The agency has a perceived reputation of being homophobic and very conservative. He made it through the background investigation and psychological exam. The last step was an interview with the under-sheriff, a captain, and a lieutenant. Now, I can tell you he was concerned about how it would all go, especially about his sexual orientation, but he approached the interview with total confidence. This applicant had been a cadet with a neighboring agency. The last question he was asked was why he wanted to work for the sheriff's department and not the agency where he served as a cadet. The applicant responded with something like, "Well, I think the other agency would have a problem with my sexual orientation, but *I know it won't be a problem here.*" He looked each of the interviewers directly in the eye as he said this and at that moment demonstrated that this "secret" was no secret and would have no power against him. He demonstrated confidence and comfort with himself and made it known that his being gay was not an issue. Granted, this applicant was applying for an agency in a state with full employment protection, but by putting the agency on notice, he not only took away any question, he insulated himself from potential discrimination right up front. In his particular case, I think this was a brilliant move.

Now if, for whatever reason, you don't end up coming out formally during the hiring process, plan ahead for how you are going to handle the normal types of questions about your personal life that you will encounter once hired and on the job. As would likely occur in any job, your co-workers will want to get to know you, so answering the "normal" questions about what you did on your weekend or if you are married or seeing anyone should be expected. Of course, you can ignore the questions or brush them off, but of course, the risk of being labeled a "non-team player" or someone who doesn't fit in will go way up. Ultimately, you will have to decide for yourself how to respond, but in all cases don't lie. Don't create a fictitious opposite gender friend or spouse, because at some point and place, someone from your workplace will see you out with your true partner and then your lie will be discovered. Rumors will then spread about you and you risk being labeled as dishonest. The question for you is: which would play out as a worst case, coming out as gay or being labeled as dishonest?

So, to the original question of when you should come in the hiring process. Clearly it's a personal decision, but my recommendation is to be yourself—your real self. Respond to the many questions you will face honestly and openly. You don't need to volunteer information you are not comfortable with, but don't deny who you are, don't lie, and don't hide anything. In the end, you won't truly be happy working for an organization that is homophobic or un-accepting of gay people, so if you are eliminated in the hiring process because you are LGBT, then so be it. There are a growing number of professional law enforcement organizations out there who will embrace this aspect of your identity.

Are you going home for the holidays this year? Is telling your family that you are L, G, B, or T on your mind? This is a question we get asked frequently by readers who are in the process of "coming out" and as this year's holiday season approaches, I thought it would be timely to share some thoughts about coming out at the holiday dinner table. I've written before about a friend who told me how he came out at Thanksgiving. He was home from college and knew he wanted to tell his parents he is gay as he had already come out to his friends at school. Relatives had flown in from different cities and him mom was busy planning the picture-perfect Thanksgiving dinner. My friend tried hard to find the perfect moment when he had enough courage and when his mom had time to listen without distraction. All of a sudden, it was Thanksgiving and dinner was being served. The conversation was brisk and often muffled by the sound of utensils striking the family china and serving spoons hitting the plate. Feeling frustrated and nervous, my friend said, "Mom, could you please pass the mashed potatoes? By the way, I'm gay." I'm sure the sudden silence that followed was deafening and the brisk halt in conversation awkward. Let me recommend another strategy.

First of all, we all know that the holidays are some of the most stressful times in family life. While they are supposed to be time to reunite, celebrate, and to be together as a family, there is often tremendous stress involved for everyone. Coming out is a special and significant event that requires great consideration of time and place. The Thanksgiving or Christmas dinner table is not the right time or place. While I recognize that every situation is different, I don't think a holiday event is the right time or place to share such a personal and important part of your life. For almost everyone I've ever talked to, telling your parents you are gay is one of the most challenging conversations to have. You want to be sure there is time for your parents and other relatives to process what you are sharing, to ask you questions if they wish, and to think about what you shared without the many distractions the holidays bring.

Coming out to a parent or relative should be a special time between you and that loved one. Set aside time for just the two or three of you that allows time for reaction, discussion, tears of joy or sadness, whatever the case may be. Allow enough time for everyone involved to process the experience and always have a way to escape if the situation doesn't go as planned. The last thing you want over a holiday is to be trapped in the same house with no place to go.

Another related question we often get is whether you should bring your boyfriend or girlfriend home to be with you when you share your news. Again, I think this is a bad idea. You are putting everyone, including your boyfriend or girlfriend, in a bad situation if things don't go well. The first step is to tell your parents about yourself alone. If things go well, then consider the best time to introduce your partner. Remember, parents need time to come out as well. They need to work through how to share the news with relatives and "surprising everyone" on a holiday has too much risk for everyone. After coming out, ask your parents about bringing your partner home for the holidays. If they are not comfortable, then you can make a decision about whether to go or not, but just showing up puts everyone involved in a potentially awkward place. This is all about protecting you, your own feelings, and those of your partner. Again, I think introducing your partner to your parents is an event best scheduled away from the holidays. Allow time for your parents to really get to know your partner without the distraction of preparing a meal for 30.

With all of this said, I'm all about coming out. Make it a priority and take the time to plan it out carefully. This is an important part of yourself that desires a holiday of its own. There is no need to share this major event with the mashed potatoes or any other dish at the Thanksgiving dinner table.

BECOMING A ROLE MODEL

Like it or not, if you are the only, or one of a few, out gay or lesbian law enforcement employee in your workplace, you are automatically appointed to the position of role model for your department. This responsibility will likely and easily extend beyond the walls of your department and into the community. Law enforcement officers play a variety of leadership roles inside the department and in the community. Agencies typically use personnel of various ethnic backgrounds to act as leaders and liaisons with various ethnicity-based community groups. The same need exists in law enforcement within the gay community. Having an openly gay or lesbian law enforcement officer in an agency that serves an identifiable gay community is a tremendous asset for the department. For all of these reasons, it's imperative that you be the best role model you can be for everyone in your department and in your community. Consider the reasons that shaped the fear that prevented you from coming out until now: the negative stereotypes and exaggerated behaviors, the negative images of gay and lesbians exploited by the media, and the continuous anti-gay sentiment that echoes in the churches of the Religious Right. The way to change all that is through living examples of the truth, found in positive role models like you.

The reality is that the stereotypes that have defined how a gay person looks and acts or how a lesbian dresses and behaves are based on a very small number of gay and lesbian people. Most gay and lesbian people would fold into the average crowd without notice. I'm not suggesting that we should avoid being individuals or standouts, but I am suggesting that, as a positive role model in law enforcement, it is up to you to show your fellow officers what it really means to be gay or lesbian. The most important thing is to always be a good person, a good friend, and a good law enforcement officer, first and foremost. Be known for being a good person, a dedicated professional, and a reliable partner, who happens to be gay or lesbian.

I'm reminded of a fellow employee who is a lesbian and who has been out for many years. She has also been very active in promoting GLBT issues in the community. I often refer to her as the "granite chipper" because she is very much an in-your-face kind of person. When introducing herself, she will often include the fact that she is a lesbian before even saying her name. There is no doubt that the gay rights movement is where it is today because of dedicated granite chippers, but I don't think that is the best approach for gay and lesbian role models in law enforcement. Causing a change in law enforcement is most effectively done slowly and methodically, through strong and effective leadership. My belief is that strong, positive gay and lesbian role models, who are good cops first, is the key to gaining acceptance for future GLBT officers.

Realize too that once you do come out in a workplace that is interested in making a difference, both within the workplace and in the community, you will likely be asked to take on a more formal leadership role. Our state commission on peace officer standards and training recently produced a workplace harassment training program for one of the monthly training programs that are distributed on DVD. The training focused on workplace harassment related to gay and lesbian officers and was the first of its kind. I was totally impressed by the leadership, professionalism, and courage of the gay and lesbian officers who participated in the video by talking about their own experiences. This is the kind of work that needs to be done in our profession, and every gay and lesbian law enforcement officer has the opportunity to play a part in helping the profession grow in its acceptance and understanding of gay and lesbian officers, just as racial minority and female officers did decades ago.

BEING OUT AND GETTING IN

Yes, you can be out and still have a successful law enforcement career. That is what this book is all about, and, like the people sharing the stories within it, there are many highly successful law enforcement professionals who happen to be members of the GLBT community. A theme I've tried to communicate throughout this book is the idea that what is most important about being gay or lesbian in law enforcement is that you are a good person and a good cop, first and foremost. Sexuality is only one innate, albeit very important, aspect of who you are. In all circumstances, be true to yourself and who you are. With that said, there are some ideas to consider when getting into law enforcement in this day and age, as law enforcement continues to evolve and gradually becomes more accepting of its GLBT members.

Much of my advice for getting into law enforcement is the same for GLBT members as it is for anyone else. The search for a job and the subsequent hiring process is really a two-way street for both the employing department and the applicant. It's important to realize that, while much of law enforcement work is the same, communities and workplaces differ greatly. Policing styles can vary greatly, so taking some time to think about the type of policing you want to do is important. An equally important aspect to consider is the organizational culture and history with gay and lesbian employees. Law enforcement is a job that you really have to want to do, and it requires a lot of commitment and effort, so take the time to do it right.

Before getting too far in to the hiring process, I recommend riding along with at least two different officers on two different shifts at the department at which you are interested in working. In addition to learning about the kind of policing provided by the department, you should pay very close attention to how the officers conduct themselves. Pay particular attention to how they talk, the words they use, and to any slurs that seem to be commonplace. Ask the officer why he likes working at the department and about the positive and negative aspects of the agency. As an applicant, remember that you too will be interviewed by the officer you are riding with. Avoid making judgments and do more listening than talking.

As stated before, know the laws regarding discrimination in the workplace. Some states include sexual orientation as a protected group, but many still do not. Some organizations may have department policies that provide protection from discrimination as well. The risk, of course, with working for an organization that has no policy or any protection at the state level is that your employment could be terminated for being a homosexual. To find out about the laws in your state, go to the website for the Human Rights Campaign at http://www.hrc.org.

One popular way of getting into law enforcement in California is to put yourself through the police academy. This gives you an advantage over others applicants who would need to complete an academy before going to work. Some states have centralized academies that may not allow anyone to put themselves through without having a law enforcement job in place. Other states, like California, have decentralized academies that are regional training centers and allow self-sponsored students. The basic curriculum in these academies is essentially the same, but the environment can vary a great deal. Again, I highly recommend doing some research before registering at one of these training centers. If the academy is affiliated with a college, research the college's policy on discrimination to see if sexual orientation is included in the list of protected groups and if the policy applies to the police academy program.

I recommend thinking about attending the academy in the same way as going to work in a new job. While in the police academy, what matters first is that you are a good student and a good person. Academy students develop very close relationships during the training experience. It is common for students to get to know each other even outside of academy life. It would be tough to be true to yourself and true to your fellow students while lying about who you are. It isn't necessary to include the fact that you are gay or lesbian when introducing yourself on the first day of class, but if someone asks at some point, be prepared to answer truthfully. Ideally, you will never be asked because it isn't appropriate in a professional setting; however, the closeness of the relationships that do form in the academy invite even this level of intimacy. Understand that the academy is not a social event and you should concentrate on studying, learning, and performing. Like any workplace, your sexual orientation is not an appropriate topic for discussion or speculation in the academy. It has no bearing on how well you learn and on how you perform. Just be a good student and a good person first, always.

HOW TO FIND THAT SOMEONE SPECIAL

Before I came out, one of the "hallmark holidays" I resented the most was Valentine's Day. I never had a relationship to celebrate and was secretly a bit jealous of all of my friends who did. And while I still find this holiday somewhat annoying, I will admit that I always enjoy planning something for just my partner and me to enjoy together. But realizing the positive aspects of this holiday didn't come immediately after coming out. I had to first find a partner.

One of the intimidating parts of coming out, especially if someone comes out later in life, is where to meet people and how to start dating. If you consider that LGBT people make up 10% of the total population, with an even lower percentage of LGBT who are "out," it might feel like slim pickings. Let me assure you, there are plenty of good gay men and women out there for you to meet. The real question is how to get started.

The most important thing about entering the dating scene is to be your true self. What I mean by that is be who you are at whatever point in life you happen to be. If you are 50 years old and just came out, be 50 and don't worry about whether or not you will be attractive to someone else. I can assure you, there are men out there of all ages who are searching for you. If you are 50 and are attracted to younger guys, there are younger guys who are attracted to older men. Avoid going through a mid-life crisis and feeling like you have to act and dress like you are 20. Just be you and put yourself out there as you are.

Now of course, you might feel like you could lose a few pounds or spruce up your wardrobe before diving into the LGBT social scene and that's fine. Exercise is good for everyone, and so if your body image motivates you to get in shape, more power to you. Just don't make yourself into something you are not. Now, for where to start…

I'm a huge fan of online dating sites. Aside from meeting my partner on one, I think they are a great place, especially when you are new to the dating scene, to meet people in a low-risk and comfortable situation. You can talk with people to see who might have something in common without having to deal with crowds, noise, and alcohol. It's a great opportunity to break the ice, talk about attitudes, experiences, and what you are looking for with minimal risk. Of course, there are online dating sites of all kinds, some of which cater to hook-ups more than long-term relationships. There are even apps for your mobile device, like Grinder and Scruff, that will help you locate others like you while on the road. In my opinion, Gay.Com is still the best online dating site for those looking for more than a one-time 20-minute date.

Gay.com now offers more of a community feel to its website. You can create a profile that certainly includes your sexual interests, but that also includes a lot more of what others might be looking for in a potential part-ner. You can enter as much or as little information about yourself as you wish and the good news is that you can get online and try it for no cost. Of course, for the additional features, you will need to purchase a subscrip-tion, but in my mind, it's worth it.

Online dating does come with its own set of risks and I always remind people to use your common sense when meeting other people in person for the first time. I know it may shock you, but some people don't use their real picture in an online profile. I can tell you from experience that I was only disappointed once by someone who I met who was clearly not the person they represented themselves to be in a picture. The other basics around online dating include always meeting in a public place for the first time. Don't provide any personal identifying data online that could subject you to identity theft and don't share your home address until after you meet and feel comfortable.

Whether you are "out" or not, there is no reason to feel alone this Valentine's Day. There are lots of people out there looking for all kinds of relationships, from friendships to a spouse. Take a chance and go online and look around. You might just be the one someone else has been looking for their entire life.

IDEAS FOR ATTRACTING LGBT APPLICANTS

When I started my law enforcement career in 1978, the first two women were hired by my department for regular patrol assignments. News of this unique hire covered the front page of the local newspaper, literally from top to bottom. As these two pioneers proved themselves, efforts were made to hire more women, but recruiting wasn't easy since before that time women were not ever considered for uniformed patrol jobs. Eventually, law enforcement figured out that in order to attract women to the job, agencies needed to present role models and to target their recruitment to women's groups where likely candidates might be. The same strategy can be effective for recruiting LGBT employees.

There are, however, a few essential things that must be done before posting recruitment fliers. By and large, law enforcement still has a bad reputation for being homophobic and unwelcoming of out gay people, especially gay men. While this may not be a fair generalization, it is nevertheless the current reality. Agencies can begin to change this perception by taking a few key actions.

1. Prospective LGBT applicants want to know that their employment is protected from discrimination based on their sexual orientation. This requires at the very least a published discrimination policy inclusive of sexual orientation and gender identity, a local ordinance, or ideally a state law.

2. Applicants can be made to feel welcome and encouraged to apply to an agency that also includes LGBT people in its mission statement or values. The Los Angeles County Sheriff's Department offers an

ideal model statement that includes not tolerating homophobia within its organization. Agency leaders should include LGBT in the same conversations that appreciate race, nationality, ethnicity, and gender.

3. Agency executives must demonstrate a sincere desire to recruit "out" LGBT employees. This desire must be communicated clearly and regularly through the ranks to those individual employees charged with recruiting and hiring new employees. This also means that everyone involved in the hiring process, including background investigators and psychologists, must be committed to this effort. Homophobia can be hidden in biased decision-making that weeds out LGBT applicants for reasons not connected to sexual orientation.

4. Once these initial organizational changes are made, recruiters will have the tools they need to go out into the community and target LGBT populations.

The initial recruitment effort will involve changing the stereotype about law enforcement's lack of interest and support for LGBT employees. This is done simply by talking with LGBT groups, sharing the agency policies and practices described above, and showing a sincere interest in attracting qualified LGBT people. Ideally, existing LGBT law enforcement employees will serve as live role models and as evidence that an LGBT person can be successful in the agency.

Like all other targeted recruitment efforts, recruitment should include high schools, colleges, and community events. For the recruitment of LGBT applicants, recruiters should seek out high school gay-straight alliance groups, LGBT youth centers, and high school gay student clubs. These groups can typically be found by searching the internet or by contact the local LGBT center. Visit these groups and talk about law enforcement career opportunities. Speak directly about the organization's desire to have "out" LGBT employees.

Other excellent places to recruit are local and regional Gay Pride festivals. Invest in both and have personnel there just like you would for any other type of community event. Have informational fliers that speak specifically about the organization's desire to hire "out" LGBT employees and include evidence that the workplace is safe from discrimination based on sexual orientation. Remember that it may take a few times at these events before perceptions change, so be persistent. A regular presence and consistent message will create the change in perception needed to attract LGBT applicants.

There are a variety of LGBT publications in which agencies could consider advertising career opportunities. For example, in the California Bay Area, the *Bay Area Reporter* and *North Bay Bohemian* both reach large LGBT populations. *The Advocate* is a national magazine that could reach a very broad audience. There are also many LGBT law enforcement associations that would share career opportunities. Click on "Organizations" at the top of this page for links to the ones we know about.

It really is as simple as reaching out to the LGBT community and talking sincerely about wanting to include LGBT people in the ranks of law enforcement. Actions of course speak louder than words, so take advantage of every opportunity to fly the agency's rainbow flag. Participate and be visible in LGBT community events and venues. And finally, reach out for help and suggestions.

CREATING AN ACCEPTING WORKPLACE

This section is especially for law enforcement leaders, including chiefs and sheriffs. It is my hope that every chief and every sheriff in the country will take the time to read about this subject here, or from someone else, for it is the agency executive who holds the real power for creating organizational change.

Imagine yourself as a chief or sheriff. You think you know the personnel who work for you pretty well. When you hired them, you reviewed their background investigation packets and you looked at the results of the psychological exam, and you know of no one in your department who is gay. One night, at about two in the morning, your work cell phone rings. Your graveyard shift watch commander is on the other end with bad news. He tells you that one of your 24-year-old male officers was found dead in his apartment. The apparent cause of death is suicide from a shot fired out of the officer's issued duty weapon. Of course, you are stunned. The next day, you find out that there was no note left. Investigators searched the officer's apartment for clues. They found no sign of an estranged wife or girlfriend. In fact, there were no pictures of the officer with any women at all. The only pictures on the wall were of the officer on the job, posing a many cops do, with various co-workers in uniform, at parties, and on the job. You've always known this officer to be fully dedicated to the job, in love with law enforcement, and a hard worker. You recall that you never met this officer's girlfriend and never saw him at any of the department's social events, other than by himself. He always seemed happy. Why would an officer who loved law enforcement so much kill himself?

The scenario above is based on a true story. The investigators surmised, based on the evidence found in the officer's apartment, that at least some of the motivation for the officer's suicide was that he was gay and felt trapped between his love of law enforcement, his real self, and his fear of being rejected by all those people he loved so much should he come out.

Most chiefs and sheriffs currently in office started their careers 20 or more years ago, in a time when most gays and lesbians working in law enforcement were completely invisible. AIDS was identified as the "gay disease" and was seen as a death sentence. While attending the basic academy, these chiefs and sheriffs likely received training, new at the time, on bloodborne pathogens, and were told that AIDS is a deadly disease that posed a threat to law enforcement officers who were exposed to the blood of drug users and gays. These chiefs and sheriffs graduated from high school and college in a time when there was no such thing as a gay-straight alliance. It was a time when bullying and gay-bashing was acceptable or at least totally overlooked. The gay rights movement was almost non-existent, and most GLBT activity was conducted underground. Except for some very progressive and liberal cities, like San Francisco, out gay law enforcement officers were unheard of because they likely didn't stay employed once they came out or were discovered. There was no such thing as an anti-discrimination law that protected homosexual employees.

In California, even some chiefs have found themselves locked away in the closet. A chief of a small local department was forced to come out when his partner moved in and rumors started to emerge and then run out of control in his department. This chief's coming out story made the front page of many newspapers across the country, naming him the first out gay police chief in the country. Although he may have been the first gay chief a newspaper found, he certainly wasn't the first and only gay chief on the job. Some chiefs and sheriffs would just as well pretend that no gay or lesbian officers work in their departments and that there is no need to even pay attention. I would like to think that, at the most, these chiefs and sheriffs are indifferent, but the reality is that homophobia in law enforcement exists at a greater level than in most other segments of society. But law enforcement can no longer afford to be indifferent, and GLBT law enforcement officers are no longer invisible. As gay and lesbian communities emerge and become more identifiable and more out, law enforcement will need to respond just as it has to other minority communities as they emerged. These agencies will look to build a staff that reflects the gay and lesbian community by seeking out gay and lesbian officers to serve. In an organization where homophobia is prevalent or even a small part of the agency's culture, attracting gay and lesbian employees is sure to be a great challenge unless change is made way ahead of time.

What is the culture like in your department? If Alfred Kinsey was right, conservatively, one out of every ten employees in your department is a homosexual. In a staff of 50 employees, that means at least five are members of the GLBT community. But if sexual orientation is invisible, why doesn't a "don't ask, don't tell" policy work? Why should a department be more sensitive or pay more attention to the GLBT minority? After all, it likely accounts for ten percent or less of the personnel roster. The answers are simple. No department can afford to lose the investment already made in the hiring and training of its personnel. No department can afford to risk a federal lawsuit for workplace harassment or discrimination. And no department can afford to lose good talent. A loss like this is more than monetary; it is bad for morale, the image of the department, and the community at large. By forcing employees to keep their sexual orientation a secret, you will eventually force the employee to make a choice between work and his personal happiness. It's not about paying more or special attention to the GLBT members of the department; it's about making sure that they are treated equally and that they are made to feel as welcome and comfortable as any heterosexual member of the department. The kinds of considerations that are required are no different than those needed for any other group that is different from the majority.

Perhaps the best way to get started with assessing the climate within your department is to ask the leaders within your department some basic questions.

- Is our department as accepting of gay, lesbian, and bisexual personnel as it is of heterosexual employees?

- Would a gay, lesbian, or bisexual employee feel comfortable bringing his or her partner to a department social function?

- Would an equally qualified gay, lesbian, or bisexual employee be promoted as often as a heterosexual employee?

- Would gay, lesbian, or bisexual members of your community know with confidence that they would be considered for employment by your agency, regardless of their sexual orientation?

- Would the words "fag," "faggot" or the phrase "that's so gay" be used by one of your employees within the walls of the department and go unnoticed or unchecked?

Leadership in changing organizational culture clearly starts at the top, with the chief or sheriff. The first person who should check his biases at the door is the chief or sheriff. The agency executive must be the walking role model of acceptance and inclusion, and that requires getting past any internal homophobia. How is this done? As I have already written, avoid thinking pornographically about sexual orientation. The first step is to look at every interaction with the individual equally, fairly, and without any bias. Remember, it's not about who a person sleeps with or what a couple does together that matters, it is about what every healthy relationship has in common: trust, respect, love, and commitment. At work, what matters is how effectively the person performs on the job, how good of a person he is, and how he contributes to the betterment of the organization and community as a whole.

Why not simply adopt the United States military's policy of "don't ask, don't tell"? The answer is quite simple. This policy effectively keeps gay and lesbian employees in the closet. It forces individuals to make a choice between loving their career or having a loving personal life. Worse yet, this policy forces an otherwise honest and trustworthy member of law enforcement to violate the golden rule of the law enforcement profession; it forces the individual to lie. Closeted officers will commonly say and do things to create the perception they are straight. One lie leads to the next, and eventually the closeted officer is living a life that is a total lie, in both his professional circles as well as in personal ones. The United States military adopted this policy in an attempt to demonstrate some neutrality or at least to appear less discriminatory toward homosexuals. The reality is that this policy is completely discriminatory and sets up individuals to fail. For example, if under a "don't ask, don't tell" policy, an officer is discovered to be homosexual by a friend or co-worker and word of this discovery is spread by the friend or co-worker, even though the employee himself did not tell, the end result can be the same. The pressure to remain hidden and undiscoverable in order to comply with this type of policy is tremendous and completely unfair. No other member of an organization would be made to suffer such pressure because of an innate aspect of who they are. "Don't ask, don't tell" policies are entirely discriminatory and detrimental to everyone, including the organization because, in one way or the other, it forces talent to eventually leave the profession.

Here is a list of things to do for every agency executive who wants to make change to ensure that personnel who are gay or lesbian will feel accepted and respected.

- Put into department policy the same protections for sexual orientation and gender identity that likely already exist for gender, race, nationality, and ethnicity. Send a clear and strong message that discrimination, harassment, or any other form of behavior that demeans based on sexual orientation is prohibited.

- Establish a practice of responding to and investigating complaints of harassment based on sexual orientation that is equal to any other type of harassment complaint.

- Review organizational mission statements, vision statements, and values to ensure that what is in writing is consistent with organizational culture and practice. Make strong statements in these documents valuing individuals and diversity.

- Talk about the issues and don't shy away from openly discussing sexual orientation as an aspect of diversity within the organization. As a leader, it's important that you demonstrate comfort with the issue.

- Education and awareness is the best way to overcome fear about differences in sexual orientation. Based on your agency's climate, explore options for training that can provide information to ease any fears that may be present.

- Reach out to the gay and lesbian community with recruitment efforts. Remember what the true intent of affirmative action always has been: to open up employment opportunities to minority groups that stereotypically wouldn't consider themselves eligible for the job.

- Don't expect change overnight. Changing organizational culture is something that takes time and continuous effort. Be patient but persistent.

- Remember that to understand and accept someone else does not require you to agree with them.

- The most important and powerful thing a chief or sheriff can do is to lead by example. Remember that the top executive establishes the formal values of an organization by how the executive acts and in what decisions are made. Actions do speak louder than the written word.

The best way to get help with establishing an accepting workplace for GLBT officers is to use the resources within your own department. Your own GLBT personnel will be fully aware of the current work environment and will be in a good place to advise you on change that may be needed. If you don't know of any GLBT officers in your department, don't be shy about reaching out for help. There are many GLBT law enforcement professional associations that can be accessed through the internet. The website for this book, http://www.comingoutfrombehindthebadge.com, has a list of professional GLBT law enforcement organizations that can help. In addition, there is a recommended reading list with books that will give anyone a better understanding of this topic.

SOME THOUGHTS ABOUT DIVERSITY TRAINING

When I hear the phrase "diversity training," the first thought that comes to my mind is someone lecturing to me about why I should feel sorry for whatever minority group they represent. As offensive as this may sound coming from a guy who belongs to one of those groups, it is a reaction reminiscent of the many bad training classes I've attended on the topic of diversity. Most of these training sessions were scheduled and presented as a reaction to some event or hot political issue occurring at the time. None of these training presentations were ever connected to one another and were viewed as an answer for the bias of the day present in the organization. I've counseled many organizations on the subject of diversity training, but I continue to see the same mistakes made over and over again. Here are my thoughts about diversity training within the law enforcement profession.

First of all, it is important to think about diversity training more as a human relations issue in general rather than simply a focus on individual minority groups. Law enforcement officers interact with people of all types, both inside and outside of the department. It is critical that the topic of human relations training incorporates both venues. Keep in mind that many organizations have suffered many more civil liabilities stemming from internal conflicts and relationships than from any conflict arising from outside the department walls. As a second thought, training in human relations is as perishable as any physical skill. There is no one magic approach or highly effective program that will forever inoculate an organization against bias, prejudice, and outright hate. Try to think of human relations training as an ongoing conversation that never ends. This approach will link together whatever efforts the department makes in a way that eventually establishes an organizational value around human differences and relationships. From a liability perspective, it will also demonstrate a pro-active and ongoing effort to create and foster a safe and comfortable workplace for everyone.

I recommend that organizations develop a human relations committee or team to look after this department value. The team should be made up of a cross-section of employees, both sworn and civilian, management and line employee. Ideally, it would represent the diversity within the organization, but most important of all, it should include employees who are committed to the success of the organization and not those with an axe to grind. This committee should not exist merely as a place for disgruntled employees to vent, but rather it should exist to help move the organization forward. There are plenty of other venues for unhappy people to put forth their own agendas. My belief is that the chief or sheriff should be a member of this committee and share the role of committee chair with another non-management member.

Human relations training should start with a discussion about why employees should even talk about this subject. This is the step most commonly missed by organizations that make an effort in this area. The agency executive should lead this discussion. Don't talk about specific biases, prejudice, or make any assumptions about attitudes that may or may not be present in the organization. Simply start out by making a statement about organizational values related to people, differences, relationships, and the development of more effective human relations inside and outside of the agency. Discuss the formation of a standing committee and define its purpose. Depending on the level of trust present within the organization, it may be necessary to resolve any suspicions or perceived ulterior motives that may be present. Be patient and do a lot of listening to whatever concerns may be expressed.

Once a committee is selected, spend some time laying out a plan for how to assess organizational climate, including the comfort level with discussing issues of difference, such as sexual orientation. If people are not even comfortable or trusting enough to talk about diversity, then a lot of preliminary work needs to be done. Here is a sequence of steps I recommend for a new committee.

1. Set up a regular meeting schedule and ensure employees are given release time from their regular jobs to attend.

2. Set up a process for publishing minutes from the meetings, but avoid making this process a huge burden. Minutes are important to avoid any perception of secrecy. Remember that trust is a crucial element throughout every aspect of this effort.

3. Assess the climate in the workplace. This includes assessing aspects of diversity that are both visible and invisible within the department. How do the numbers compare to the diversity within the community?

4. Assess attitudes and biases within the department, both real and perceived. Do employees feel comfortable discussing differences and other issues related to diversity?

5. Review organizational history related to human relations issues. Think about complaints that have been made and the presence of the players involved in those complaints within the organization. Are there any wounds that still remain open from these complaints?

Based on the information gathered from these questions, establish a starting point for the discussion. In other words, if employees are afraid or hesitant to discuss differences, then work needs to be done to build trust. Begin the discussion with talk about what people have in common (goals, department values, department mission, and department vision). There must be trust and an agreement to even talk about human relations issues before any training can begin. Without trust and agreement, employees are likely to throw up a wall of resistance in the form of personal protection, and little will be accomplished.

If, on the other hand, employees feel trust and agree with the value of discussing diversity, the organization can move forward more easily with a discussion of the differences that exist among employees in the department. Remember that maintaining trust is extremely important throughout this ongoing discussion or training effort. Before tackling what biases individuals have, it is important for people to understand how biases and prejudices are created. Think about starting out with training that addresses the origin of biases and the socialization process we all experience through growing up with our families, with our friends, and within our different generations. Bias and prejudice is something learned, and that means it can be unlearned. The genesis of bias and prejudice is fear, both of that which is unknown as well as of that which is created through fiction. Once employees understand the origins of bias and accept the fact that whatever biases they have are acquired through a learned process, they may be more comfortable with the idea of participating in training experiences that will help unlearn those biases.

Keep in mind that many employees may feel vulnerable when participating in a discussion about their biases. Some may fear being labeled as a racist if they openly self-identify their own biases. Even though the term "racist" has no connection with the term "bias," this is a common fear that must be addressed in the trust-building process. One of the rules of engagement for any human relations training effort must be confidentiality. What is said in the training room must stay inside the training room. It is essential that employees not feel like they are walking on eggshells during these training sessions. Discussions about the origins of bias and prejudice may not always be pretty, but they are important to have, so try to create a trusting, professional environment that is comfortable and open. Remember, the goal is not to force a change of an individual's values per se, but more to create an understanding and acceptance of our differences in such a way that the individual may choose to make a change.

Once all of this foundational work is done, you are ready to use the information about the diversity within the organization and the community, together with the information about biases present within the organization, to shape a training plan. Remember that bias and prejudice is something that is often learned through negative experiences and misinformation. Training, therefore, can be used to create positive experiences and a flow of accurate information, with the intent of creating a change in attitudes and biases. The training committee should prioritize the overall needs of the department and set out a plan to address individual diversity topics. There may be temptation at this point to run forward with enthusiasm, but I highly recommend a slower, methodical, and long-term approach. Be cautious about burn-out and overwhelming employees with diversity training. While this topic is important, officer safety, physical skills, and other topics carry equal weight. A department can be highly effective by simply integrating human relations training into the department's training plan on a periodic and continuous basis. Remember that organizations evolve and personnel rosters change. Topics may need to be revisited periodically in a way that brings new members of the organization into the same ongoing conversation.

When designing training for the department, quality is more important that quantity. In other words, it is more important to spend money on one great speaker than two mediocre ones. I highly recommend use of an outside facilitator to at least get the human relations conversation started. I've found that peers teaching each other can be the most difficult classes to pull off, and this is especially true with this topic. If there is someone in-house who is respected, knowledgeable, and trustworthy, then employ them to the fullest extent to make the program work. It's much less important that the facilitator be someone from a minority group than it is that they have the knowledge, skills, and abilities to be a good facilitator. In fact, it might be better if the training facilitator didn't come from a minority group in order to avoid any possible perception of a private agenda or one-sided perspective.

When it comes to providing training and exposure to individual groups, look to your own community for help. You will know which group could most effectively represent the topic group and which ones will be best received by department personnel. Of course, look inside, as well, for members of different groups to help organize and facilitate the training dealing with their own group. This can be particularly effective because it gives law enforcement personnel a chance to not only learn about a particular group, but to learn about being a member of that group while working in law enforcement. It also enlists participation and buy-in from within the organization. The best part of this approach is that it will likely cost the department budget nothing and will go a long way in bringing people together. In all cases, be sure the presenters understand the mission of the training. This mission should minimally include providing an experience that increases understanding of the group and that promotes an acceptance of the group by law enforcement. It would be disastrous for any group to come in and present a "Woe is me; here are all the reasons you should feel sorry for me" story. It would be equally problematic for the presenter to use the training session as a way to present and confront all of the bad history the individual has had with law enforcement. The presenters and audience need to be on the same side and have the same goals.

With respect to diversity training and sexual orientation, remember that this topic may be the most challenging for department personnel. Set a tone that is non-threatening and does not pose a forced change. Allow employees to learn through experience and exposure, and remember that one training session is not likely to change years of bigotry. Keep the training focused on department values and missions and consider emphasizing the idea that to understand and accept someone does not require you to agree with them. Another important idea to keep in mind is that bias associated with sexual orientation differs by generation. Think about the time and place and about the experience your personnel have had as they grew up in high school and college. Consider the fact that an officer who graduated from high school in the early '80s likely had little or no exposure to mainstream homosexuals, whereas an officer who graduated 10 or 20 years later grew up with gay-straight alliances on their high school campus.

If planned correctly, human relations training could become your department's most fascinating and engaging training topic. Think about it; people are interesting and law enforcement is entirely a people-oriented business. Don't take shortcuts, and give your personnel the edge they need to be highly effective in performing the work of your business, that of serving the people in your community.

SECTION IV

RECOMMENDED BOOKS

There are many excellent books and organizations that will support the discussion of coming out and continue where this book leaves off. I've read most of these books, and I support their message.

Is It a Choice? 300 Questions Commonly Asked of Gays and Lesbians.
By: Eric Marcus. Published by: Harper.
This is the book I sent to my parents as an owner's manual for their new gay son. It can be read a little at a time and deals very directly with stereotypes and common fears. I recommend this book to anyone with a friend or family member who is coming out.

Victory: The Triumphant Gay Revolution
By: Linda Hirshman. Published by: Harper Perennial.
This book offers an optimistic look back at LGBT history.

The Right Side of History: 100 Years of LGBTQ Activism
By: Adrian Brooks. Published by: Cleis Press.
One great way to learn about history is through storytelling. This book includes events told by different authors that include major landmarks in the LGBT civil rights movement.

Journeys across the Rainbow: Inspirational Stories for the Human Race
By: David Jensen and Dale Colclasure. Published by: Rainbow Pride Press.
While preparing to write this book, I read a number of anthologies from various types of people about their coming out experiences. This book goes beyond coming out stories and evoked a strong emotional reaction from me. The stories are incredible and will make you feel really good.

One Teacher in 10, second edition
By: Kevin Jennings. Published by: Alyson Books.
This is anthology from teachers who came out on the job. Teachers and police officers have a lot in common, and I found this book to be very supportive and inspiring.

Gay, Straight, and the Reason Why: The Science of Sexual Orientation
By: Simon LeVay. Published by: Oxford University Press.
If you are fascinated by the science of sexuality, this is the book for you. It is very science-heavy, but provides a fascinating insight into where attraction comes from.

The Meaning of Matthew: My Son's Murder in Laramie, and a World Transformed
By: Judy Shepard. Published by: Plum.
This book is really unlike the others and has nothing to do with coming out, but I include it as recommended reading because of how Matthew Shepard's story impacted me. This book was written by Matthew's mother and not only tells the truth about what happened to Matthew, but also provides some insight into the person Matt Shepard was.

The Way Out
By: Chris Nutter. Published by: HCI.
This is a newer book about coming out and offers some different perspectives. It tells a tough story and is definitely worth reading.

A Matter of Justice
By: Robin Buhrke. Published by: Routledge.
When the idea of writing a book about coming out in law enforcement first came to my mind, this book is what I had in mind. However, the stories in this book represent a different generation of law enforcement officers who came out in the early and mid-90s. What I discovered in reading these stories was that our profession has grown in a very positive way since then. It made me feel good about how far we have come.

Discrimination and Harassment by Law Enforcement Officers in the LGBT Community
Discrimination against Law Enforcement Officers on the Basis of Sexual Orientation and Gender Identity: 2000 to 2013
By: UCLA Williams Institute. Published by: University of Southern California.
These are the two studies mentioned in this book in the section on homophobia in law enforcement. The Williams Institute is recognized as a leader in the study of discrimination related to gender and sexual orientation.

Out to Protect Grants and Scholarships

In 2009, I created Out to Protect Incorporated, a national non-profit organization that support LGBT law enforcement professionals. Our mission is to create a greater awareness of the lesbian, gay, bisexual, and transgender professionals working in law enforcement. We do this by encouraging LGBT people to "come out" and by providing education and awareness.

Out to Protect offers scholarships for LGBT students attending a basic law enforcement training program, such as a basic police academy, corrections academy, or 9-1-1 dispatcher academy. The organization also offers grants for law enforcement agencies to provide LGBT awareness training. This includes offering speakers and panels for this kind of training. You can learn more about Out to Protect at www.outtoprotect.org

Gay and Lesbian Peace Officer Associations

One of the wonderful things about the law enforcement profession is the camaraderie that is available at all levels, including sexual orientation. Most of the organizations listed below offer membership to any active peace officer or law enforcement employee. Some of these groups, such as the Gay Officers Action League, present periodic conferences with incredible guest speakers. I recommend these groups for networking and support.

We have a complete list of active LGBT law enforcement organizations on our own website at www.comingoutfrombehindthebadge.com.

GAY AND LESBIAN ORGANIZATIONS

While you may have felt at one time that you were the only gay or lesbian person in law enforcement, hopefully by now you have realized you are one of thousands. I hope you have also come to realize that there is a very visible community ready to embrace and support you. The organizations I've included on this list are just some of the best ones I've come to know and can recommend to any fellow officer. I encourage you to look at their Web sites and reach out.

Gay Lesbian Straight Education Network:

http://www.glsen.org/cgi-bin/iowa/home.html

Gay and Lesbian Alliance against Defamation: http://www.glaad.org

Gay Straight Alliance Network: http://www.glaad.org

Human Rights Campaign: http://www.hrc.org

Lambda Legal Project: http://www.lambdalegal.com

Matthew Shepard Foundation: http://www.matthewshepard.org

Matthew's Place: http://www.matthewsplace.com

Parents and Friends of Lesbians and Gays: http://www.pflag.org

The Trevor Project: http://www.thetrevorproject.org

Greg Miraglia is the dean of criminal justice training at Napa Valley College in California. He served three law enforcement agencies as a dispatcher, reserve police officer, supervisor, division manager, and, most recently, as a deputy police chief. With over 30 years of academy teaching experience, he is recognized as an expert in human relations, workplace harassment and discrimination prevention, and hate crimes education. Mr. Miraglia is the creator and primary teacher of the LGBT Studies Program at Napa Valley College. He is an active member of the board of directors for the Matthew Shepard Foundation, the national program coordinator of the Stop the Hate program, and the host and producer of the Outbeat News radio program on PBS radio station KRCB in Santa Rosa, California. He has a master's degree in education administration, a bachelor's degree in business, and is a graduate of the California P.O.S.T. Master Instructor Development Program.

http://www.comingoutfrombehindthebadge.com